WRITING
SOLID
CODE

WRITING
SOLID
CODE

Microsoft's

Techniques for

Developing

Bug-Free

C Programs

STEVE MAGUIRE

Foreword by Dave Moore
Director of Development, Microsoft Corporation

Microsoft
P R E S S

PUBLISHED BY
Microsoft Press
A Division of Microsoft Corporation
One Microsoft Way
Redmond, Washington 98052-6399

Library of Congress Cataloging-in-Publication Data
Maguire, Stephen A.
    Writing solid code : microsoft's techniques for developing bug-free
  C programs / Stephen A. Maguire.
      p.   cm.
    Includes bibliographical references and index.
    ISBN 1-55615-551-4
    1. C (Computer program language) 2. Development.
  I. Title.
  QA76.73.C15M335   1993
  005.1'4--dc20   93-15659
                                                     CIP

Printed and bound in the United States of America.

3 4 5 6 7 8 9   AGAG   8 7 6 5 4 3

Distributed to the book trade in Canada by Macmillan of Canada, a division of Canada Publishing Corporation.

Distributed to the book trade outside the United States and Canada by Penguin Books Ltd.

Penguin Books Ltd., Harmondsworth, Middlesex, England
Penguin Books Australia Ltd., Ringwood, Victoria, Australia
Penguin Books N.Z. Ltd., 182-190 Wairau Road, Auckland 10, New Zealand

British Cataloging-in-Publication Data available.

Acquisitions Editor: Mike Halvorson
Project Editor: Erin O'Connor
Technical Reviewer: Wm. Jeff Carey

To my wife, Beth,
and to my parents, Joseph and Julia Maguire,
for all their love and support.

CONTENTS

> With the growing complexity of software and the associated climb in bug
> rates, it's becoming increasingly necessary for programmers to produce
> bug-free code much earlier in the development cycle, before the code is
> first sent to Testing. The key to writing bug-free code is to become more
> aware of how bugs come about. Programmers can cultivate this aware-
> ness by asking themselves two simple questions about every bug they en-
> counter: "How could I have prevented this bug?" and "How could I have
> automatically detected this bug?" The guidelines in this book are the re-
> sults of regularly asking these two questions over a number of years.

If your compiler could detect every bug in your program—no matter the
type—and issue an error message, ridding your code of bugs would be
simple. Such omniscient compilers don't exist, but by enabling optional
compiler warnings, using syntax and portability checkers, and using automated unit tests, you can increase the number of bugs that are detected for
you automatically.

A good development strategy is to maintain two versions of your program:
one that you ship and one that you use to debug the code. By using debugging assertion statements, you can detect bugs caused by bad function arguments, accidental use of undefined behavior, mistaken assumptions made
by other programmers, and impossible conditions that nevertheless somehow show up. Debug-only backup algorithms help verify function results
and the algorithms used in functions.

Assertions wait quietly until bugs show up. Even more powerful are subsystem integrity checks that actively validate subsystems and alert you to bugs before the bugs affect the program. The integrity checks for the standard C memory manager can detect dangling pointers, lost memory blocks, and illegal use of memory that has not been initialized or that has already been released. Integrity checks can also be used to eliminate rare behavior, which is responsible for untested scenarios, and to force subsystem bugs to be reproducible so that they can be tracked down and fixed.

The best way to find bugs is to step through all new code in a debugger. By stepping through each instruction with your focus on the data flow, you can quickly detect problems in your expressions and algorithms. Keeping the focus on the data, not the instructions, gives you a second, very different, view of the code. Stepping through code takes time, but not nearly as much as most programmers would expect it to.

It's not enough that your functions be bug-free; functions must be easy to use without introducing unexpected bugs. If bug rates are to be reduced, each function needs to have one well-defined purpose, to have explicit single-purpose inputs and outputs, to be readable at the point where it is called, and ideally to never return an error condition. Functions with these attributes are easy to validate using assertions and debug code, and they minimize the amount of error handling code that must be written.

Given the numerous implementation possibilities for a given function, it should come as no surprise that some implementations will be more error-prone than others. The key to writing robust functions is to exchange risky algorithms and language idioms for alternatives that have proven to be comparably efficient yet much safer. At one extreme this can mean using unambiguous data types; at the other it can mean tossing out an entire design simply because it would be difficult, or impossible, to test.

Some programming practices are so risky they should never be used. Most such practices are obviously risky, but some seem quite safe, even desirable, because they fill a need without apparent hazard. These treacherous coding practices are the wolves in sheep's clothing. Why shouldn't you reference memory you've just released? Why is it risky to pass data in global or static storage? Why should you avoid parasitic functions? Why it is unwise to rely on every nit-picky detail outlined in the ANSI standard?

A programmer can follow every guideline in this book, but without the proper attitude and a set of good programming habits, writing bug-free code will be much harder than it needs to be. If a programmer believes that a bug can simply "go away," or that fixing bugs "later" won't be harmful to the product, bugs will persist. If a programmer regularly "cleans up" code, allows unnecessary flexibility in functions, welcomes every "free" feature that pops out of a design, or simply "tries" haphazard solutions to problems hoping to hit upon something that works, writing bug-free code will be an uphill battle. Having a good set of habits and attitudes is possibly the most important requirement for consistently writing bug-free code.

FOREWORD

I first met Steve Maguire in 1986, when we hired him to work on Macintosh Excel. He impressed me then as a particularly conscientious and dedicated programmer. At that time, I was the development manager for Microsoft Multiplan, Word, and Chart. The company was growing rapidly, and so were problems with both our products and our development process. Steve was instrumental in solving some of those problems and with this book becomes the recorder of many good practices we developed in response to those problems. But I'm getting ahead of myself.

I was hired by Bill Gates and Charles Simonyi in 1981 to work in Microsoft's business applications group. Back then, that meant 7 programmers working on one business application—Microsoft Multiplan. Another 30 programmers were working on our language and operating systems products. The rest of the 100 people in the company were in technical writing, sales, marketing, and administration. At that time, all 7 Multiplan programmers were crammed into one large room in an office building in downtown Bellevue, Washington. We weren't even in the same building with the rest of the developers, who were working on MS-DOS and Basic. They were two blocks away. But that wasn't a big problem. We were a small company with a vision of what we wanted to accomplish: a computer on every desk running Microsoft software.

The system we used to develop Multiplan was pretty sophisticated for PC development in those days. We wrote the core product in C—most programs then were written in assembly or Pascal. We did our editing and compilation on a PDP-11 running Unix. The C code was compiled into p-code and downloaded to the target machines. We had to build p-code interpreters for each microprocessor in use at that time.

By the end of 1983, we had interpreters working for the 8080/Z80, the 6502, the Z8000, the 68000, the TI 99/a, and the 8086. And by that time, we had application specialists working on each of our primary business applications—a spreadsheet, a word processor, a simple database record manager, and a business graphics package. We had assembly language and environment specialists working on the interpreters. We also had a group working on the compiler and development tools. Except for a small dependence on the minuscule operating system services, the 30-member application development team was self-contained, building its own development tools, compilers, interpreters, and product code.

In 1981, our primary focus had been on shipping original equipment manufacturer products. We would work with an OEM, customizing our products to fit the OEM's machine and sales channels. Then we would ship the OEM a disk and photo-ready copies of the manual. The OEM would do all of the manufacturing of the product, the sales, and the support.

By 1982, we had started to switch to a retail emphasis. The OEM focus had allowed us to travel light. We'd needed only a few marketing folks to sell the products to the OEMs, a few developers to build the products, and a few technical writers to write the manuals. Testing, project management, product manufacturing, product shipping, product support, and sales had been provided by the OEM. With the switch to a retail focus, we had to develop all of these specialized product development and support functions at Microsoft.

Early on, we developed products for IBM and Apple PCs. Our first retail products were Multiplan for IBM-DOS and Multiplan for the Apple II. But we still developed many OEM products. We worked on spreadsheet, word processing, business graphics, and database products for Unix, Xenix, the TI 99/a, the Tandy M100, the MSX (an 8-bit home computer in Japan), non-IBM-compatible MS-DOS machines, the Commodore 64, the Atari, the Apple III, the Apple Lisa, the Apple Macintosh, OS/2, Windows, and many other specialized hardware environments. Some of these environments had several variants themselves. Before the IBM-compatible became the dominant machine, we'd had to tailor our applications for every MS-DOS machine that was built. We'd had a different product for the Tandy, the Wang, the Paradyne, the Consumer Devices, the Eagle, the Victor, the Olivetti, the DEC Rainbow, and many other MS-DOS machines. While dealing with this system specialization, we were developing numerous specialized foreign language versions of our business applications.

Our early products were only English language versions. Today we build over 30 language products that we adapt, or more often tailor, to the target language/culture, including Arabic, Australian, Bahas, Chinese, Czechoslovakian, Danish, Dutch, English (UK), Finnish, French, French

Canadian, German, Greek, Hebrew, Honguel (Korean), Italian, Japanese, Norwegian, Portuguese, Russian, Spanish, Swedish, Turkish, US English, and more.

By 1985, some of the complexity of product development had been eliminated by the success of the IBM PC. The variety of video standards we'd had to support had been reduced to the primary IBM-compatible modes (CGA and monochrome). But video support started to get out of hand again around 1988. IBM had developed the EGA video extensions, then they developed the VGA, and it was soon followed by the SVGA and all of its variants.

Support for the other hardware peripherals also grew more complex. We had to support over 200 variations of laser and dot matrix printers. Fortunately, input devices didn't get too varied. There was the IBM standard keyboard and the extended keyboard. And most pointing devices followed the Microsoft mouse standard.

Today a lot of the complexity and variations in the hardware have simply gone away or have been incorporated into one complex but complete interface. We have to build products for only two primary systems—Windows and the Mac. But new levels and magnitudes of complexity have emerged to replace the complexities of hardware support. Now developers need to be conversant with message-based GUI programming and with object-oriented design and programming. They need to support product extensibility through Object Linking and Embedding (OLE) in Windows and through Publish and Subscribe on the Mac. And they need to support consistent access to features across product families and consistent methods of programmability across product families.

In 1984, the increase in the complexity of our products and the high standards involved in building retail products led us to start up a quality assurance group. We called this group Testing in 1984, and we call this group Testing today, although our testing group has grown from 5 testers in 1984 to over 500 testers. Our testing group today is really an advanced quality assurance group that looks out for our customer's interests.

Before we'd had a testing group, the business applications developers had relied on the OEM customer to test the product to find bugs. This arrangement worked out well until we started to ship the retail product directly to end users, before we'd shipped it to any OEM customers. For an interval, before the testing group was going strong, the developers had to test the retail products themselves. The developers who lived through that experience learned that they had to be very careful not to introduce bugs as they wrote and debugged the code. They found out the hard way how costly it was to release a product that had bugs in it.

But as the testing group got bigger, the development groups got more and more dependent on the testing group to find bugs. The development groups soon adopted the attitude that the testing group was responsible for finding all bugs. This led to such serious problems—slipped schedules, buggy features, incomplete features, even canceled products—that something had to be done. Many developers felt no shame if bugs were found in their code after the product had shipped. They'd ask indignantly, "Why didn't Testing find that bug before we shipped?" Testing should have responded, "Why did you put that bug in the product in the first place?"

Eventually, the developers began to realize that Testing can never find all of the bugs in a piece of software. The bugs might be in the design, or in the specifications, or in the analysis of the customer's needs. And testers can't do complete code coverage or path coverage in their tests. Bugs might be hidden in obscure and rarely tested code. Bugs can be temporarily masked by the operations of other parts of the program—or by the testing environment. These are the kinds of bugs that testers have a hard time finding. Because of these factors, a testing group will usually find only 60 percent of the bugs in a product.

The developers can bring more knowledge and tools to reviewing and testing the code. When the developers set their minds and their tools to it, they can find over 90 percent of the bugs in the code. If the developers give the responsibility for finding the bugs to the testers, the users of the product will find 40 percent of the bugs. If Development and Testing both work to find the bugs, the users will end up finding less than 4 percent of the bugs. And that 4 percent could be found by the users during the beta test of the product.

In early 1989, many of the development managers and leads met to discuss the problem. Out of that meeting came a realization and an attitude change: Finding and fixing bugs was Development's responsibility. Development had been letting bugs slip past them. Now it became their responsibility again to prevent bugs from being released to Testing and then on to the customers. The development teams set off on the goal of having a "nearly shippable product every day." This means that when a feature is marked complete, any bugs found in it will have to be fixed before any new work is attempted. Work in progress will be brought to a standstill if serious bugs are found in features marked complete.

We labeled this new attitude "zero defects." The code would be built, reviewed, and tested by Development and delivered to Testing with zero defects. Fortunately, a few of the development groups had already been experimenting with many of the techniques for developing zero defect code. We started to actively share those techniques among all the development groups. Steve Maguire did a lot of troubleshooting from group to group in those days, and he has set down many of our techniques for writing solid, bug-free code in this book.

Microsoft improved and is always improving its product development process along with its development tools. In 1981, there were the developers, the writers of the manuals, and small sales, marketing, and administrative groups. Now we have product marketing, channel marketing, sales, support, testing, user education (technical writing and publishing), program management, and many other specialists. With today's complex structure of special groups at Microsoft, we want to ensure that the techniques for developing solid code aren't lost, misunderstood, or forgotten. Steve Maguire's book should help both us and you keep those techniques alive.

Today I'm the director of development and testing for Microsoft. Part of my job is to inventory and disseminate best practices. I'm very grateful to Steve for taking the time to write a book so enjoyable to read that will help managers and programmers develop world-class code. Steve has captured and described many of the techniques that are used at Microsoft to develop solid, shippable code. It will become recommended reading for all Microsoft programmers.

David M. Moore
Director of Development, Microsoft
Redmond, Washington
January 1993

PREFACE

In 1986, after 10 years of consulting and working for small companies, I went to work for Microsoft specifically to get experience in writing Macintosh applications. I joined Microsoft's Excel team, the group responsible for the company's graphical spreadsheet application.

I'm not sure what I was expecting the code to look like—glamorous or elegant, I suppose. What I found was plain, everyday code, nothing much different from what I'd seen before. To be sure, the spreadsheet had a wonderful user interface—it was much easier and more intuitive to use than any of the character-based spreadsheets of the time. But what impressed me even more was the implementation of an extensive debugging system built into the product.

The system automatically alerted programmers and testers to bugs, much the way warning lights in the cockpit of a Boeing 747 alert pilots to failures—the debugging system was not so much testing the code as it was *monitoring* it. None of the concepts in the debugging system were new, but I was struck by the sheer extent to which they were employed, and by how effective the system was in detecting bugs. It was an eye-opener. It didn't take me long to discover that most of Microsoft's projects had extensive internal debugging systems—and that there was a heightened awareness among the programmers of bugs and their causes.

I worked on Macintosh Excel for two years before I left to help another Microsoft group, whose code was turning up with a higher than usual number of bugs. I found that during the two years in which I had been focused on Excel, Microsoft had tripled in size and many of the programming concepts that were well-known among the older groups had not spread to the newer groups during the rapid growth. Instead of having a heightened awareness of error-prone coding practices, the newer programmers had a normal awareness—about what I'd seen among programmers in the years before I joined Microsoft.

About six months after I'd moved to the new group, I was talking to a fellow programmer and mentioned that somebody should document the concepts behind writing bug-free code so that the principles could spread to the newer groups. The other programmer looked at me and said, "You don't seem to mind writing documents; why don't *you* write down the details? In fact, why don't you write a book and see if Microsoft Press will publish it? After all, none of this information is proprietary; it simply makes programmers more aware of bugs."

I didn't give that suggestion much thought then, mainly because I didn't have the time and I'd never written a book before—the closest I'd come to authorship was cowriting a programming column for *Hi-Res Magazine* in the early 1980s. Not quite the same thing.

But as you can see, the book did get written, and for a simple reason: In 1989 Microsoft canceled an unannounced product because of a runaway bug list. Now, runaway bug lists weren't new—several of Microsoft's competitors had already canceled projects because of them. But this was the first time that Microsoft had ever canceled a project for that reason. It was also the latest in a string of buggy products, and management had finally said, "Enough is enough" and taken a series of steps to get bug counts back down to their previous levels. Still, nobody was given responsibility for putting the details down on paper.

By this time the company was nine times larger than when I'd started, and I didn't see how the company's coding could return to its previous low bug levels without explicit, recorded guidelines, particularly when I considered the growing complexity of Windows and Macintosh applications. That's when I decided, finally, to write this book.

Microsoft Press agreed to publish it.

And here it is.

I hope you enjoy reading the book. I've tried to keep it informal and entertaining.

ACKNOWLEDGMENTS

I'd like to thank everybody at Microsoft Press who helped make this book a reality, and in particular the two people who held my hand throughout the writing process. First I would like to thank Mike Halvorson, my acquisitions editor, for letting me take the project at my own speed and for patiently answering this first-time book author's many questions. I would especially like to thank Erin O'Connor, my manuscript editor, who gave me early feedback on the chapters, and without whose help this book simply would not exist. Erin also encouraged me to relax into my own style, and it certainly didn't hurt that she laughed at the text's little jokes. Jeff Carey gave the ideas and the code a good going over, and Kathleen Atkins made many good suggestions.

I'd also like to thank my father, Joseph Maguire, who in the mid-1970s introduced me to those first microcomputers: the Altair, the IMSAI, and the Sol-20. He is responsible for getting me hooked on this business. Evan Rosen, with whom I worked at Valpar International from 1981 to 1983, was a great influence on me, and his knowledge and insight show up in this book. Paul Davis, with whom I've had the pleasure to work during the past 10 years on various projects all over the country, has also shaped my thinking in significant ways.

I'd like to thank all the people who took the time to read through draft copies of this book to give me technical feedback: Mark Gerber, Melissa Glerum, Chris Mason, Dave Moore, John Rae-Grant, and Alex Tilles. I'd especially like to thank Eric Schlegel and Paul Davis for not only reviewing draft copies of the book but also giving me early help in hammering out the details.

Seattle, Washington
October 22, 1992

INTRODUCTION

Several years ago I picked up a copy of T$_E$X: *The Program*, by Donald Knuth, and what I read in the preface astounded me:

> I believe that the final bug in T$_E$X was discovered and removed on November 27, 1985. But if, somehow, an error still lurks in the code, I shall gladly pay a finder's fee of $20.48 to the first person who discovers it. (This is twice the previous amount, and I plan to double it again in a year; you see, I really am confident!)

I have no idea whether Knuth paid anybody $20.48 or even $40.96; that's not important. What *is* important is the confidence Knuth had in the quality of his code. How many programmers do you know who would seriously claim that their programs are totally bug-free? How many would publish such a claim and back it up with a finder's fee?

Programmers could make such claims if they truly believed that their testing groups had found all their bugs. But that's the problem. How many times have you heard programmers say, "I hope Testing has found all the bugs" right before the code is boxed, shrink-wrapped, and shipped to dealers? They cross their fingers and hope for the best.

Programmers today aren't sure their code is bug-free because they've relinquished responsibility for thoroughly testing it. It's not that management ever came out and said, "Don't worry about testing your code—the testers will do that for you." It's more subtle than that. Management expects programmers to test their code, but they expect testers to be more thorough; after all, that's Testing's full-time job.

The purpose of this book is to show how programmers can take back the responsibility for writing bug-free code. That doesn't necessarily mean writing perfect code the first time—it means creating a product that's bug-free before it first goes into testing. Some programmers may laugh incredulously at such an idea, but this book demonstrates techniques and provides guidelines that programmers can use to work toward that goal.

THE TWO CRITICAL QUESTIONS

The most critical requirement for writing bug-free code is to become attuned to what causes bugs. All of the techniques and guidelines presented in this book are the result of programmers asking themselves two questions over and over again, year after year, for every bug found in their code:

◆ How could I have *automatically* detected this bug?

◆ How could I have *prevented* this bug?

The easy answer to both questions would be "better testing," but that's not automatic, nor is it really preventive. Answers like "better testing" are so general they have no muscle—they're effectively worthless. Good answers to these questions result in specific techniques that eliminate the kind of bug you've just found.

This book is devoted to techniques and guidelines that have been found to reduce or completely eliminate entire classes of bugs. Some of its points smack right up against common coding practices, but before dismissing them with "everybody breaks that guideline," or "nobody does that," stop and think it through for yourself. If "nobody does that," why not? Make sure the reasons are still valid. Practices that made sense when FORTRAN was the hot new language may not make sense now.

That's not to say that you should blindly follow the guidelines in this book. They aren't rules. Too many programmers have taken the guideline "Don't use *goto* statements" as a commandment from God that should never be broken. When asked why they're so strongly against *goto*s, they say that using *goto* statements results in unmaintainable spaghetti code. Experienced programmers often add that *goto* statements can upset the compiler's code optimizer. Both points are valid. Yet there are times when the judicious use of a *goto* can greatly improve the clarity and efficiency of the code. In such cases, clinging to the guideline "Don't use *goto* statements" would result in worse code, not better.

The guidelines in this book are no different: They're meant to be followed most of the time, and they're meant to be broken when you can get better results by breaking them.

In addition to the guidelines and techniques, most of the chapters in this book contain a section at the end called "Things to Think About." Questions in this section of a chapter explore new areas that haven't been covered in the earlier parts of the chapter. The questions aren't exercises—they don't test your comprehension of the chapter. I've tried to introduce at least one new concept in every question, and I've provided a complete set of answers in order to pass on as much information as possible. If you usually skip over exercises, consider reading the answers in Appendix C so that you won't miss any of the guidelines or techniques I've introduced there.

Building atop Existing Foundations

Programmers who have been using C for a while know that they should use parentheses around arguments in macro definitions; they know that strings have unseen null characters; they know that C arrays start with element *0*, not *1*; and they know that you must use *break* statements to prevent *switch* cases from falling into each other. These and other misunderstandings about the C language are common sources of bugs, but you won't find these bugs under discussion in this book unless such discussion is part of another point I'm making. I have tried to focus on the little-known, or rarely published, techniques for writing bug-free code, techniques that you won't usually find in programming textbooks or hear about in programming courses.

Nor have I tried to rehash guidelines already covered so well in *The Elements of Programming Style*, the programming classic written by Brian Kernighan and P. J. Plauger. Although Kernighan and Plauger use FORTRAN and PL/I in their examples, their guidelines—with a few exceptions—are applicable to any programming language, including C. *Writing Solid Code* builds on the groundwork laid by *The Elements of Programming Style* and follows a similar format.

Finally, although this book is written for professional programmers working on real projects with real deadlines, it's also suitable for students in advanced C programming courses. Few students will ever work on a compiler once they finish their compiler course, but all will have to focus on writing bug-free code. It's my hope that this book will help give students the skills they'll need to write solid, production quality code once they graduate.

WHAT'S A "MACINTOSH"?

Sometimes it almost seems that a book won't be taken seriously unless it mentions the PDP-11, the IBM 360, or some other old piece of hardware. So there, I've mentioned them, and I won't mention them again in this book. The systems you will hear a lot about in this book are MS-DOS, Microsoft Windows, and especially the Apple Macintosh—because those are the systems I've written code for most recently.

You'll also hear a lot about the history of the Microsoft Excel and Microsoft Word applications in this book. Excel is Microsoft's graphical spreadsheet, originally written for the Macintosh and later significantly re-written, cleaned up, and enhanced for Windows.

Throughout the book, I talk about my experiences as a Macintosh Excel programmer, but I must confess that I spent most of my time either porting Windows code to the Macintosh sources or implementing look-alike features that Windows Excel already had. I had little to do with the phenomenal success of the product.

My only strategic contribution to Macintosh Excel was to convince Microsoft to kill it, and to instead build the Macintosh version directly from the much-improved Windows version's sources. Macintosh Excel 2.2 was the first version based on Windows Excel, sharing 80% of the code with its sibling. This was great for Macintosh Excel users because with the 2.2 release they saw a big jump in features and quality.

Word is Microsoft's word processing application. Actually, there are three versions of Word: Word for MS-DOS, which is character-based; Word for the Macintosh; and Word for Windows. As I write, the three products are still built from separate sources, but the versions are similar enough that most users can move among them without much difficulty. Eventually, all versions of Word will be built from common sources. The work is in progress.

WHAT ABOUT THE CODE?

You don't need to be an MS-DOS, Microsoft Windows, or Apple Macintosh expert to follow the book's code—the code is written in straightforward C that should compile and run with any ANSI C development system.

However, if you're a mainframe or minicomputer programmer with-out much experience on microcomputers, be aware that protected memory support is still rare in microcomputer operating systems. You can read and write through *NULL* pointers, trash your stack frame, and spew garbage throughout memory—even memory belonging to another application— and the hardware will stand by quietly while you do it. If you find yourself thinking, "The hardware will catch that bug," consider yourself lucky to have such a helpful system. Not all programmers are so fortunate.

In several places I've shown ANSI C library functions that don't quite match the standard's requirements. For example, the ANSI version of the *memchr* function declares the character *c* as an *int*:

```
void *memchr(const void *s, int c, size_t n);
```

Internally, *memchr* treats the character as an *unsigned char*, but the character is declared as an *int* for backward compatibility with pre-ANSI, unprototyped source code. Since I use ANSI C throughout the book, I have dropped that backward compatibility detail and instead have used the more accurate types for clarity and stronger prototype checking. In Chapter 1, I'll explain in more detail why this is desirable, but for now, just remember that not all of the "standard" functions follow the standard precisely. You'll see that the interface for *memchr* is often written with the character declared as a *char*, not an *int*:

```
void *memchr(const void *pv, unsigned char ch, size_t size);
```

WHAT ARE THOSE GOBBLEDYGOOK NAMES?

By now you've probably flipped through the pages of this book and noticed the many strange-looking variable and function names used in the code. Names like *pch, ppb, and pvResizeBlock* are common.

Although names like *pch* look funny and are hard to pronounce, they are filled with information—once you understand the "Hungarian" naming convention developed by Charles Simonyi in the early 1970s. The premise behind the Hungarian naming convention is that conveying information is far more important in naming your variables than being able to stand up and read your code aloud during a program review.

The details of the simplified Hungarian naming convention I use in this book are pretty easy. For variables of each data type in your program, you use an abbreviation for the type as part of the variable name. There's nothing earth-shattering about that—programmers have long called their characters *c* or *ch*, their bytes *b*, their integers *i*, and so on. The Hungarian convention merely enforces this practice for all data types in a program. For example,

```
char    ch;       /* a plain old character */
byte    b;        /* a byte, which is an unsigned char */
flag    f;        /* flags that are always TRUE or FALSE */
symbol sym;       /* some sort of symbol structure */
```

The convention doesn't specify what the data type abbreviations should be—only that they be used consistently throughout the program.

Pointer variables pose an interesting problem in that they must point to something. The Hungarian naming convention handles this problem by requiring that all pointer variable names start with the letter *p* followed by the abbreviation for the data type that the pointer references. If you were to declare pointers to the data types above, you would have the following names:

```
char    *pch;         /* character pointer */
byte    *pb;          /* byte pointer */
flag    *pf;          /* etc. */
symbol *psym;
```

Pointers to other pointers aren't any different from pointers to regular data types—you still attach a *p* to the front of the data type that's being pointed to. The name for a pointer to a character pointer would be a *p* tacked to the front of a *pch*:

```
char **ppch;          /* pointer to a character pointer */
```

This piling up of data types makes Hungarian difficult to read, but the naming convention allows programmers to append a descriptive word or two—each starting with a capital letter—to the abbreviation for the variable type. Not only does this improve readability, but it also makes it possible to distinguish similarly typed variables from each other. The *strcpy* function, for example, takes two character pointers as arguments, so one possible prototype for the function would be

```
char *strcpy(char *pchTo, char *pchFrom);    /* prototype */
```

This brings up another point. Because the purpose of the Hungarian naming convention is to increase comprehension, the convention puts more emphasis on what the data types represent than on how they are actually declared. The two arguments to *strcpy* are character pointers, but more important, they are pointers to zero-terminated strings. Naming *strcpy*'s arguments as *pch*s would be correct, but using *str*s would be more meaningful:

```
char *strcpy(char *strTo, char *strFrom);        /* prototype */
```

*str*s are still character pointers, but when you see the names, you know they're special character pointers—they point to strings.

Function and array names follow the same convention—they start with the type returned and are followed by a descriptive tag. In formal Hungarian, function names always start with a capital letter, but in this book I have regularized the convention for consistency; there's no difference in capitalization conventions among function names, array names, and variable names. If the standard *malloc* and *realloc* functions were written using Hungarian-style names, they might be prototyped as

```
void *pvNewBlock(size_t size);                   /* prototype */
```

and

```
void *pvResizeBlock(void *pv, size_t sizeNew);  /* prototype */
```

One benefit of using Hungarian names is that they make it easy to decipher pointer expressions. For example, you'll see many pointers to pointers in this book, particularly *ppb*'s

```
*ppb = pbNew;
```

Although this code may look unreadable at first, once you realize that you can cancel *s and *p*s in such expressions, you can easily understand what is going on. If you cancel the * with one *p* in the expression above, you get

```
pb = pbNew;
```

Since the types match—they're both *pb*s—you know that the expression is correct. &s and ->s also cancel with *p*s. Consider these statements:

```
pb = &b;
```

```
b = psym->bLength;
```

If you cancel the *p* and the *&* in the first statement, you get a *byte* assigned to a *byte*, and you know the expression is valid. In the second statement, if you cancel the *p* with the ->, you also get a *byte* assigned to a *byte*: *b = sym.bLength*. This "type calculus," as it is called, makes it easier to tear apart complex pointer expressions.

Although I've left a lot unsaid about the Hungarian naming convention, the basic outline here should be enough for you to follow the code in this book.

Hungary for More?

The simplified form of Hungarian used in this book doesn't do justice to the full-blown version developed by Charles Simonyi. Is *pch[]* an array of *pchs*, or is it a pointer to an array of characters? With the simplified Hungarian I've used you'd have to refer to the declaration to be sure, but the complete Hungarian convention clears up this ambiguity and many others. I chose to use a simplified version of Hungarian because of, well, its simplicity, and because the ambiguous cases never come up in this book. I apologize to Charles Simonyi for presenting only a suggestion of his well-thought-out naming convention.

Hungarian is not for everybody. Some people think it's the best thing since structured programming; others hate Hungarian with a passion. Both camps have their reasons. If Hungarian looks interesting to you and you'd like to find out more about it, you can find a thorough discussion of the convention in Charles Simonyi's doctoral thesis: "Meta-Programming: A Software Production Method" (Stanford University, 1977; Xerox Palo Alto Research Center, 1977).

JUST WHAT IS A BUG?

Before we move on to Chapter 1's hypothetical bug-catching compiler, I should explain a little bit about the kind of "bug" this book is preoccupied with. I know you know what a bug is—I don't need to define "bug" for anybody reading this book. But in this book I make a distinction between two classes of bugs: those you introduce while working on a feature and those that remain in your code after you believe the code is finished.

Many software houses use source code control systems to simplify program development. A programmer checks out a file he or she needs to modify, much the way you would check out a book at the library. The only difference is that the programmer checks out a *copy* of the file, not the file itself. This allows the programmer to implement new features without actually touching the master source files. Once the programmer has finished implementing a feature and is sure that the code is free of bugs, the file is checked back in, and the source code control system updates the master files accordingly.

With this arrangement, it really doesn't matter how many bugs the programmer introduces into the code while implementing new features, provided, of course, that all bugs are fixed before the new code is checked into the master sources.

When I say "bug" in this book, I mean bugs that make it into the master sources, where they hurt the product and affect the customer. I don't expect programmers to write flawless code every time they sit at the keyboard, but I do believe that it's possible to keep bugs out of the master sources.

The guidelines and techniques in the following chapters describe how to write such bug-free code.

1

A HYPOTHETICAL COMPILER

Think about this for a moment: How buggy would your programs be if the compiler could pinpoint every problem in your code? I'm not just talking about syntax errors, but about every problem, no matter how obscure.

Suppose you had an off-by-one bug and the compiler could somehow detect it and give you an error like this one:

```
->line 23:  while (i <= j)
                     ^^
  Off-by-one error: This should be '<'
```

Or what if it could find mistakes in your algorithms:

```
->line 42:  int itoa(int i, char *str)
                ^^^^
  Algorithm error: itoa fails when i is -32768
```

Or suppose it could tell you when you're passing bad arguments:

```
->line 318:   strCopy = memcpy(malloc(length), str, length);
                             ^^^^^^
   Invalid argument: memcpy fails when malloc returns NULL
```

OK, so maybe this is a bit farfetched, but if the compiler could do this, how easy do you think it would be to write bug-free programs? Wouldn't it be trivial—at least compared to what programmers normally go through?

If you were to aim a spy satellite camera at a typical software house, you'd find programmers hunched over their keyboards tracking down reported bugs. Elsewhere, you might find testers attacking the latest internal release, bombarding it with inputs to catch new bugs. You might even find testers checking to be sure that none of the old bugs have sneaked back into the code. If you think searching for bugs this way takes a lot of effort compared to using the hypothetical compiler to catch errors, you're right; it also requires a lot of luck.

Luck?

Yes, luck. When a tester finds a bug, isn't it because he or she happened to notice that some number was wrong, or that a feature didn't behave as expected, or that the program crashed? Take another look at the hypothetical compiler errors. Would a tester see the off-by-one bug if the program appeared to work despite the problem? What about the other two errors?

It may sound scary, but testers hurl inputs at programs and hope that lurking bugs will somehow show themselves. "Yeah, but our testers are more sophisticated than that. They use code coverage tools, automated test suites, random monkey programs, display snapshots, and a bunch of other stuff." That may be true, but look at what those tools do. Coverage analysis tells testers what parts of your program aren't being tested; the testers use that information to devise new inputs to your program. And the other tools are automated forms of the "pound and observe" strategy.

Don't misunderstand me, I'm not saying that what testers do is wrong. I'm saying that it's hard to test a program as a black box because all a tester can do is stuff things into the program and watch what pops out. It's like trying to determine whether somebody is insane. You ask questions; you listen to answers; and you make a judgment call. In the end, you're never really sure because you don't know what's going on inside the other person's head. You always wonder, "Did I ask enough questions? Did I ask the *right* questions?"

Don't rely on black-box testing. Try to mimic that hypothetical compiler. Eliminate luck and take every opportunity to catch bugs automatically.

WATCH YOUR LANGUAGE

When was the last time you read an advertisement for a leading word processor? If the folks on Madison Avenue wrote it, it probably sounded something like this: "Whether you're writing a note to Johnny's teacher or working on the next Great American Novel, WordSmasher can handle it. Effortlessly. And to catch typing mistakes that creep into your masterpiece, there's a mind-boggling 233,000-word spelling dictionary—*51,000* more words than in the nearest competitor's. So run down to your dealer and pick up a copy. WordSmasher. The most revolutionary writing tool since the ballpoint pen."

As users, we've been trained by constant marketing propaganda to believe that the bigger the spelling dictionary, the better. But that isn't true. You can find the words *em*, *abel*, and *si* in any paperback dictionary, but do you really want your spelling checker to allow those words when *me*, *able*, and *is* are so common? If you see *suing* in something I write, the odds are astronomical that I meant *using*. It doesn't matter that *suing* is a real word; in my writing, it's an error.

Fortunately, high-quality spelling checkers will let you delete troublesome words like *em* from their dictionaries so that you can flag an otherwise legal word as an error. Good compilers are no different—they will let you flag otherwise legal C idioms as errors because the idioms are so often used in a mistaken way. Such a compiler could detect the misplaced semicolon in the *while* loop below:

```
/* memcpy -- copy a nonoverlapping memory block. */

void *memcpy(void *pvTo, void *pvFrom, size_t size)
{
    byte *pbTo   = (byte *)pvTo;
    byte *pbFrom = (byte *)pvFrom;

    while (size-- > 0);
        *pbTo++ = *pbFrom++;

    return (pvTo);
}
```

You can tell from the indentation that the semicolon is a mistake, but what the compiler sees is a *while* statement with a null body, and that's perfectly legal. Now there are times that you want null statements and times that you don't. To catch the unwanted null statements, compilers often provide an optional warning that, if you use it, will automatically alert you to bugs like this one. And for those times when you intend to use a null statement, you can, but you must make it explicit and use *NULL*:

```
char *strcpy(char *pchTo, char *pchFrom)
{
    char *pchStart = pchTo;

    while (*pchTo++ = *pchFrom++)
        NULL;

    return (pchStart);
}
```

This works because *NULL* is a legal C expression. Even better, the compiler won't generate any code for a *NULL* statement because it is just a constant. The result: The compiler allows explicit *NULL* statements but flags unintentional null statements as errors, automatically. Disallowing one kind of null statement is not that different from deleting the word *zeros* from your spelling dictionary because you want to be consistent about using the alternative spelling *zeroes*.

Another common problem is the unintentional assignment. C is flexible and lets you use assignments anywhere you can write an expression, but if you aren't careful, this extra flexibility can trip you up. Take a look at this common bug:

```
if (ch = '\t')
    ExpandTab();
```

Although it's clear that the code is supposed to compare the tab character to *ch*, it's actually assigning the character to *ch*. And of course the compiler won't generate an error because the code is legal C.

Some compilers help you catch this bug by letting you disable simple assignments in && and *||* expressions and also in the control expressions of the *if, for,* and *while* constructs. The idea behind this feature is that if a programmer is going to accidentally type = instead of ==, the odds are good that it's going to be in one of these five spots.

The option doesn't stop you from making assignments, but to circumvent the warning you must explicitly compare the result against another value, usually *0* or the null character. So, going back to the *strcpy* example above, instead of writing the loop as

```
while (*pchTo++ = *pchFrom++)
    NULL;
```

which would generate a warning, you would write:

```
while ((*pchTo++ = *pchFrom++) != '\0')
    NULL;
```

Best of all, modern commercial-grade compilers won't generate extra code for the comparison because it is redundant and can be optimized away. You can count on the optimization for compilers that have this optional warning. Again, the idea is to disallow risky, though legal, usage when there is a safer alternative.

Another class of bugs falls into the category of "argument bugs." Years ago, when I was still learning C, I used to call *fputc* this way:

```
fprintf(stderr, "Unable to open file %s.\n", filename);
  :
  :
  :
fputc(stderr, '\n');
```

That might look OK, but the arguments to *fputc* are in the wrong order. For some reason, I had "learned" that the stream pointer (*stderr*) was always the first argument to any of the stream functions. That isn't true, so I often passed garbage to those routines. Fortunately, ANSI C provides an automatic compile-time method to catch these bugs: function prototypes.

Because the ANSI standard requires that all library functions have prototypes, you can find the prototype for *fputc* in the *stdio.h* header file. It should look something like this:

```
int fputc(int c, FILE *stream);
```

If you include *stdio.h* in a file and then call *fputc*, the compiler will compare each argument you pass with what is expected, and if the types differ, it will generate an error. In my case, since I was passing a *FILE ** argument in place of an *int*, the prototype would have automatically caught my early *fputc* bugs.

ANSI C may require prototypes for standard functions, but it does not require them for functions that you or I might write; they're strictly optional. If you want to detect calling bugs in your own code, you must create your own prototypes and keep them up to date.

Now I've heard programmers complain about having to maintain prototypes, particularly when they're moving a project from traditional C to ANSI C. The complaint is somewhat justified, but look at it this way: If you don't use prototypes, you have to rely on conventional testing methods and hope you catch any calling bugs in your code. You have to ask yourself which is more important, saving yourself some maintenance effort, or being able to catch bugs the moment you compile your code. If you're not sure, consider that using prototypes can result in better code generation. The reason: The ANSI standard permits compilers to make optimizations based on prototype information.

Strengthen Your Prototypes

Unfortunately, prototypes won't alert you to calling bugs where you have swapped two arguments of the same type. For instance, if the *memchr* function had this prototype,

```
void *memchr(const void *pv, int ch, int size);
```

you could swap the character and size arguments and the compiler wouldn't issue a warning. But by using more accurate types in your interfaces and prototypes, you can strengthen the error checking that prototypes provide. For example, the prototype below would alert you to a bug if you had reversed the character and size arguments:

```
void *memchr(const void *pv, unsigned char ch, size_t size);
```

The drawback to using more accurate types is that you must often cast your arguments to the correct type—even if they are in the correct order—to silence noncritical type-mismatch warnings.

In traditional C, the compiler doesn't have much information about functions outside the file it is currently compiling, yet it must generate calls to those functions, and the calls obviously must work. Compiler writers have solved this problem by using a normalized calling convention, which works, but it often means that the compiler must generate extra code to adhere to the convention. But if you use the "require prototypes for all functions" compiler warning option, the compiler can use whatever calling convention it deems most efficient since it knows the argument lists for every function in the program.

The null statement alert, erroneous assignment warning, and prototype checks are just a few of the options found in many C compilers; often there are more. The key point of optional compiler warnings is that they alert you to possible bugs, in much the way the spelling checker alerts you to possible misspellings.

Peter Lynch, arguably the best mutual fund manager of the 1980s, once said that the difference between investors and gamblers is that investors take every opportunity, no matter how small, to tilt the advantage their way; gamblers, in his view, rely on luck. Apply that concept to your programming and enable every optional compiler warning; view the warnings as a risk-free, high-return investment in your program. Don't ask, "Should I enable this warning?" Instead ask, "Why shouldn't I enable it?" Turn on every warning unless you have an excellent reason not to.

———◆———

Enable all optional compiler warnings.

———◆———

lint—It's Not That Bad

A more thorough method of detecting bugs with almost no effort is to use *lint*. Originally, *lint* was a tool that scanned C source files and reported warnings for any code that didn't look portable. But today, most *lint* utilities are much more thorough and will flag not only portability problems but also any C idioms that, while portable and perfectly legal, are likely to be wrong. The unintentional null statement, erroneous assignment, and calling bugs of the previous section fall into this category.

Unfortunately, many programmers still view *lint* as a portability checker that spews out numerous warnings they care nothing about. The tool has a reputation for not being worth the trouble. If you're one of the programmers who feel that way about *lint,* maybe you should reevaluate your opinion. After all, which tool more thoroughly approximates the hypothetical compiler I talked about earlier: your real compiler or *lint*?

Actually, once you have put your sources into *lint*-free shape, keeping them *lint*-free is simple—you simply run *lint* over your changes before you merge them into the master sources. In a week or two, you'll be writing *lint*-free code without giving it much thought. When you reach that point, you gain all the advantages that *lint* provides, without all the headaches.

———◆———

Use lint *to catch bugs that your compiler may miss.*

———◆———

BUT MY CHANGES WERE TRIVIAL

I was having lunch with one of the technical reviewers for this book, and he asked me if I was going to include a section on unit tests. I told him no because while unit tests are related to writing bug-free code, they really fall into a different category: how to write tests for your code.

He said, "No, you misunderstand. I mean are you going to point out that programmers should actually run their unit tests before merging their changes into the master sources? One of the programmers on my team just let a bug slip into our master sources because he didn't run the unit test after making his changes."

That was surprising because most project leads at Microsoft expect programmers to run their unit tests before merging in their changes.

"Did you ask him why he didn't run the test?" I said.

My friend looked up from his lunch. "He said that he didn't write any new code—he just moved existing code around. He said he didn't think he needed to run the test."

The story reminded me of a programmer who once didn't even bother to compile one of his changes before merging the code into the master sources. I found out about it, of course, because I couldn't compile the project without getting an error. When I asked the programmer how he could miss a compiler error, he said, "The change was so trivial, I didn't think I could make a mistake."

Neither of these bugs should have made it into the master sources because both could have been caught automatically, with almost no effort. Why do programmers make such mistakes? Mainly it's because they get overconfident of their ability to write correct code.

Sometimes it may seem that you can skip steps designed to keep bugs out of your code, but any time you take a shortcut, you're asking for trouble. I doubt that there are many programmers who would "finish" a feature without even compiling the code—I know of just that one incident—but the temptation to bypass unit tests is stronger, especially for simple changes.

If you find yourself about to bypass a step that could easily detect bugs for you, stop yourself and instead make use of every tool you have at your disposal. Unit tests are meant to catch bugs, but they can't do their job if you don't run them.

———◆———

If you have unit tests, use them.

———◆———

NO MORE EGG ROLLS

How many programmers do you know who prefer to spend their time tracking down and fixing bugs instead of writing new code? I'm sure there are such programmers, but I've never met one. The programmers I know would give up takeout Chinese food for life if you promised them that they'd never have to track down another bug.

As you write code, keep that hypothetical compiler in mind and take advantage of every opportunity to catch bugs automatically or with little effort. Think about compiler errors, *lint* errors, and unit test failures. How much skill does it take to find such errors? Almost none. How many bugs would make it into your product if none of the bugs required much skill or effort to detect?

If you want to find bugs quickly and easily, use those features of your tools that tell you where the bugs are. The sooner you know where the bugs are, the sooner you can fix them and move on to more interesting work.

QUICK REVIEW

◆ The best way to eliminate bugs in your code is to find them as early and as easily as possible. Look for ways to catch bugs automatically, with minimal effort.

◆ Strive to reduce the amount of programmer skill necessary to catch bugs. Optional compiler or *lint* warnings don't require any programmer skills to catch bugs.

THINGS TO THINK ABOUT

1. Suppose you're using the compiler option to disable assignments in *while* conditions. Why would that catch the precedence bug in the code below?

```
while (ch=getchar() != EOF)
    ⋮
```

2. You saw how you could use the compiler to catch unintentional null and assignment statements. Suggest ways that the compiler could optionally warn of the common problems below. How would you bypass the warnings?

    a. *if (flight == 063)* where you think you're testing for Flight 63 when in fact, because the leading *0* forces *063* to be an octal number, you're testing for Flight 51.

    b. *if (pb != NULL & *pb != 0xFF)* where you accidentally typed *&* instead of *&&*, causing **pb != 0xFF* to be executed even if *pb* is *NULL*.

    c. *quot = numer/*pdenom;* where in spite of your intentions the */** is interpreted as the start of a comment.

    d. *word = bHigh<<8 + bLow;* which, because of precedence rules, is interpreted as *word = bHigh<<(8 + bLow);* despite your intentions.

3. How could the compiler automatically alert you to possible "dangling-*else*" bugs? How would you silence the warning?

4.   Take another look at this coding error:

```
if (ch = '\t')
    ExpandTab();
```

Instead of disabling simple assignments in *if* statements, you could use another popular way of catching this bug. You could reverse the operands of the assignment operator:

```
if ('\t' = ch)
    ExpandTab();
```

That way, if you type = instead of ==, the compiler will squawk because you can't assign something to a constant. How thorough is this solution? Why is this approach not as automatic as the compiler switch?

5.   The C preprocessor can also cause unexpected results. For example, the *UINT_MAX* macro is defined in *limits.h*, but if you forget to include the header file, the *#if* directive below will quietly fail — the preprocessor will replace the undefined *UINT_MAX* with *0*, and the test will incorrectly fail:

```
    :
    :
#if UINT_MAX > 65535u
        :
        :
#endif
```

How could the preprocessor alert you to this bug?

PROJECT: To ease the task of maintaining prototypes, some compilers will automatically generate prototypes for you as they compile your program. If your compiler doesn't have such an option, write a utility to do this for you. How would having a standard coding convention make it easier to write such a utility?

PROJECT: If your compiler doesn't already support the warnings discussed in this chapter (including the exercises), encourage your compiler vendor to support them. Also urge your compiler vendor to provide a method of selectively enabling or disabling specific warnings in addition to letting you enable or disable classes of errors. Why would this be desirable?

2

ASSERT YOURSELF

Using the compiler to catch bugs automatically is great, but I'll bet that if you reviewed the outstanding bugs in your project, you'd find that the compiler would catch just a small percentage of them. What's more, I'll bet that if you isolated each bug, you'd find that the code would work correctly most of the time.

Remember this code from Chapter 1?

```
strCopy = memcpy(malloc(length), str, length);
```

This code will work in every case except the one in which *malloc* fails. When that happens, *malloc* will pass a *NULL* pointer to *memcpy*, and *memcpy* can't handle that. If you're lucky, you'll crash and see the bug long before you ship; if you're not, one of your customers surely will.

The compiler can't catch this bug or any like it. Nor can the compiler catch bugs in your algorithms, verify your assumptions, or in general check the validity of data being passed around.

Finding these kinds of bugs is hard. It takes a skilled programmer or tester to consistently root them out. But finding these kinds of bugs automatically is easy, if you know how.

A TALE OF TWO VERSIONS

Let's jump right in and see how you could catch the *memcpy* bug above. The easiest solution is to have *memcpy* check for *NULL* pointers and abort with an error message if it finds one. Here's how:

```
/* memcpy -- copy a nonoverlapping memory block. */

void *memcpy(void *pvTo, void *pvFrom, size_t size)
{
    byte *pbTo   = (byte *)pvTo;
    byte *pbFrom = (byte *)pvFrom;

    if (pvTo == NULL  ||  pvFrom == NULL)
    {
        fprintf(stderr, "Bad args in memcpy\n");
        abort();
    }

    while (size-- > 0)
        *pbTo++ = *pbFrom++;

    return (pvTo);
}
```

Nobody is going to slip a *NULL* pointer past this function. The only problem is that the tests double the size of the code and slow it down. If you're thinking this is a case in which the cure is worse than the disease, I think you're right; the tests aren't practical. That's where the C preprocessor comes in handy.

What if you kept two versions of your program? One fast and sleek that you ship, and the other slow and fat because it contains the extra checks. You would maintain both versions in the same sources and use the C preprocessor to conditionally include or exclude the checks.

For example, you might compile the *NULL* pointer tests only when *DEBUG* is defined:

```
void *memcpy(void *pvTo, void *pvFrom, size_t size)
{
    byte *pbTo   = (byte *)pvTo;
    byte *pbFrom = (byte *)pvFrom;

    #ifdef DEBUG
        if (pvTo == NULL  ||  pvFrom == NULL)
        {
            fprintf(stderr, "Bad args in memcpy\n");
            abort();
        }
    #endif

    while (size-- > 0)
        *pbTo++ = *pbFrom++;

    return (pvTo);
}
```

The idea is to maintain both debug and nondebug (that is, ship) versions of your program. While writing code, you compile the debug version and use it to catch bugs automatically as you add features. Later, when you've finished, you compile a ship version, shrink-wrap it, and send it to dealers.

Of course, you wouldn't really want to wait until the last minute to run the code you intend to ship—that would be silly. But throughout development, you should exercise the debug version, mainly because, as we'll see in this chapter and the next, running the debug version can drastically reduce the time required to develop the program. Imagine how robust your application would be if every function did some minimal error checking, testing for conditions that should never happen.

The trick, of course, is to ensure that the debug code is strictly extra code that isn't necessary in the final product. There are some gotchas, but I'll cover them as they arise.

———◆———

Maintain both ship and debug
versions of your program.

———◆———

INTRODUCING ASSERT

Let's be honest here. The debug code I put in *memcpy* looks awful and over-whelms the function. I don't know many programmers who would stand still for that, even if it were for a good cause. That's why some clever pro-grammer decided to hide all that debug code in a macro named *assert*, which is defined in the ANSI *assert.h* header file.

assert is nothing more than a repackaged form of the *#ifdef* code we saw before, but when you use the macro, it takes one line instead of seven:

```
void *memcpy(void *pvTo, void *pvFrom, size_t size)
{
    byte *pbTo   = (byte *)pvTo;
    byte *pbFrom = (byte *)pvFrom;

    assert(pvTo != NULL  &&  pvFrom != NULL);

    while (size-- > 0)
        *pbTo++ = *pbFrom++;

    return (pvTo);
}
```

assert is a debug-only macro that aborts execution if its argument is false. You can see in the code above that if either pointer is null, the *assert* will fire.

assert is not a macro you just throw together; you must define it care-fully so that it won't cause important differences between the ship and de-bug versions of your program. *assert* should not disturb memory, initialize data that would otherwise be uninitialized, or cause any other side effects. You want your debug program to behave exactly like the ship version. That's why *assert* is a macro and not a function; if it were a function, calling it could cause unexpected memory or code swapping. Remember, the pro-grammers who use *assert* view it as a harmless test that they can safely use no matter what state the system is in.

You should also be aware that once programmers learn to use asser-tions, they often redefine the *assert* macro. For instance, instead of having *assert* abort execution when an error occurs, programmers sometimes rede-fine *assert* so that the macro hops into a debugger at the point of the error. Some versions of *assert* even give you the choice of continuing the pro-gram's execution as though the failure never happened.

If you decide to define your own version of the assertion macro, consider using a name other than *assert* so that you leave the standard macro untouched. In this book, I'll be using a nonstandard assertion macro, so I've given it the name *ASSERT* to make it stand out in code. The major difference between the *assert* and *ASSERT* macros is that *assert* is an expression that you can use freely in your code, but *ASSERT* is a statement, which restricts its use. With *assert* you can write

```
if (assert(p != NULL), p->foo != bar)
    :
    :
```

but if you try that with *ASSERT*, you'll get a syntax error. That's intentional. Unless you plan to use assertions in expression contexts, you should define *ASSERT* as a statement so that the compiler will generate an error if you mistakenly use it in an expression. Remember, every bit helps in the war against bugs. Why allow flexibility that you don't use?

Here is one way you could define the *ASSERT* macro:

```
#ifdef DEBUG

    void _Assert(char *, unsigned);    /* prototype */

    #define ASSERT(f)          \
        if (f)                 \
            NULL;              \
        else                   \
            _Assert(__FILE__, __LINE__)

#else

    #define ASSERT(f)    NULL

#endif
```

You can see that if *DEBUG* is defined, *ASSERT* will expand to an *if* statement. The *NULL* statement in the *if* may seem strange, but you need both the *if* and the *else* statements to prevent unexpected dangling-*if* problems. And you might think that you need a final semicolon after the closing *)* in the call to *_Assert*, but you don't because you provide the final semicolon when you use *ASSERT*:

```
ASSERT(pvTo != NULL  &&  pvFrom != NULL);
```

When *ASSERT* fails, it calls *_Assert* with the file name and line number provided by the preprocessor through the *_FILE_* and *_LINE_* macros. *_Assert* prints an error message to *stderr* and then aborts:

```
void _Assert(char *strFile, unsigned uLine)
{
    fflush(stdout);
    fprintf(stderr, "\nAssertion failed: %s, line %u\n",
            strFile, uLine);
    fflush(stderr);
    abort();
}
```

You need the calls to *fflush* to write out any buffered output before you execute *abort*. You want to *fflush stdout* before flushing *stderr* in case they both point to the same device. This ensures that *fprintf* will display the error message only after all other output to *stdout*.

Now if you called *memcpy* with a *NULL* pointer, *ASSERT* would catch the bug and display something like

```
Assertion failed: string.c, line 153
```

This shows another difference between *assert* and *ASSERT*. The standard macro would display a message like the one above, but it would also display the test that failed. For example, the *assert* that comes with one compiler I normally use would display this message:

```
Assertion failed: pvTo != NULL  &&  pvFrom != NULL
File string.c, line 153
```

The only problem with including the expression is that every time you use *assert* it generates a textual representation of the condition for *_Assert* to print. And the question is, where does the compiler store the string? Macintosh, MS-DOS, and Windows compilers normally store strings in the global data area, but on a Macintosh, that typically limits you to a total of 32K for data. In MS-DOS and Windows, you have 64K. In large programs such as Microsoft Word and Microsoft Excel, assertion strings can gobble up that memory in no time.

There are work-arounds, but the easiest one is to omit the expression string in the error message. After all, you'll know what the problem is once you look at line 153 of *string.c,* and you'll see it in context.

If you want see how to define a standard *assert*, look at the *assert.h* file included with your system. The Rationale section of the ANSI standard also talks about *assert* and shows one possible implementation. P. J. Plauger also discusses the subtleties of implementing the standard *assert* in his book *The Standard C Library* (Prentice Hall, 1992).

Regardless of how you ultimately define your assertion macro, use it to validate the arguments passed to your functions. If you check data at every entry point, bugs won't live long before getting noticed. The best part is that you will catch these bugs automatically, as they occur.

———◆———

Use assertions to validate function arguments.

———◆———

"Undefined" Means "Steer Clear"

If you were to stop and read the ANSI C definition for the *memcpy* routine, you would see that the very last line reads, "If copying takes place between objects that overlap, the behavior is undefined." Other books describe this uncertainty somewhat differently. For example, in *Standard C* (Microsoft Press, 1989), P. J. Plauger and Jim Brodie say, "The elements of the arrays can be accessed and stored in any order."

In short, these books say that if you rely on *memcpy* to behave in a particular way when you call it with overlapping blocks, you're making an assumption about behavior that can vary from one compiler to the next or even between releases of the same compiler.

I'm sure there are programmers who deliberately exploit undefined behavior, but I think most programmers intelligently avoid doing this. Those who don't should learn to. Most programmers view undefined behavior as illegal behavior, and that's where assertions come in handy. If you called *memcpy* when you meant to call *memmove*, wouldn't you want to know about it?

You can beef up *memcpy* by adding an assertion to verify that the two blocks never overlap:

```
/* memcpy -- copy a nonoverlapping memory block. */

void *memcpy(void *pvTo, void *pvFrom, size_t size)
{
```

(continued)

```
byte *pbTo   = (byte *)pvTo;
byte *pbFrom = (byte *)pvFrom;

ASSERT(pvTo != NULL  &&  pvFrom != NULL);
ASSERT(pbTo >= pbFrom+size  ||  pbFrom >= pbTo+size);

while (size-- > 0)
    *pbTo++ = *pbFrom++;

return (pvTo);
}
```

How that one-line overlap check works may not be obvious, but it's easy to figure out if you think of the two blocks of memory as cars in line at a stop light. There you know that the cars don't overlap if the back bumper of one car is in front of the front bumper of the other car. The check implements that idea: *pbTo* and *pbFrom* are the back bumpers of the two blocks, and *pbTo+size* and *pbFrom+size* are the spots just in front of the front bumpers of the blocks. That's all there is to it.

Don't Let This Happen to You

In late 1988, the release date for one of Microsoft's cash-cows, Word for MS-DOS, slipped three months and noticeably affected the bottom line of the company. (That's the problem with temperamental cows.) The frustrating aspect of the slip was that for three months the Word team had thought they were going to ship "any day now."

The Word group was relying on a key component from an application tools group. The tools group kept telling the Word group that the code was almost done, and the people in the tools group truly believed what they were saying. They didn't realize that their code was filled with bugs.

One notable difference between the Word code and the code from the tools group was that the Word code was (and is) loaded with assertions and debug code. The tools group used almost no assertions in their code, so the tools programmers had no good way to determine how buggy their code actually was. Bugs just kept trickling in, bugs that could have been detected months earlier if assertions had been used.

And by the way, if you don't see why all this overlapping stuff is important, just think about the case in which *pbTo* is equal to *pbFrom+1* and you move at least 2 bytes—*memcpy* won't work correctly.

So in the future, stop and review your code for undefined behavior. If you find undefined behavior, either remove it from the design or include assertions to notify programmers when they use undefined behavior.

Dealing with undefined behavior is particularly important if you provide code libraries (or operating systems) to other programmers. If you have ever developed such libraries, you know that other programmers will make use of all sorts of undefined behavior as they "try things" to get the result they want. The consequences really show up when you release a new and improved library. Invariably, you find that while your library is 100 percent compatible with the last version, half the applications crash when they try to use it. The reason: The new library is not 100 percent compatible with the old "undefined behavior."

◆————

Strip undefined behavior from your code, or use assertions to catch illegal uses of undefined behavior.

————◆

THE CODE THAT CRIED "DANGER"

While we're on the subject, I'd like to talk some more about that *memcpy* overlap assertion for a moment. Here it is again:

```
ASSERT(pbTo >= pbFrom+size  !!  pbFrom >= pbTo+size);
```

Suppose you called *memcpy* and the assertion above failed. When you looked it up, would you know what was wrong if you'd never seen an overlap check before? I know I probably wouldn't. But that's not to say that the code is tricky or unclear—it is, after all, a straightforward overlap check. But being straightforward and being obvious are not the same thing.

Take my word for it, there are few things more frustrating than to track an assertion to somebody else's code and then have no idea why the assertion landed there. Instead of fixing the problem, you waste time just trying to figure out what the problem is. That's not all. Programmers do, on occasion, write buggy assertions, but it's hard to tell whether you should fix the program or fix the assertion if you can't figure out what the assertion is checking for.

Fortunately, it's easy to solve this problem—just add comments to assertions that don't make their purposes evident. I know this sounds obvious, but it's amazing how rarely programmers do this. They go to all the trouble to protect you from danger, but then they don't tell you what the danger is. It's as if you were walking through the woods and saw a big red DANGER sign nailed to a tree. But *what* danger? Falling trees? Abandoned mine shafts? Bigfoot? Unless you tell people what the danger is (or unless it's obvious), you're not helping them. People in the woods will ignore the

Not for Errors

When programmers start using assertions, they sometimes use them incorrectly to detect real errors, not illegal conditions. For example, look at the assertions in this *strdup* function:

```
/* strdup -- allocate a duplicate of a string. */

char *strdup(char *str)
{
    char *strNew;

    ASSERT(str != NULL);

    strNew = (char *)malloc(strlen(str)+1);
    ASSERT(strNew != NULL);
    strcpy(strNew, str);

    return (strNew);
}
```

In this code, the first assertion is a correct use because it tests for an illegal condition that should never occur if the program is working correctly. The second assertion is quite different—it is testing for an error condition that definitely will show up in the final product and that must be handled. This assertion is incorrect and should be replaced with code to handle the error condition.

sign. Similarly, programmers will ignore any assertions they don't understand—they'll assume that the assertions are wrong and rip them out. So
add comments to unclear assertions.

Even better, if the bug has a probable solution, note that. When a programmer calls *memcpy* with overlapping blocks, there's a good chance that
this is exactly what he or she wants to do, unaware of the overlap restriction. A comment can point out that *memmove* should be used for overlapping blocks:

```
/* Blocks overlap? Use memmove. */
ASSERT(pbTo >= pbFrom+size  ||  pbFrom >= pbTo+size);
```

You don't need to write tomes. One approach is to use a short, well-
thought-out question. That can be far more informative than an entire para-
graph that methodically explains every detail. But be careful—don't
suggest a solution unless you're sure it will help other programmers. You
don't want your comments to mislead people.

———◆———

Don't waste people's time. Document
unclear assertions.

———◆———

ARE YOU MAKING ASSUMPTIONS AGAIN?

Sometimes when you write code, you need to make assumptions about the
target environment, but not always. For example, the *memset* routine below
makes no assumptions about the target environment and should work with
any ANSI C compiler:

```
/* memset -- fill memory with a "byte" value. */

void *memset(void *pv, byte b, size_t size)
{
    byte *pb = (byte *)pv;

    while (size-- > 0)
        *pb++ = b;

    return (pv);
}
```

But for many environments, you can write a faster *memset* routine by
packing a larger data type with the fill value and then using the packed
value to fill memory using fewer stores. For example, on the 68000, the
memset routine below could fill up to four times faster than the portable version on the previous page:

```
/*  longfill -- fill memory with a "long" value. Returns a
 *  pointer to the first long value after the last long
 *  that is filled.
 */
long *longfill(long *pl, long l, size_t size);   /* prototype */


void *memset(void *pv, byte b, size_t size)
{
    byte *pb = (byte *)pv;

    if (size >= sizeThreshold)
    {
        unsigned long l;

        l = (b << 8) | b;    /* Pack a long with 4 bytes. */
        l = (l << 16) | l;

        pb = (byte *)longfill((long *)pb, l, size / 4);
        size = size % 4;
    }

    while (size-- > 0)
        *pb++ = b;

    return (pv);
}
```

The routine above is fairly straightforward, except possibly for the test
against *sizeThreshold*. If it's not obvious why this test is desirable, consider
that it takes time to pack a *long* with four copies of a *byte*. There is also some
overhead in calling the *longfill* function. The test against *sizeThreshold* ensures that *memset* won't fill using *longs* unless doing so would be faster than
not doing so, even accounting for the extra overhead.

The only problem with this new version of *memset* is that it makes a
number of assumptions about the compiler and the operating system. The
code explicitly assumes that *longs* use 4 bytes of memory and that bytes are
8 bits wide. These assumptions are true for many computers, and they're

almost universally true (right now) for microcomputers. Still, that doesn't mean you should blithely let the code operate on its assumptions, because if there's one thing you can count on, it's that what is true today will probably not be true a few years from now.

Some programmers would "improve" the routine by writing it so that it's more portable:

```
void *memset(void *pv, byte b, size_t size)
{
    byte *pb = (byte *)pv;

    if (size >= sizeThreshold)
    {
        unsigned long l;
        size_t sizeLong;

        l = 0;
        for (sizeLong = sizeof(long); sizeLong-- > 0; NULL)
            l = (l << CHAR_BIT) | b;

        pb = (byte *)longfill((long *)pb, l,  size / sizeof(long));
        size = size % sizeof(long);
    }

    while (size-- > 0)
        *pb++ = b;

    return (pv);
}
```

This code may look more portable since it makes heavy use of the *sizeof* operator, but looks don't mean anything; you would still have to review the code if you moved it to a new environment. If you tried the code on a Macintosh Plus, or on any other 68000-based computer, the program would crash if *pv* initially pointed to an odd address. That's because *byte ** and *long ** are not convertible types on the 68000—you can't store a *long* at an odd address without getting a hardware crash.

So what should you do?

In this case, you simply shouldn't try to write *memset* as a portable function, but should instead accept that it is nonportable and protect yourself against change. For the 68000, you can avoid the odd-aligned problem by *byte*-filling until you're even-aligned, and only then switch to the *long*-fill. And although being even-aligned is sufficient, you will get even better performance on the newer 68020-, 68030-, and 68040-based Macintoshes if the *long*-fills are aligned on 4-byte boundaries. As for the other assumptions, you can verify them using assertions and conditional compilation:

```
void *memset(void *pv, byte b, size_t size)
{
    byte *pb = (byte *)pv;

    #ifdef MC680x0
    if (size >= sizeThreshold)
    {
        unsigned long l;

        ASSERT(sizeof(long) == 4  &&  CHAR_BIT == 8);
        ASSERT(sizeThreshold >= 3);

        /* byte-fill until long aligned. */
        while (((unsigned long)pb & 3) != 0)
        {
            *pb++ = b;
            size--;
        }

        /* Now pack a long and long-fill the rest. */
        l = (b << 8) | b;
        l = (l << 16) | l;

        pb = (byte *)longfill((long *)pb, l,  size / sizeof(long));
        size = size % sizeof(long);
    }
    #endif  /* MC680x0 */

    while (size-- > 0)
        *pb++ = b;

    return (pv);
}
```

As you can see, I've bracketed the machine-specific code with the *MC680x0* preprocessor definition. Not only will this preprocessor definition keep the nonportable code from being accidentally used on a different target, but by searching for every occurrence of *MC680x0*, you can isolate all target-specific code.

I've also added a straightforward assertion to verify that *long*s use 4 bytes of memory, and that *byte*s are 8 bits wide. These assumptions aren't likely to change, but you never know.

Finally, I've added a loop to align *pb* before the call to *longfill,* and since the loop can execute up to three times regardless of the value of *size,* I've also added an assertion to check that *sizeThreshold* is at least 3. (It should be higher, but it must be at least 3, or the code won't work.)

With these changes, the routine is explicitly marked nonportable, and all the assumptions have been eliminated or verified with an assertion. These measures make the function much less likely to be used incorrectly.

———◆———

Either remove implicit assumptions, or
assert that they are valid.

———◆———

Owning the Compiler Is Not Enough

Some applications groups at Microsoft are now finding that they have to review and clean up their code because so much of it is littered with things like *+2* instead of *+sizeof(int),* the comparison of unsigned values to *0xFFFF* instead of to something like *UINT_MAX,* and the use of *int* in data structures when they really meant to use a 16-bit data type.

It may seem to you that the original programmers were being sloppy, but they thought they had good reason for thinking they could safely use *+2* instead of *+sizeof(int).* Microsoft writes its own compilers, and that gave programmers a false sense of security. As one programmer put it a couple of years ago, "The compiler group would never change something that would break all of our code."

That programmer was wrong.

The compiler group changed the size of *int*s (and a number of other things) to generate faster and smaller code for Intel's 80386 and newer processors. The compiler group didn't want to break internal code, but it was far more important for them to remain competitive in the marketplace. After all, it wasn't their fault that some Microsoft programmers made erroneous assumptions.

CAN THE IMPOSSIBLE HAPPEN?

The inputs to a function don't always come in as formal parameters. Sometimes you get only a pointer to the inputs. Take a look at this simple decompression routine:

```
byte *pbExpand(byte *pbFrom, byte *pbTo, size_t sizeFrom)
{
    byte    b, *pbEnd;
    size_t size;

    pbEnd = pbFrom+sizeFrom; /* Point just beyond end of buffer. */
    while (pbFrom < pbEnd)
    {
        b = *pbFrom++;

        if (b == bRepeatCode)
        {
            /* Store "size" copies of "b" at pbTo. */
            b = *pbFrom++;
            size = (size_t)*pbFrom++;

            while (size-- > 0)
                *pbTo++ = b;
        }
        else
            *pbTo++ = b;
    }

    return (pbTo);
}
```

This code copies one data buffer to another, but in the process it looks for packets of compressed characters. If it finds the special byte *bRepeatCode* in the data, it knows that the next 2 bytes are a character to repeat and the number of times to repeat it. Although it's simplistic, you could use the routine in something like a programmer's editor, in which text often has many consecutive tab or space characters for indentation.

To make *pbExpand* more robust, you could assert that *pbFrom*, *pbTo*, and *sizeFrom* are valid on entry, but you can do more than that. You can validate the buffer data as well.

It always takes 3 bytes to encode a run, so the compression routine never packs just two consecutive characters; and while it could pack three, there's no real benefit in that. It strictly packs runs of four or more characters.

There is one exception. If the original data contains *bRepeatCode,* it has to be specially handled so that when *pbExpand* comes along later, it won't go crazy thinking it's got a compressed packet. When the compression routine finds *bRepeatCode* in the original data, it bundles it into a packet in which *bRepeatCode* itself is repeated one time.

In short, for every packet, *size* must be at least 4, or else the byte must be *bRepeatCode* and *size* must be 1. You can use assertions to verify this:

```
    .
    .
    .
{
    /* Store "size" copies of "b" at pbTo. */
    b = *pbFrom++;
    size = (size_t)*pbFrom++;

    ASSERT(size >= 4  ||
          (size == 1  &&  b == bRepeatCode));
    .
    .
    .
```

If this assertion fails, either *pbFrom* points to garbage or the compression routine has a bug in it. In either case, it's a bug that might not otherwise be obvious.

———◆———

Use assertions to detect impossible conditions.

———◆———

THE SILENT TREATMENT

Suppose you were hired to write the software for a nuclear reactor and you had to handle the case in which the core overheats.

Some programmers might attack this case by automatically dumping water into the core, inserting cooling rods, or doing whatever it is you do when you're trying to cool a reactor. And as long as the program had everything under control, it wouldn't alert the staff to the problem.

Another programmer might choose to always alert the reactor staff whenever the core overheats. The computer could still automatically take care of things, but the operators would always know about it.

Which way would you implement the code?

I doubt there would be much disagreement on this one; you would alert the operators. That the computer can restore the reactor to normal operation is irrelevant. Cores don't overheat spontaneously—something unusual has to happen for things to go awry, and when they do, somebody had better figure out what that unusual something is so that it doesn't happen again.

Surprisingly, programmers, and particularly experienced programmers, write code every day that quietly fixes problems whenever something unexpected happens. They even code that way intentionally. And you probably do it yourself.

Of course, what I'm driving at is defensive programming.

In the last section, I showed you code for *pbExpand*. That function uses defensive programming. This revised version doesn't—look at the loop conditions:

```c
byte *pbExpand(byte *pbFrom, byte *pbTo, size_t sizeFrom)
{
    byte    b, *pbEnd;
    size_t size;

    pbEnd = pbFrom+sizeFrom; /* Point just beyond end of buffer. */
    while (pbFrom != pbEnd)
    {
        b = *pbFrom++;

        if (b == bRepeatCode)
        {
            /* Store "size" copies of "b" at pbTo. */
            b = *pbFrom++;
            size = (size_t)*pbFrom++;

            do
                *pbTo++ = b;
            while (--size != 0);
        }
        else
            *pbTo++ = b;
    }

    return (pbTo);
}
```

Even though this code more accurately reflects the algorithm, few experienced programmers would actually code the algorithm this way. You'd have a better chance of getting them into a two-person Cessna that had no seat belts and no doors. The code feels too risky.

They'd think, "I know *pbFrom* should never be greater than *pbEnd* in that outer loop, but what happens if that ever *does* happen? Hmm. I'd better make sure the loop shuts down if this impossible case ever comes up."

They'd use the same logic for the inner loop. Even though *size* should always be greater than or equal to *1*, using a *while* loop instead of a *do* loop keeps the code from crashing if *size* is ever *0* on entry.

It seems reasonable, even smart, to protect yourself from these impossible scenarios. But what if *pbFrom* somehow bounces past *pbEnd*? Are you more likely to spot this bug in the risky version on the previous page or in the defensive version we saw earlier?

The risky version will probably crash since *pbExpand* tromps about decompressing everything in memory. You're definitely going to notice that. The defensive version, on the other hand, exits before *pbExpand* can do much, if any, damage. You still might notice the bug, but I wouldn't bet my money on it.

Defensive programming is often touted as a better coding style, but *it hides bugs*. Remember, the errors we're talking about should never happen, and by safely handling them, you make it harder to write bug-free code. This is especially true when you have a bouncing pointer such as *pbFrom*, one that gets bumped by different amounts each time through the loop.

Does that mean you should stop programming defensively?

The answer of course is no. Programming defensively hides bugs, but it does serve a valuable purpose. The worst thing a program can do is crash and lose data that a user might have spent hours creating. And in a less-than-ideal world in which programs do crash, anything you can do to prevent data loss is worthwhile. Defensive programming works toward achieving this goal. Without it, your code would be a house of cards ready to crumble with the slightest change in your hardware or operating system. At the same time, you don't want to hide bugs by programming defensively.

Suppose *pbExpand* gets called with invalid arguments. Specifically, suppose that *sizeFrom* is a bit too small and the last byte of the data buffer happens to be *bRepeatCode*. Since this will look like a compressed packet, *pbExpand* will read 2 bytes too many from the data buffer and bump *pbFrom* beyond *pbEnd*. The result? The risky version of *pbExpand* will probably crash, and the defensive one will probably save the user from losing data, although it can still wipe out as much as 255 bytes of unknown data. You want both behaviors, but in different versions of your program. You want the debug version to alert you to the bug, and you want the ship version to recover safely, with no loss of data. The solution is to write your code using defensive programming the way you always have but use an assertion to alert you if things go haywire:

```
byte *pbExpand(byte *pbFrom, byte *pbTo, size_t sizeFrom)
{
    byte    b, *pbEnd;
    size_t  size;

    pbEnd = pbFrom+sizeFrom;  /* Point just beyond end of buffer. */
    while (pbFrom < pbEnd)
    {
        b = *pbFrom++;
        .
        .
        .
    }
    ASSERT(pbFrom == pbEnd);

    return (pbTo);
}
```

This assertion simply verifies that the code terminated correctly. In the ship version, the defensive code helps protect the user if anything goes wrong, but in the debug version, the bug is still reported. If that's not having your espresso and drinking it too, I don't know what is.

Still, you don't need to be obsessive about this. If *pbFrom* were always bumped by 1 each time through the loop, it would take a stray cosmic ray to knock it beyond *pbEnd* and cause problems. In such cases, assertions don't buy you anything, so leave them out. Look at your code and use your common sense.

One last point. Loops are only one area in which programmers routinely program defensively. No matter where you employ the defensive style, ask yourself, "Am I hiding bugs in this code by using defensive programming?" If you might be, add assertions to alert you to those bugs.

---◆---

*Don't hide bugs when you
program defensively.*

---◆---

Two Algorithms Are Better Than One

Checking for bad inputs and flawed assumptions is only part of what you can do to trap bugs in your programs. Just as another function can pass garbage to your function, yours can return garbage to its callers. You never want to do that.

Since both *memcpy* and *memset* simply return one of their parameters, there's little chance that you'd accidentally return garbage in those routines. But in a more complex routine, you might not be so sure of your results.

For example, I recently wrote a 68000 disassembler as part of a development tool for Macintosh programmers. Speed wasn't critical for the disassembler, but it was vital that it work correctly, so I chose to implement the code using a simple table-driven algorithm that I could easily test. I also used assertions to automatically catch any bugs that I missed while testing the code.

If you've ever looked at an assembly language reference book, chances are good that it described every instruction in painstaking detail. And as a part of that thoroughness, it showed a bit-pattern for each instruction. For instance, if you looked up the *ADD* instruction in a 68000 reference manual, you would see that it has this bit-pattern:

	15	14	13	12	11	10	9	8	7	6	5	4	3	2	1	0
ADD:	1	1	0	1	Register			Op-Mode			Effective Address					
											Mode			Register		

You can ignore the register and mode fields of this instruction—we're interested in only the bits that are explicitly *0* or *1*—in this case, the upper 4 bits of the instruction. You figure out whether you have an *ADD* instruction by stripping away the nonexplicit bits and checking to see whether the upper 4 bits are *1101*, or hex *0xD*:

```
if ((inst & 0xF000) == 0xD000)
    it's an ADD instruction...
```

The *DIVS* instruction (used for signed division) has 7 explicit bits in its pattern:

	15	14	13	12	11	10	9	8	7	6	5	4	3	2	1	0
DIVS:	1	0	0	0	Register			1	1	1	Effective Address Mode			Register		

Again, if you just strip out the nonexplicit register and mode fields, you can tell whether you have a *DIVS* instruction by using

```
if ((inst & 0xF1C0) == 0x81C0)
    it's a DIVS instruction...
```

You can use this mask-then-test technique to isolate every assembly language instruction, and once you know you've got an *ADD* or a *DIVS*, you can call a decode function to make sense of those register and mode fields that we've been ignoring.

That's how the disassembler works in the tool I developed.

Of course, I don't have 142 different *if* statements to check for every possible instruction. Instead I have a table containing a mask, pattern, and decode function for each instruction. The lookup algorithm loops over this table, and if it matches an instruction, it calls the corresponding routine to decode the register and mode fields.

Here's a part of that table, and the code that uses it:

```
/* idInst is a table of masks and patterns that
 * identify a bit-pattern as a specific type of
 * instruction.
 */

static identity idInst[] =
{
    { 0xFF00, 0x0600, pcDecodeADDI  }, /* mask, pat, function */
    { 0xF130, 0xD100, pcDecodeADDX  },
    { 0xF000, 0xD000, pcDecodeADD   },
    { 0xF000, 0x6000, pcDecodeBcc   }, /* short branches */
    { 0xF1C0, 0x4180, pcDecodeCHK   },
    { 0xF138, 0xB108, pcDecodeCMPM  },
    { 0xFF00, 0x0C00, pcDecodeCMPI  },
    { 0xF1C0, 0x81C0, pcDecodeDIVS  },
    { 0xF100, 0xB100, pcDecodeEOR   },
        :
        :
        :
```

```
    { 0xFF00, 0x4A00, pcDecodeTST   },
    { 0xFFF8, 0x4E58, pcDecodeUNLK  },
    { 0x0000, 0x0000, pcDecodeError }
};


/*  pcDisasm
 *
 *  Disassemble one instruction and fill in the opc opcode
 *  structure. pcDisasm returns an updated program counter.
 *
 *  Typical use: pcNext = pcDisasm(pc, &opc);
 */

instruction *pcDisasm(instruction *pc, opcode *popcRet)
{
    identity      *pid;
    instruction   inst = *pc;

    for (pid = &idInst[0]; pid->mask != 0; pid++)
    {
        if ((inst & pid->mask) == pid->pat)
            break;
    }

    return (pid->pcDecode(inst, pc+1, popcRet));
}
```

As you can see, *pcDisasm* is not a large function. It uses a simple algorithm that reads the current instruction, picks it out of the table, and then calls a decode routine to fill in the *opcode* structure that *popcRet* points to. As a final task, *pcDisasm* returns an updated program counter. This is necessary because not all 68000 instructions are the same size. The decode routines will, if necessary, read the extra parts of an instruction and then return the new program counter to *pcDisasm,* which passes it on.

Now back to the original point that you can't always be sure your routine won't return garbage.

With a function such as *pcDisasm,* it's hard to tell whether you're returning valid data. Even though *pcDisasm* itself might be properly identifying an instruction, the decode routines could be spewing garbage and you'd have a tough time spotting that. One way to trap such bugs is to put assertions into every decode routine. I'm not saying you shouldn't do that, but an even more powerful approach would be to put the assertions into *pcDisasm* since it is the bottleneck routine for all of the decode functions.

The question is, How? How would you automatically check that the decode routines are correctly filling in the *opcode* structure? You'd have to write code to validate that structure. And how would you do that? Well, basically, you'd have to write a routine that compares a 68000 instruction to the contents of an *opcode* structure. In other words, you'd have to write a second disassembler.

I know that may sound crazy, but is it really?

Look at what Microsoft Excel does in its recalculation engine. Since speed is critical to the success of a spreadsheet, Excel uses a complex algorithm to make sure that it never recomputes a formula in a cell in which it doesn't need to. The only problem is that because the algorithm is so complex, it's hard to modify without introducing bugs. The Excel programmers didn't like this difficulty, so they wrote a second recalc engine that runs only in the debug version of the program. After the smart engine stops calculating, the debug engine kicks in and slowly but thoroughly recomputes every cell that has a formula in it. An assertion fires if there are any differences between the results of the two recalculation engines.

Microsoft Word has a similar problem. Since speed is also critical in the page layout code of a word processor, the Word programmers wrote the layout code in hand-tuned assembly language. That was great for speed, but it was lousy in terms of keeping bugs out of the code. And, unlike the code for Excel's recalculation engine, which doesn't change very often, the layout code for Word changes regularly as new features are added to Word. To automatically catch layout bugs, the Word programmers write C versions of every hand-tuned assembly language routine. If the two routines disagree, an assertion fires.

In the same way, it made sense to use a debug-only disassembler to validate the primary disassembler in the tool I was working on.

I won't bore you with the details of how I implemented *pcDisasmAlt*, the second disassembler, but it was logic rather than table driven. In brief, I used nested *switch* statements to successively peel away significant bits until I had isolated the exact instruction. The code on the next page shows how I used *pcDisasmAlt* to validate the primary disassembler.

```
instruction *pcDisasm(instruction *pc, opcode *popcRet)
{
    identity     *pid;
    instruction  inst = *pc;
    instruction  *pcRet;

    for (pid = &idInst[0]; pid->mask != 0; pid++)
    {
        if ((inst & pid->mask) == pid->pat)
            break;
    }

    pcRet = pid->pcDecode(inst, pc+1, popcRet);

#ifdef DEBUG
    {
        opcode opc;

        /* Check both outputs for validity. */
        ASSERT(pcRet == pcDisasmAlt(pc, &opc));
        ASSERT(compare_opc(popcRet, &opc) == SAME);
    }
#endif

    return (pcRet);
}
```

Normally, you should slip your debug checks into existing code without their getting in the way. I couldn't quite manage that here—I had to declare the *pcRet* local variable so that I could validate the pointer that *pid->pcDecode* returns. This is OK since it doesn't violate the cardinal rule "You should always execute debug code in addition to and not instead of ship code." That may seem blatantly obvious right now, but once you start using assertions and debug code you'll find that there are times when you'd rather execute debug code instead of ship code. We'll see an example of this in Chapter 3, but for now, let me say this: Resist the urge. I had to modify *pcDisasm* to make the debug checks, but all the ship code is still executed.

I won't pretend that you should write two versions of every function in your program. That would be about as ridiculous as wasting the time to make every function as efficient as possible. I do believe that most programs have key functionality that must work no matter what else goes wrong. In a spreadsheet, it's the recalculation engine. In a word processor, it's the page layout engine. In a project manager, it's the task scheduler. In a database, it's the search/extraction engine. And in every program, it's the code that guarantees that the user will never lose data.

As you write code, keep an eye out for opportunities to validate your results. Bottleneck routines are particularly good places in which to look. And be sure to use a different algorithm, if possible, not just a second implementation of the same algorithm. By using a different algorithm, you not only find implementation bugs, but you also increase your odds of finding bugs in the algorithms themselves.

———◆———

Use a second algorithm to validate
your results.

———◆———

Hey, What Goes On Here?

Earlier in the chapter, I said that you must use care when defining the *ASSERT* macro. In particular, I said that the macro mustn't move memory, call other functions, or cause any unexpected side effects. If all of that is advisable, why did I use the assertions below in the *pcDisasm* function?

```
/* Check both outputs for validity. */
ASSERT(pcRet == pcDisasmAlt(pc, &opc));
ASSERT(compare_opc(popcRet, &opc) == SAME);
```

The reason that *ASSERT* must not call functions is that the macro could possibly disturb the surrounding code in an unexpected way. But in the code above, *ASSERT* isn't calling the functions; I am—the programmer who used *ASSERT*. I knew that it was safe to call functions in *pcDisasm* without causing problems, so I had no qualms about calling functions within assertions.

STOP BUGS AT THE STARTING LINE

Up to now, I've been ignoring the register and mode bits of instructions, but what if special encodings for those fields change the underlying instruction? For example, the pattern for the *EOR* instruction looks like this:

	15	14	13	12	11	10	9	8	7	6	5	4	3	2	1	0
EOR:	1	0	1	1	Register			1	Mode		Effective Address					
											Mode			Register		

and the pattern for the *CMPM* instruction looks remarkably similar:

	15	14	13	12	11	10	9	8	7	6	5	4	3	2	1	0
CMPM:	1	0	1	1	Register			1	Size		0	0	1	Register		

Notice that if the Effective Address Mode field of the *EOR* instruction is *001*, the EOR instruction will look like the *CMPM* instruction. The problem, of course, is that if *EOR* is placed earlier in the *idInst* table, it will incorrectly pluck out any *CMPM* instructions that come through.

The good news is that because *pcDisasm* and *pcDisasmAlt* use different algorithms, you will get an assertion failure the first time you disassemble a *CMPM* instruction. This happens because *pcDisasm* will fill the *opcode* structure with an *EOR* instruction but *pcDisasmAlt* will correctly (we hope) fill it with a *CMPM* instruction. When the two structures are compared in the debug code, you will get an assertion failure. This is an example of the power of using different algorithms in your debug functions.

The bad news is that you'll catch this bug only if you try to disassemble a *CMPM* instruction. I'd like to think that your external test suites would be thorough enough to catch this bug, but remember what I said in Chapter 1: You want to catch bugs automatically, at the earliest possible moment, and without relying on the skills of others.

So while you could push this off onto your testing group, don't. Despite what many programmers believe, testers are not there to test your code. That's your job. If you disagree, just name one other job in which it's acceptable to do slipshod work simply because somebody else is going to review it for mistakes. Why should programming be an exception? If you want to consistently write bug-free code, you must grab the reins and take charge. So let's start here.

Whenever you notice something risky about your code, ask yourself, "How can I automatically catch this bug at the earliest possible moment?"

By habitually asking yourself this question, you will find all sorts of ways to make your programs more robust.

You can detect bugs in the table by scanning it in *main* just after you initialize your program. You do this by looking at every table entry to verify that no earlier entry will incorrectly intercept its instruction. The code to check the table for such bugs is short, but it's not necessarily clear:

```
void CheckIdInst(void)
{
    identity *pid, *pidEarlier;
    instruction inst;

    /* For each instruction in the table... */
    for (pid = &idInst[0]; pid->mask != 0; pid++)
    {
        /* ...verify that no earlier entries collide with it. */
        for (pidEarlier = &idInst[0]; pidEarlier < pid;
                pidEarlier++)
        {
            inst = pid->pat | (pidEarlier->pat & ~pid->mask);
            if ((inst & pidEarlier->mask) == pidEarlier->pat)
                ASSERT(bitcount(pid->mask) <
                        bitcount(pidEarlier->mask));
        }
    }
}
```

This check works by comparing the current instruction with each of the instructions that appear earlier in the table. All of the instructions have "don't care" bits—they are the register and mode bits that are masked out. But what if those "don't care" bits just happen to form the bit-pattern for an earlier instruction in the table? In that case, you would have a collision between two table entries. Which entry should be placed earlier in the table?

The answer is simple. If two entries in the table match the same instruction, the entry with more explicit bits should appear earlier in the table. If this isn't intuitively evident to you, take another look at the patterns for *EOR* and *CMPM*. If both of those patterns matched the same instruction, which would you choose as the "right" match? Why? Since the masks have one bit set for each explicit 0 or 1 bit in the pattern, you can tell which entry is more specific by comparing the number of bits set in each mask.

It's more difficult to tell whether two instructions collide. The idea is to take the pattern of one entry and force its "don't care" bits to exactly match the pattern of each of the earlier entries. This is the value that is assigned to *inst* in the code. By design, *inst* has to match the pattern of the current entry since you're changing only bits that don't matter, but if *inst* also matches the pattern of an earlier entry, the two entries collide and you must compare their masks.

A Word of Caution

Once you start using assertions, you will probably see your bug counts climb dramatically. This can alarm people if they're not prepared for it.

I once rewrote a buggy code library that several groups at Microsoft were sharing. The original version didn't have any assertions, but I loaded the new version with them. I got an unexpected surprise. When I released the new library to the groups, one programmer got angry and demanded that I give back the original version. I asked him why.

"We installed the library, and we started getting lots of bugs," he said.

"You mean the library is causing bugs?" I was shocked.

"It seems to be. We're getting a lot of assertions that we didn't used to have."

"Have you looked at any of those assertions?"

"Yes we have, and they were bugs in our code, but there are so many assertions that they can't all be valid. We don't have time to waste tracking down phantom problems. I want the old library back."

Well, I didn't think he was seeing phantom bugs, so I asked him to continue to use the library until he found an erroneous assertion. He was upset, but he agreed, and in the end, he found that all the bugs were in the project and not in the library.

That programmer panicked because I hadn't told anybody that I had added assertions to the library, and nobody was expecting to get failures. If I had told people to expect assertion failures, I could have kept that programmer from panicking. But programmers aren't the only people who panic. Because companies gauge the progress of projects by the number of features left to implement and by the number of outstanding bugs, any time the number of either of those climbs dramatically, everybody involved with the project gets nervous. If you can, alert people and prevent this anxiety.

By calling *CheckIdInst* at startup, you will catch collision bugs the very first time you execute the program—you won't need to disassemble a single instruction. You should look for similar types of startup checks in your own code because they can quickly alert you to bugs that otherwise might go unnoticed for some time.

---◆---

Don't wait for bugs to happen; use
startup checks.

---◆---

ASSERTIONS ARE FOREVER

In this chapter, you've seen how you can use assertions to automatically catch bugs in your code. And while this is a valuable tool that can help you find that "last" bug much sooner than before, you can overuse it as you can any tool. It's up to you to determine where to draw the line. For some programmers, asserting that the denominator is not zero before every division operation might be critical; for others, it would be ridiculous. Use your best judgment.

Another thing: You should leave assertions in your code for the life of the project—don't strip them out once you've shipped your program. Those assertions will be valuable again when you start adding features for the next version.

QUICK REVIEW

◆   Maintain shipping and debugging versions of your program. Shrink-wrap the shipping version, but use the debugging version as much as possible to catch bugs quickly.

◆   Assertions are a shorthand way to write debugging checks. Use them to catch illegal conditions that should never arise. Don't confuse such conditions with error conditions, which you must handle in the final product.

◆   Use assertions to validate function arguments and to alert programmers when they do something undefined. The more rigidly you define your functions, the easier it will be to validate the arguments.

◆ Once you've written a function, review it and ask yourself, "What am I assuming?" If you find an assumption, either assert that your assumption is always valid, or rewrite the code to remove the assumption. Also ask, "What is most likely to be wrong in this code, and how can I automatically detect the problem?" Strive to implement tests that catch bugs at the earliest possible moment.

◆ Textbooks encourage programmers to program defensively, but remember that this coding style hides bugs. When you write defensive code, use assertions to alert you if the "can't happen" cases do happen.

THINGS TO THINK ABOUT

1. Suppose you have to maintain a shared library and you want to include assertions but you don't want to release the library sources. How could you define *ASSERTMSG*, an assertion macro that displays a meaningful message instead of the file name and line number? For instance, the *memcpy* routine might display this assertion:

```
Assertion failure in memcpy: The blocks overlap
```

2. Each time you use *ASSERT,* the *__FILE__* macro generates a unique file name string. That means that if you use 73 assertions in the same file, the compiler will generate 73 identical copies of the file name string. How could you implement the *ASSERT* macro so that the file name string would be defined just once per file?

3. What's wrong with the assertion in the function below?

```
/* getline -- read a \n delimited line into a buffer. */

void getline(char *pch)
{
    int ch;           /* ch must be an int. */

    do
        ASSERT((ch = getchar()) != EOF);
    while ((*pch++ = ch) != '\n');
}
```

4.   When programmers add new elements to an enumeration, they sometimes forget to add new cases to the appropriate *switch* statements. How could you use assertions to help detect this problem?

5.   *CheckIdInst* verifies that the *idInst* table entries are in the correct order, but out-of-order entries aren't the only kind of problem that can occur in the table. With so many numbers, it would be easy to mistype the value of a mask or pattern. How could you enhance *CheckIdInst* to help automatically catch typing mistakes?

6.   Earlier we saw that when the Effective Address Mode field of the *EOR* instruction is *001*, it is really a *CMPM* instruction. There are other restrictions in the *EOR* instruction. For example, the 2-bit mode field can never be *11* (that would make it a *CMPA.L* instruction), and if the Effective Address Mode field is *111*, the Effective Address Register field must be either *000* or *001*. Since *pcDecodeEOR* should never be called with these non-*EOR* combinations, how would you add assertions to it to catch bugs in the table?

7.   How could you use a second algorithm to verify the *qsort* function? How could you verify a binary search routine? And how about verifying the *itoa* function?

PROJECT: Contact the company who wrote your operating system and encourage them to provide a debugging version for programmers. This, by the way, is good for both parties because OS companies want people to write applications for their operating systems. It's in their best interest to make it easier to bring products to market.

3

FORTIFY YOUR SUBSYSTEMS

You can have 50,000 fans attending a football game, but you need only a handful of people to check tickets—provided, of course, that they stand at the gates. Your program has such gates; they're the entry points to your subsystems.

Think of the file system you use. You open files, close them, read and write them, and create them. That's five basic operations, but the code to support those operations is often large and complex. You use the entry points without worrying much about file directories, free space maps, or how to read from or write to a specific hardware device whether it's a disk drive, a tape drive, or a network connection.

Or what about a memory manager? You allocate memory, release it, and sometimes change its size. But again, there can be a lot of support code behind those operations.

In general, a subsystem hides its implementation details, which can be quite complex, and instead provides a few key entry points that programmers use to communicate with the subsystem. If you were to add some debugging checks to the entry points of such a subsystem, you could get substantial error checking without having to make many, if any, changes to the rest of your program.

Suppose you were asked to write the *malloc*, *free*, and *realloc* routines for a standard C runtime library. (Somebody has to write these things.) You could fill the code with assertions. You could thoroughly test it. And you could write a superb programmer's guide. But you and I both know that programmers are still going to have problems when they use the code. What can you do to help?

Here's a suggestion: When you've finished writing a subsystem, ask yourself, "How are programmers going to misuse this subsystem, and how can I detect these problems automatically?" Ideally, you would have asked this question before you began coding, to eliminate risky designs, but ask it again anyway. For a memory manager, you can rely on programmers to

- Allocate a block and use the uninitialized contents

- Free a block, but continue to reference the contents

- Call *realloc* to expand a block and when it moves continue to reference the contents at the old location

- Allocate a block but "lose" it because the pointer isn't saved

- Read or write beyond the boundaries of a block

- Fail to notice error conditions

These are not wildly hypothetical problems—they show up all the time. Worse, they're usually hard to spot because they aren't repeatable. You crash once, never to see the problem again—at least not until one of your users calls up in a huff and asks you to please fix the bug that keeps clobbering her in some common scenario.

These bugs are hard to spot, but that doesn't mean you can't improve things. Assertions are worthwhile, but you have to execute them if they're to report problems. Look at the problems above and tell me how assertions in your memory manager would catch them. They wouldn't.

In this chapter, I'm going to talk about additional techniques you can use to ferret out subsystem bugs that you would otherwise have trouble spotting. I'll be using the C memory manager as a model, but you can apply the points to any subsystem, whether it's a simple linked list manager or a shared text-retrieval engine.

Now You See It, Now You Don't

Normally, you would build tests directly into your subsystems, but I'm not going to do that here for two reasons. The first is that I don't want to clutter the book's examples with the code for implementing *malloc*, *free*, and *realloc*. The second is that you sometimes don't have the source code for subsystems that you use. Of the half-dozen compilers I'm using to test the examples in this book, only two provide the sources for their standard libraries.

Instead of building the tests into sources that you may not have, or that are undoubtedly different from what I have, I'm going to put scaffolding around the memory management routines in the form of cover functions. This is, after all, what you would have to do if you didn't have the sources to a subsystem. And while I'm at it, I'm going to adopt the naming convention I use throughout the rest of this book.

Let's start with the cover function for *malloc*. It looks like this:

```
/* fNewMemory -- allocate a memory block. */

flag fNewMemory(void **ppv, size_t size)
{
    byte **ppb = (byte **)ppv;

    *ppb = (byte *)malloc(size);
    return (*ppb != NULL);              /* Success? */
}
```

This may look more complicated than *malloc*, but that's largely because of the noise introduced by the *void* ** argument pointer. If you look at how a programmer would call this function, you can see that it is as clear, if not more clear, than a call to *malloc*. Instead of writing

```
if ((pbBlock = (byte *)malloc(32)) != NULL)
    successful -- pbBlock points to the block
else
    unsuccessful -- pbBlock is NULL
```

you would write

```
if (fNewMemory(&pbBlock, 32))
    successful -- pbBlock points to the block
else
    unsuccessful -- pbBlock is NULL
```

which would achieve the same thing. The only difference between the two functions is that *fNewMemory* separates the "success?" and "pointer" outputs whereas *malloc* fuses them into one dual-purpose output. In both cases, *pbBlock* points to the block if it was allocated or is *NULL* if the block wasn't.

In the last chapter, I said that you should either eliminate undefined behavior or use an assertion to verify that it doesn't happen. If you apply that advice to *malloc*, you should see that there are two undefined items you have to handle. First, it's meaningless (according to the ANSI standard) to ask *malloc* to allocate a zero-length block. Second, if *malloc* returns a block, it leaves the contents uninitialized—the block may be filled with zeros, or it may contain random garbage. You just don't know.

Handling a request to allocate a zero-length block is simple. You check for it with an assertion. But what about the other problem? How can you assert that a block's contents are, or are not, valid? It doesn't make sense. That leaves you with just one option: Eliminate the undefined behavior. The obvious approach is to have *fNewMemory* zero-fill blocks the moment it allocates them. That would work, but in a correct program, the contents of the blocks shouldn't matter. Burdening your ship program with unnecessary fills is something you should avoid.

Unnecessary fills can also hide bugs.

Suppose you allocate memory for a data structure but you forget to initialize one of the fields—or alternatively, a maintenance programmer extends the structure and forgets to add the initialization code for the new fields. That's a bug, but you may not notice it if *fNewMemory* sets the field to *0* or any other possibly useful value.

Still, you don't want to leave the contents undefined because that makes bugs hard to reproduce. What if a bug showed up only when the garbage happened to be one particular value? You would miss the bug much of the time and periodically crash for no apparent reason. Imagine how hard it would be to reach zero-bugs if every bug happened only some of the time—programmers (and testers) would go crazy trying to track down problems. The key to exposing bugs is to eliminate random behavior wherever you find it.

Exactly how you do this depends on the subsystem and the random behavior involved. For *malloc* you can eliminate randomness by filling the block—but only in debug versions of your program. That solves the problem without putting a ball and chain on the code you release. But remember, you don't want to hide bugs. The idea is to fill the blocks using a weird value that looks like garbage but that makes bugs apparent.

I use the value *0xA3* for Macintosh programs. I chose this value by asking myself a number of questions: What would force a bad pointer to show itself? What about a bad counter or index? What if the contents of the block were executed?

On some Macintosh models, you can't reference 16-bit or 32-bit values using an odd pointer, so I knew that the value should be odd. I also knew that I was more likely to spot a bad counter or index if it were large and caused noticeable delays or forced the system to misbehave. Finally, of all the weird-looking, odd-valued, and large numbers you can represent in a byte, I chose *0xA3* because if the block were somehow executed, the undefined machine language instruction *0xA3A3* would instantly crash in a clean, predictable way—you'd get an "undefined A-Line trap" error in the system debugger. This last point may seem nit-picky, but why not use every opportunity, however remote, to automatically catch bugs?

The value you choose for your machine may be different. On Intel 80x86-based machines, pointers can be odd, so having an odd-valued number isn't important. But the process for choosing the value is similar: You would ask yourself how uninitialized data could be used and then look for ways to make it noticeable. Microsoft applications use *0xCC* to fill blocks because it is large and easily noticeable, and if executed, causes the code to safely drop into the debugger.

If you add both the size-check assertion and the code to fill undefined memory, *fNewMemory* becomes

```
#define bGarbage    0xA3

flag fNewMemory(void **ppv, size_t size)
{
    byte **ppb = (byte **)ppv;

    ASSERT(ppv != NULL  &&  size != 0);

    *ppb = (byte *)malloc(size);
```

(continued)

```
#ifdef DEBUG
{
    if (*ppb != NULL)
        memset(*ppb, bGarbage, size);
}
#endif

    return (*ppb != NULL);
}
```

Not only does this version of *fNewMemory* help make bugs reproducible, but it often makes them easier to track down. If you find yourself staring at a loop index with the value *0xA3A3*, or a pointer with the value *0xA3A3A3A3*, it's clear that you're looking at uninitialized data. More than once, I've been tracking down one bug, only to spot another in the process because I ran across some unexpected combination of *0xA3*s.

So look at the subsystems in your application and isolate the design points that can cause random bugs. Once you have identified these points, either remove them by changing your design, or add debugging code to minimize the amount of random behavior.

———◆———

Eliminate random behavior.
Force bugs to be reproducible.

———◆———

SHRED YOUR GARBAGE

The cover function for *free* looks like this:

```
void FreeMemory(void *pv)
{
    free(pv);
}
```

The ANSI standard says that *free* is undefined if you pass it an invalid pointer. That sounds reasonable, but how can you tell whether *pv* is valid? How can you assert that *pv* points to the start of an allocated block? The answer is that you can't, at least not without more information.

It gets worse.

Suppose your program maintains a tree of some sort and that the *deletenode* routine calls *FreeMemory* to release one of the nodes. What will happen if there is a bug in *deletenode* that causes it to release the node but fail to update the link pointers in the surrounding allocated nodes? Obviously, you will have a tree structure that contains a free node. But guess what? On most systems, that free node will still look valid.

That shouldn't be too surprising. When you call *free*, you're telling the memory manager that you don't need the memory anymore, so why should it waste time scrambling the contents?

That's a reasonable optimization, but it has the nasty side effect that free memory—which is garbage—looks like it contains valid data. Instead of having a tree with a node that will crash the system the next time you traverse the structure, you have a tree that looks valid. How likely are you to spot that problem? Unless you have the luck of a lotto winner, not very.

"No problem," you say, "I'll just add some debug code to *FreeMemory* to fill the block with *0xA3* before it calls *free*. That way, the contents are guaranteed to look like garbage and the tree manipulation routines will break when they hit the free node." Good idea, but how large is the block? Oops, you don't know that either.

You could throw up your hands at this point and declare that *FreeMemory* has beaten you. After all, you can't assert that *pv* is valid since you have no way to do it, and you can't destroy the contents of the block because you don't know how large it is.

Instead of giving up, let's assume for a moment that you have a debug function, *sizeofBlock*, that will give you the size of any allocated memory block. If you have the sources to your memory manager, you could probably write such a routine without much effort. But even if you don't, don't worry—I'll provide an implementation for *sizeofBlock* later in the chapter. Using *sizeofBlock*, you can destroy the memory before you release it:

```
void FreeMemory(void *pv)
{
    ASSERT(pv != NULL);

    #ifdef DEBUG
    {
        memset(pv, bGarbage, sizeofBlock(pv));
    }
    #endif

    free(pv);
}
```

This code not only fills the block, but it also validates *pv* as a side effect of calling *sizeofBlock*. If the pointer is bad, *sizeofBlock* will assert—it can do this because, obviously, it must know about every allocated block.

It might seem strange that I used an assertion to check that *pv* is not *NULL* even though *NULL* is a legal argument for *free*—the ANSI standard says that *free* does nothing in this case. The reason shouldn't be too surprising: I don't believe in passing *NULL* pointers to functions where it has no meaning but those conjured up for convenience; the assertion simply validates this practice. Of course, your beliefs could be different, and you may want to remove the assertion. The point I want to make is that you don't need to blindly follow the ANSI standard. Just because somebody else thought that *free* should accept *NULL* pointers doesn't mean you're forced to accept that.

realloc is another function that releases memory and creates garbage. Here is its cover function:

```
flag fResizeMemory(void **ppv, size_t sizeNew)
{
    byte **ppb = (byte **)ppv;
    byte *pbNew;

    pbNew = (byte *)realloc(*ppb, sizeNew);
    if (pbNew != NULL)
        *ppb = pbNew;
    return (pbNew != NULL);
}
```

Like *fNewMemory*, *fResizeMemory* returns a status flag to indicate whether it successfully changed the size of the block. Assuming that *pbBlock* points to allocated memory, you could resize the block this way:

```
if (fResizeMemory(&pbBlock, sizeNew))
    successful -- pbBlock points to the new block
else
    unsuccessful -- pbBlock points to the old block
```

You should note that, unlike *realloc*, *fResizeMemory* does not return a null pointer if the operation fails; it returns the original pointer, which still points to the allocated, though unchanged, block.

The *realloc* function (and so *fResizeMemory*) is interesting in that it contains elements of both *free* and *malloc*, depending on whether you're shrinking a block or expanding it. In *FreeMemory*, I destroyed the block contents just before the block was released. In *fNewMemory*, I filled the new block with weird-looking "garbage" right after calling *malloc*. You must do both to make *fResizeMemory* robust. That requires two separate blocks of debug code:

```c
flag fResizeMemory(void **ppv, size_t sizeNew)
{
    byte **ppb = (byte **)ppv;
    byte *pbNew;
#ifdef DEBUG
        size_t sizeOld;
#endif

    ASSERT(ppb != NULL  &&  sizeNew != 0);

#ifdef DEBUG
    {
        sizeOld = sizeofBlock(*ppb);

        /* If shrinking, erase the tail contents. */
        if (sizeNew < sizeOld)
            memset((*ppb)+sizeNew, bGarbage, sizeOld-sizeNew);
    }
#endif

    pbNew = (byte *)realloc(*ppb, sizeNew);
    if (pbNew != NULL)
    {
#ifdef DEBUG
        {
            /* If expanding, initialize the new tail. */
            if (sizeNew > sizeOld)
                memset(pbNew+sizeOld, bGarbage, sizeNew-sizeOld);
        }
#endif

        *ppb = pbNew;
    }
    return (pbNew != NULL);
}
```

That looks like a lot of extra code, but if you look closer you'll see that most of it is air, braces, *#ifdef* directives, and comments. But even if there were a lot of extra code, worrying about that would be wasted energy.

Debug versions don't have to have to be small and tight or have lightning fast response; they need to be usable only to the extent that programmers and testers will regularly use them. Unless the code gets so big or so slow that programmers and testers stop using it, add whatever debug code you feel is necessary to strengthen your application. If the code gets too big or too slow, make hybrid versions that contain specific sets of debug code.

The important thing is to review your subsystems and isolate the cases in which they allocate or release memory, and make sure that the memory looks like the garbage it is.

Destroy your garbage so that
it's not misused.

Using #ifdef *with Locals Is Ugly!*

Take a look at *sizeOld*, a debug-only local variable. Bracketing *sizeOld* with an *#ifdef* sequence may look ugly, but it's important that all debug code be removed from the ship versions of your program. Oh, I know, if you were to remove the *#ifdef* directive, the code would be much more readable and would function correctly in both the ship and the debug versions of your code. The only drawback? In the ship version, you would declare *sizeOld* and then never use the variable.

It may seem OK to declare *sizeOld* in the ship version of your program and then not use the variable, but there's a serious problem with that. What if a maintenance programmer fails to notice that *sizeOld* is a debug-only variable and erroneously uses it, uninitialized, in ship code? By bracketing *sizeOld*'s declaration with an *#ifdef* directive, you prevent the programmer from using the variable without getting a compiler error when the ship version of the code is built.

It may look ugly using the *#ifdef* directive to remove debugging variables, but the practice helps eliminate a source of potential bugs.

MOVERS AND SHAKERS

Suppose that instead of freeing a tree structure node, your program calls *fResizeMemory* to expand the node to accommodate a variable-length data structure. If *fResizeMemory* moves the node as it expands it, you now have two nodes: the real one at the new location and the untouched garbage left at the old location.

What would happen if the programmer who wrote *expandnode* wasn't aware that *fResizeMemory* could move the node as it expanded it? Wouldn't that programmer leave the tree structure in its old state, with surrounding nodes still pointing to the original unexpanded and valid-looking block? And wouldn't the new block end up floating out in memory space with nothing pointing to it? In effect, you would have a valid-looking but flawed tree structure—and a lost block of memory. That's not good.

Now you might think that *fResizeMemory* could destroy the original memory any time it moved a block while expanding it. A simple call to *memset* would do the trick:

```
flag fResizeMemory(void **ppv, size_t sizeNew)
{
    .
    .
    .
    pbNew = (byte *)realloc(*ppb, sizeNew);
    if (pbNew != NULL)
    {
        #ifdef DEBUG
        {
            /* If the block moved, destroy the old one. */
            if (pbNew != *ppb)
                memset(*ppb, bGarbage, sizeOld);

            /* If expanding, initialize the new tail. */
            if (sizeNew > sizeOld)
                memset(pbNew+sizeOld, bGarbage, sizeNew-sizeOld);
        }
        #endif

        *ppb = pbNew;
    }
    return (pbNew != NULL);
}
```

Unfortunately, you can't do that. Even though you know the size and location of the old block, you can't scramble the contents because you don't know what the memory manager does with its free memory. Some memory managers don't do anything with the memory, but others use it to store free-chain information, or other internal implementation data. The fact is that once you release memory, you don't own it, so you shouldn't touch it. If you do, you risk corrupting your system.

"I've covered all the other cases, so is this one worth worrying about?" I think so, mainly because programmers either don't know, or regularly forget, that *realloc* can move blocks. Detecting this problem is important.

In one extreme case, when I was adding features to Microsoft's internal 68000 cross assembler, I was asked by the Macintosh Word and Excel programmers to track down a long-time bug that would randomly crash the system. The only difficulty was that the bug showed up about as often as you get your hair cut. Individuals wouldn't get hit too often, but the bug was constantly biting somebody, and that gave it some priority. I'll spare you the details, but it took weeks, off and on, to come up with a reproducible scenario for the bug, and then it took three days to track down the actual cause.

That's a long time to find the cause of a reproducible bug, but I had no idea what was causing it, and every time I stepped through the data structures, they looked perfect. I had no idea that those perfect data structures were, in fact, garbage left by an earlier call to *realloc*.

But the real problem was not that it took me so long to find the exact cause of the bug; rather that it took so much effort to come up with a reproducible case. Not only did *realloc* have to move the block of memory as it was expanding it, but the old memory had to be reallocated and filled with new data. In the assembler, both happened rarely.

This brings up another guideline for writing bug-free code: You don't want anything to happen rarely. You need to isolate those behaviors in your subsystems that may happen and make sure that they do happen. And often. If you find rare behavior in your subsystems, be sure to do something—anything—to stir things up.

The assembler bug could have been found within hours, instead of years, if *realloc* hadn't so rarely moved blocks when it expanded them. But the question is, how can you force *realloc* to move blocks more often? The answer is that you can't, at least not unless your particular operating system provides a way. But you can simulate what *realloc* does. If a programmer calls *fResizeMemory* to expand a block, you can move it in *fResizeMemory* by creating a new block, copying the contents of the old block to the new block, and finally releasing the old block. You can do exactly what *realloc* does:

```
flag fResizeMemory(void **ppv, size_t sizeNew)
{
    byte **ppb = (byte **)ppv;
    byte *pbNew;
#ifdef DEBUG
    size_t sizeOld;
#endif

    ASSERT(ppb != NULL  &&  sizeNew != 0);

#ifdef DEBUG
    {
        sizeOld = sizeofBlock(*ppb);

        /*  If the block is shrinking, pre-fill the soon-to-be-
         *  released memory. If the block is expanding, force
         *  it to move (instead of expanding in place) by faking
         *  a realloc. If the block is the same size, don't do
         *  anything.
         */

        if (sizeNew < sizeOld)
            memset((*ppb)+sizeNew, bGarbage, sizeOld-sizeNew);
        else if (sizeNew > sizeOld)
        {
            byte *pbForceNew;

            if (fNewMemory(&pbForceNew, sizeNew))
            {
                memcpy(pbForceNew, *ppb, sizeOld);
                FreeMemory(*ppb);
                *ppb = pbForceNew;
            }
        }
    }
#endif

    pbNew = (byte *)realloc(*ppb, sizeNew);
        :
        :
}
```

Here I've added new code that is executed only if the block is expanding. By allocating the new block before releasing the old block, you know that the block will be moved unless, of course, the allocation fails. If that happens, the new code behaves like a big no-op instruction.

But notice what I've done here. Not only does the code force the block to move regularly, but—as a side effect—the code also destroys the contents of the old block. That happens when it calls *FreeMemory* to release the original block.

Now maybe you're wondering, "Since the code fakes a *realloc*, why does it still call *realloc*?" After all, you could speed things up by embedding a *return* statement in the new code:

```
if (fNewMemory(&pbForceNew, sizeNew))
{
    memcpy(pbForceNew, *ppb, sizeOld);
    FreeMemory(*ppb);
    *ppb = pbForceNew;
    return (TRUE);
}
```

You could do that, but don't—it's a bad habit to get into. Remember that debug code is *extra* code, not different code. Unless there is a compelling reason not to, you should always execute the ship code, even if it's redundant. After all, there is no better way to catch bugs in code than to execute it, and you want to execute ship code as much as possible.

Sometimes when I explain the concepts in this section to a programmer, he or she will argue that always moving memory is just as bad as never moving it—that I've gone to the other extreme. That's an astute observation and is worth talking about for a moment.

Always doing something would be as bad as never doing it if it were true for both the ship version and the debug version of your program. In this example, though, the ship version of *fResizeMemory* is practically catatonic while the debug version moves blocks with such zeal that you'd think it was on amphetamines.

It's OK if something happens rarely, as long as it's not rare in both the ship and the debug versions of your program.

———◆———

If something happens rarely, force it
to happen often.

———◆———

KEEP A JOURNAL TO JOG YOUR MEMORY

The problem with the memory manager—from a debugging viewpoint—is that you know the size of a block when you first create it but you lose that information almost immediately unless you keep a record of it somewhere. You've already seen how valuable the *sizeofBlock* function can be, but imagine how useful it would be to know how many blocks are allocated and where they fall in memory. If you knew that, I could hand you an arbitrary pointer and you could tell me whether it was valid. Consider how useful that would be, particularly for validating pointer arguments to functions.

Suppose you had a function *fValidPointer* that took a pointer and a size and returned *TRUE* if the pointer actually pointed to *size* bytes of allocated memory. You could then write special-purpose, more-stringent versions of popular routines. For instance, if you found that you often fill parts of allocated memory, you could bypass the lenient *memset* function and instead call your own *FillMemory* routine, which would rigorously validate the pointer argument:

```
void FillMemory(void *pv, byte b, size_t size)
{
    ASSERT(fValidPointer(pv, size));

    memset(pv, b, size);
}
```

By calling *fValidPointer*, you ensure that *pv* points to a valid block and that there are at least *size* bytes from *pv* to the end of that block. That's a far stronger test than *memset*'s null pointer check. This is an example of trading both size and speed for extra security.

Or, if you choose, you can call *FillMemory* in your debug versions but call *memset* directly in the ship versions. You do that by globally including a ship-version macro like this one:

```
#define FillMemory(pb,b,size)  memset((pb),(b),(size))
```

But I'm getting off the point.

What I'm saying is that if you keep extra information in the debug versions of your programs, you can often provide much stronger error checking.

So far, I've shown you how to use *sizeofBlock* to fill memory in *FreeMemory* and *fResizeMemory*, but filling memory is a "weak" way to find bugs compared to what you can do if you keep a record of every allocated memory block.

Again, I'm going to assume the worst-case scenario: that you can't derive any information about allocated memory blocks from the subsystem itself. For the memory manager, this worst case means that you can't derive the size of a block, that you can't tell whether a pointer is valid, and that you can't even tell whether a block exists or how many there are. If you need this information, you have to provide it, and that means keeping an allocation log of some sort. How you keep the log doesn't matter, but you must have the information handy when it's called for.

Here's one possible way to maintain such a log: When you allocate a block in *fNewMemory*, allocate an extra block for a log entry; when you release a block in *FreeMemory*, release the log information; and when you change the size of a block in *fResizeMemory*, update the log information to reflect the new size and location of the block. These three actions can be isolated in, not surprisingly, three debug interfaces:

```
/* Create a memory record for the new block. */
flag fCreateBlockInfo(byte *pbNew, size_t sizeNew);

/* Release the information stored about a block. */
void FreeBlockInfo(byte *pb);

/* Update the information about an existing block. */
void UpdateBlockInfo(byte *pbOld, byte *pbNew, size_t sizeNew);
```

How these routines maintain the log information isn't too important, provided, of course, that they don't slow the system down to the point that it's unusable. You can find code in Appendix B that implements these memory log functions.

Modifying *FreeMemory* and *fResizeMemory* to call the appropriate memory log routines is straightforward. *FreeMemory* becomes

```
void FreeMemory(void *pv)
{
    #ifdef DEBUG
    {
        memset(pv, bGarbage, sizeofBlock(pv));
        FreeBlockInfo(pv);
    }
    #endif

    free(pv);
}
```

In *fResizeMemory*, you call *UpdateBlockInfo* if *realloc* successfully changes the size of the block. If *realloc* fails, there isn't anything to update. The tail part of *fResizeMemory* becomes

```
flag fResizeMemory(void **ppv, size_t sizeNew)
{
    :
    :
    pbNew = (byte *)realloc(*ppb, sizeNew);
    if (pbNew != NULL)
    {
        #ifdef DEBUG
        {
            UpdateBlockInfo(*ppb, pbNew, sizeNew);

            /* If expanding, initialize the new tail. */
            if (sizeNew > sizeOld)
                memset(pbNew+sizeOld, bGarbage, sizeNew-sizeOld);
        }
        #endif

        *ppb = pbNew;
    }
    return (pbNew != NULL);
}
```

Modifying *fNewMemory* is a bit more complicated, and that's why I've saved it for last. When you call *fNewMemory* to allocate a block, the system must allocate two blocks: one for your request and one for the log information. For the call to succeed, both allocations must succeed; otherwise, you'll have a memory block with no log information to back it up. That's important because without that log information you'll get an assertion failure if you call any function that validates its pointer arguments.

In the code on the next page, you'll see that if *fNewMemory* allocates the memory requested but fails to allocate the memory for the log entry, it will release the first memory block and fake a memory failure. This keeps the memory system and the log information synchronized.

```
flag fNewMemory(void **ppv, size_t size)
{
    byte **ppb = (byte **)ppv;

    ASSERT(ppv != NULL  &&  size != 0);

    *ppb = (byte *)malloc(size);

    #ifdef DEBUG
    {
        if (*ppb != NULL)
        {
            memset(*ppb, bGarbage, size);

            /*  If unable to create the block information,
             *  fake a total memory failure.
             */
            if (!fCreateBlockInfo(*ppb, size))
            {
                free(*ppb);
                *ppb = NULL;
            }
        }
    }
    #endif

    return (*ppb != NULL);
}
```

That does it.

Now that you have a total record of the memory system, you can easily write functions like *sizeofBlock* and *fValidPointer* (see Appendix B) or anything else you find useful.

—————◆—————

*Keep debug information to allow
stronger error checking.*

—————◆—————

DON'T WAIT FOR BUGS TO CALL

Up to this point, every change I've suggested helps you notice bugs when they happen. That's good, but it's not automatic. Think about the *deletenode* routine I talked about earlier. If that code called *FreeMemory* to release a node and left dangling pointers in the tree, would you have any chance of spotting the problem if those pointers never got used? No, you wouldn't. Or what if I had a bug in *fResizeMemory* such as forgetting to call *FreeMemory*?

```
if (fNewMemory(&pbForceNew, sizeNew))
{
    memcpy(pbForceNew, *ppb, sizeOld);
    /* FreeMemory(*ppb); */
    *ppb = pbForceNew;
}
```

The Uncertainty Principle and Other Specters

Sometimes when I explain the concept of using debugging checks to a programmer, he or she expresses a concern that adding such test code is intrusive. Heisenberg's Uncertainty Principle always comes up.

There is no question that the debug code will create differences between the ship and the debug versions of your code, but as long as you're careful not to change the underlying behavior of the code, those differences shouldn't matter. The debug version of *fResizeMemory* may move blocks more frequently, but that doesn't change the code's basic behavior. Similarly, *fNewMemory* may allocate more memory than you request (for the log information), but again, that shouldn't affect your code's behavior. If you count on *fNewMemory* or *malloc* to give you exactly 21 bytes when you ask for that amount, you're in trouble, with or without the debug code. To maintain alignment restrictions, memory managers routinely allocate more memory than you ask for.

Another objection is that the debug code itself will increase the size of an application, which therefore uses more RAM. But remember, the purpose of the debug version is to catch bugs, not to make the maximal use of memory. It's OK if you can't load the largest possible spreadsheet, or edit the largest possible document, or do whatever memory-hogging thing it is that your application does. The worst case is that you'll run out of memory sooner than you normally would, forcing the program to exercise your error handling code more often. The best case is that the debug code will catch bugs quickly with little or no real testing effort.

I would have introduced a subtle bug. It's subtle because nothing obvious will go wrong. But every time you execute the code you will "lose" a memory block because the only pointer to it is destroyed when you assign *pbForceNew* to *ppb*. Will the debug code help catch this bug? Not at all.

Bugs such as this one differ from the bugs I talked about earlier in that nothing illegal ever happens. Just as roadblocks are worthless if the crooks never try to leave town, the debug code I've shown so far is worthless for catching bugs when the data isn't used. That doesn't mean the bugs don't exist. They do. It just means that you can't see them—they're "lying low."

To find these bugs, you do the programmer's equivalent of a house-to-house search. Instead of waiting for the bugs to show themselves, you add debug code to actively search for these kinds of problems.

In the first case, you have a dangling pointer to a block that is no longer allocated. In the second case, you have a block that is allocated but that has no pointer to it. These bugs would normally be hard to find, but not if you've been keeping debug information.

Think about how you find errors in your bank statement: You have a list of the funds you think you've allocated; the bank has a list it thinks you've allocated; you find errors by comparing the two lists. The way you find dangling pointers and lost blocks is no different. You compare the list of known pointers, which is stored in your data structures, to the list of known allocations, which is stored in the debug information. If you find pointers that don't reference allocated blocks, or blocks that don't have any pointers to them, you've got problems.

But programmers—especially experienced programmers—balk at the idea of checking every pointer stored in every data structure because tracking them down seems difficult, if not impossible. The reality, though, is that even poorly written programs clump pointers into classes of allocations.

For example, the 68000 assembler I talked about earlier might allocate memory for 753 symbol names, but it doesn't keep track of them by means of 753 global variables. That would be silly. Instead, it uses an array, a hash table, a tree, or possibly a simple linked list. There may be 753 symbol names, but looping over any of these data structures is simple and takes little code.

To compare the list of pointers stored in the data structures to the list of allocations stored in the debug information, I've defined three functions that work together with the information gathering routines described in the last section—you can find their implementations in Appendix B:

```
/* Mark all blocks as "unreferenced." */
void ClearMemoryRefs(void);

/* Note that the block pointed to by "pv" has a reference. */
void NoteMemoryRef(void *pv);

/* Scan the reference flags looking for lost blocks. */
void CheckMemoryRefs(void);
```

The way you use these routines is straightforward. First, you call *ClearMemoryRefs* to set the debug information to a known state. Next, you scan your global data structures and call *NoteMemoryRef* for each pointer to allocated memory, both to validate the pointer and to mark that the block was referenced. Once you've accomplished that, every pointer should be validated and every block should have a reference mark. Finally, you call *CheckMemoryRefs* to verify that all blocks are marked; if *CheckMemoryRefs* finds an unmarked block, it asserts, alerting you to the lost block.

Let's see how you would use these routines to validate the pointers in the 68000 assembler. For simplicity's sake, let's assume that the symbol table for the assembler is maintained in a binary tree in which each node looks like this:

```
/*  "symbol" is the node definition for a symbol name.
 *  We allocate one of these nodes for every symbol
 *  defined in the user's assembly source code.
 */

typedef struct SYMBOL
{
    struct SYMBOL *psymRight;
    struct SYMBOL *psymLeft;
    char *strName;                  /* the textual representation */
    :
    :
} symbol;                           /* naming: sym, *psym */
```

I've shown only the three fields that contain pointers. The first two fields are pointers to the left and right subtrees; the third is to the null-terminated symbol string. Once you've called *ClearMemoryRefs*, you traverse the tree and note every pointer stored in it. I've isolated this code in one debug-only function:

```
void NoteSymbolRefs(symbol *psym)
{
    if (psym != NULL)
    {
        /* Validate the current node before going deeper. */
        NoteMemoryRef(psym);
        NoteMemoryRef(psym->strName);

        /* Now do the subtrees. */
        NoteSymbolRefs(psym->psymRight);
        NoteSymbolRefs(psym->psymLeft);
    }
}
```

This code traverses the symbol table in a pre-order fashion to note every pointer in the tree. Normally, because the symbol table is stored as an in-order tree, I would traverse it in an in-order fashion, but I didn't do that here because I wanted to validate *psym* before I dereferenced it. That required a pre-order search. If you do an in-order or a post-order traversal, you must dereference *psym* before you validate it, and that could lead to a crash, probably after the function wildly recurses many times. True, you would see the bug, but it's much easier to track down a controlled assertion failure than it is to isolate a random crash.

Once you've written Note-Ref routines for your other data structures, wrap them up in a single routine you can call from anywhere in your program. For the assembler, the routine might look like this:

```
void CheckMemoryIntegrity(void)
{
    /* Mark all blocks as "unreferenced." */
    ClearMemoryRefs();

    /* Note all known global allocations. */
    NoteSymbolRefs(psymRoot);
    NoteMacroRefs();
        :
        :
    NoteCacheRefs();
    NoteVariableRefs();

    /* Make sure everything is OK. */
    CheckMemoryRefs();
}
```

The only remaining question is, When do you call this routine? Obviously, you want to call it as often as you can, but when you call it really depends on your program. At a minimum, you should call the routine any time you're about to use the subsystem. Even better, you should check the subsystem any time your program is burning cycles waiting for the user to press a key, move a mouse, or twiddle a hardware switch. You might as well use the opportunity to check things out.

———◆———

Create thorough subsystem checks,
and use them often.

———◆———

IT'S OBVIOUS ONCE YOU SEE IT

In his book *Influence: How and Why People Agree to Things* (Morrow, 1984), Dr. Robert Cialdini points out that if you're a salesperson and somebody walks into your men's clothing store looking for a sweater and a suit, you should always show the person the suits first, and then the sweaters. You'll make larger sales because after you sell somebody a $500 suit, an $80 sweater is going to look inexpensive by comparison. But if you drag the person to the sweaters first, $80 is going to look outrageous and you'll probably sell a $35 sweater instead. This is obvious to anybody who takes 30 seconds to think about it, but how many people do?

In the same way, some programmers might have thought that choosing a value for *bGarbage* was trivial—pick any old number. Other programmers might have thought it unimportant whether you recursed over the symbol table's tree structure with a pre-order, in-order, or post-order traversal. But, as I pointed out earlier, some choices are better than others.

If you find yourself making an arbitrary choice about an implementation detail, stop and take 30 seconds to review the possibilities; for each one, ask yourself, "Will this cause bugs or will it help find them?" If you asked that question about the possible values for *bGarbage*, you could see that choosing *0* could cause bugs and that a value such as *0xA3* could help find them.

Design your tests carefully.
Nothing should be arbitrary.

THERE'S NO NEED TO KNOW

No doubt you'll also run across designs for subsystem tests that require various levels of knowledge about the tests in order to use them. Using *fValidPointer* is an example of this; you can't use it if you don't know that it exists. But the best tests are transparent—they work regardless of whether the programmer is aware of them.

Suppose an inexperienced programmer or somebody unfamiliar with your project joins your team. Can't he or she freely use *fNewMemory*, *fResizeMemory*, and *FreeMemory* without ever knowing about the underlying tests?

What if the new programmer is unaware that *fResizeMemory* can move blocks and introduces a bug like the one in the assembler. Does he or she need to know anything about the integrity checks for those checks to kick in and fire off an "illegal pointer" assertion?

Suppose the new programmer creates a lost memory block? Again, the checks kick in and alert him or her to the problem with a "lost memory" assertion. The new programmer may not even know what a lost memory block is; he or she doesn't need to know that for the checks to work. Even better, by tracking down the failure, the new programmer will learn about lost memory—without stealing time from an experienced programmer.

This is the power of well-designed subsystem tests—when they corner a bug, they grab it by the antennae, drag it to the broadcast studio, and interrupt your regularly scheduled program. You can't ask for better feedback than that.

Strive to implement transparent
integrity checks.

YOU DON'T SHIP THE DEBUG VERSION

I know that I've added a lot of code to the memory manager in this chapter. Some programmers might even be thinking, "This stuff seems worthwhile, but adding all these checks and including the code for log information is just too much." I have to admit that I once felt the same way.

I had a gut revulsion to adding so much inefficiency to a program, but I soon learned that I was wrong. Adding such code to the ship version of a program would kill it in the marketplace, but this code is only in the debug version. Sure, debug code slows down performance, but what's worse: having your retail product crash on your users, or having your internal debug version be somewhat slower as it helps you find bugs? You shouldn't worry too much about the efficiency of debug code. After all, your customers aren't going to be using that version.

It's important to distinguish, at the emotional level, between debug and ship versions of your program. You use the debug version to find bugs. You use the ship version to please customers. And because that's true, the coding trade-offs you make for the two versions are radically different.

Remember that as long as your product meets the size and speed needs of your customers, you can do anything you want in your debug code. If adding log routines to the memory manager helps you find all sorts of nasty bugs, everybody wins. Your users have a zippy program, and you find bugs without expending much time and energy.

An Historical Note

Microsoft used to routinely send debug versions of its applications to beta testers in order to find more bugs. They stopped doing that, at least for a while, when a "prerelease" magazine review—based on a debug beta version of a product—came out with the judgment that the program was great but was about as fast as a three-toed sloth. Consider yourself warned. Either don't release debug versions to your test sites, or make it very clear that the code is loaded with internal debug checks that affect performance. If your program has a sign-on message, it would be wise to show a disclaimer that even Geraldo Rivera could not gloss over.

Microsoft programmers routinely load their programs with debug code. Microsoft Excel, for instance, contains memory subsystem tests (which are even more thorough than those here), a cell table integrity check, artificial memory failure mechanisms so that testers can force code to execute out-of-memory error handlers, and a host of other checks. That's not to say that Excel has never shipped with bugs—it has—but almost never in code that contained thorough subsystem checks.

I know I've added a lot of code to the memory manager in this chapter, but consider this: All of the new code was built into the cover functions *fNewMemory*, *FreeMemory*, and *fResizeMemory*; nothing was added to the callers of these functions, nor was anything added to the code that implements *malloc*, *free*, and *realloc*.

Even the speed degradation isn't as bad as you might expect it to be. If Microsoft's results are typical, the debug version of your application—packed with assertions and subsystem tests—should run at about half the speed of your ship version.

◆

*Don't apply ship version constraints
to the debug version. Trade size and
speed for error detection.*

◆

FIND BUGS NOW, OR FIND THEM LATER

In this chapter, I've covered a half-dozen ways to enhance validation of a memory subsystem, but the points apply to *any* subsystem. Imagine how much harder it would be for bugs to go unnoticed in a program that thoroughly validates itself. In all likelihood, if these debugging tests had been used in the 68000 assembler I talked about, the elusive *realloc* bug that took years to find could have been found automatically within hours or days of when the code was first written. It would not have mattered whether the programmer was highly skilled or inexperienced; the tests would have caught the bug.

In fact, the tests would have caught all similar bugs. Automatically. Without the need for luck or skill.

That's how you write bug-free code.

QUICK REVIEW

◆ Look at your subsystems and ask yourself how programmers are likely to misuse them. Add assertions and validation checks to catch hard-to-spot and common bugs.

◆ You can't fix bugs if you can't repeatably find them. Look for anything that can cause random behavior and remove it from the debug version of your program. Setting "undefined" memory to a constant garbage value is one example of removing random behavior. That way, if something references the memory while it's still undefined, you'll get the same results every time you execute the offending code.

◆ If your subsystems release memory (or other resources) and create "garbage," scramble the data so that it really looks like garbage; otherwise, code somewhere may continue to use the data without your noticing it.

◆ Similarly, if your subsystems contain behavior that *may* happen, add debug code to make sure such behavior *does* happen. Making everything happen increases your odds of catching bugs in code that is normally not executed.

◆ Make sure your tests work even for programmers who are unaware of them. The best tests are those that require no knowledge of their existence.

◆ If possible, build tests into your subsystems instead of on top of them. And don't wait until the subsystem is coded to look for ways to validate it. For each design you consider, ask yourself, "How can I thoroughly validate this implementation?" If you find that it would be difficult or impossible to test the implementation, seriously consider a different design, even if that means trading size or speed for the ability to test the system.

◆ Think twice before throwing out a validation test because it would be too slow or use too much memory. Remember, the validation code won't appear in the ship version of your program. If you find yourself thinking, "This test would be too slow (or too big)," stop and ask yourself, "How can I keep this test, but make it faster (or smaller)?"

THINGS TO THINK ABOUT

1. If, while testing your code, you run across data made up of some combination of *0xA3s*, you know that you're probably looking at uninitialized data, or at data that has been released. How could you change the debug code to make it easier to determine which kind of data you've found?

2. Programmers occasionally write code that fills past the end of an allocated memory block. Describe how you could enhance the memory subsystem checks to alert you to these types of bugs.

3. Although the *CheckMemoryIntegrity* routine will catch dangling pointers, there are times when it can't find them. For instance, suppose you have a function that calls *FreeMemory* but a bug in the code leaves a dangling pointer to the free block. Now further suppose that before the pointer can be validated, something calls *fNewMemory* and reallocates the block of memory released a moment ago. What you're left with is a dangling pointer that points to allocated memory, but it's no longer the same block. That's a bug, but to *CheckMemoryIntegrity*, everything looks quite legal. If this were a common bug in your program, how could you enhance the system to detect this problem?

4. With the *NoteMemoryRef* routine, you can validate every pointer in your program, but how do you validate the block sizes? For instance, suppose you have a valid pointer to an 18-character string but the memory block is shorter than that? Or, what about the reverse case, in which your code thinks it has a 15-byte block but the log information shows that you allocated 18 bytes? That is often just as bad. How could you strengthen the integrity checks to catch these problems?

5. The *NoteMemoryRef* routine in Appendix B lets you mark a block as being referenced, but it doesn't alert you to a problem if a block is referenced five times when it should be referenced only once. For example, a doubly linked list would have two references to each node: one for the forward pointer and one for the back pointer. But in most cases, your blocks should have exactly one reference to them and if there are more, you have a bug

someplace. How could you improve the integrity checks to allow multiple references to some blocks but still assert for those for which this should never happen?

6. Throughout the chapter, I talked about debug code that you could add to the memory system to help programmers detect problems. But what about adding code to help testers? Testers know that programmers often mishandle the error conditions, so how could you give testers the ability to fake out-of-memory conditions?

PROJECT: Look at the major subsystems in your program. What kinds of debug checks could you implement to catch the common bugs associated with using those subsystems?

PROJECT: If you don't have a debug version of your operating system, get one if you can; otherwise, write your own, using cover functions. If you're feeling particularly benevolent, make your code available—in some way—to other developers.

4

STEP THROUGH YOUR CODE

I've said before that the best way to find bugs is to execute the code and then somehow spot them, either by eye or by using automated tests such as assertions and subsystem integrity checks. But while assertions and subsystem checks are valuable, they don't protect you from problems you haven't thought of in advance; in that respect, they are like the security system in your home.

If you wire your doors and windows but thieves get in through a skylight or basement opening, the alarm won't go off. If you put disturbance-sensors on your VCR, stereo, and other things you expect thieves to take but they grab your Barry Manilow collection, they're going to get away unnoticed. Similarly, if you validate your function arguments using assertions but the bugs show up in your logic, the alarms in your assertions are going to remain quiet.

In theory, you could put so many assertions and so much debug code into your programs that no bug could live long before you were alerted to its presence. In theory. In reality, including that much debug code would probably be a waste of time for most projects, and it would still require that you predetermine what the likely bugs are.

Rather than going overboard with assertions and debug checks, a better approach is to actively look for bugs when they're most likely to occur. But when is that? Isn't it when you've just written new code, or changed existing code? Sure it is. Code doesn't break spontaneously—something has to change for code to start breaking.

The best way to write bug-free code is to actively step through all new or modified code to watch it execute, and to verify that every instruction does exactly what you intended it to do.

In this chapter, I'll talk not only about why it's important to step through your code, but about how to do it effectively.

GAIN CONFIDENCE IN YOUR CODE

Recently, I was working on a feature for Microsoft's internal Macintosh development system. When I began testing the code, I found a bug and traced it to some new code written by another programmer. What puzzled me about this bug was that it was so central to the other programmer's code that I couldn't see how his feature could possibly have worked. I went to his office to ask him about it.

"I think I've found a bug in the code you just finished," I said. "Do you have time to take a quick look at it?"

He loaded the code into an editor and I showed him where I thought the problem was. When he saw the code, he was surprised.

"You're right; the code is definitely wrong. I wonder why my test didn't catch the bug?"

I was wondering the same thing. "How exactly did you test the code?"

He explained his test to me, and it seemed as if it should have caught the bug. We were both confused. "Let's set a breakpoint on the function and step through the code to see what's really going on," I suggested.

We tried to do just that, but when we set the breakpoint and hit the "run" key, the test ran to completion; it never hit the breakpoint. That's why the programmer never saw the bug. It didn't take much longer to determine why the test wasn't reaching the breakpoint—a function a few steps up the call chain had an optimization that allowed it to sometimes skip unnecessary work. In this case, it skipped the new code.

Do you remember what I said in Chapter 1 about the problems with black-box testing? I said that testers throw inputs at code and decide whether the code works by looking at the outputs—if the outputs look correct, the code works. The problem with that approach is that you can't tell what goes on between stuffing in the inputs and receiving the outputs. The programmer missed the bug above because he tested the code as a black box; he put in some inputs, got the correct outputs, and judged the code to be correct. He didn't use the extra tools available to him as a programmer.

Programmers, unlike most testers, have the ability to set breakpoints in code, step through code, and watch the process of inputs transforming into outputs. Strangely, though, few programmers make it a habit to step through their code when they test it; many don't even bother to set a breakpoint on the code to make sure that the code is executed.

Let's go back to the point I made in the introduction to this chapter: The best way to catch bugs is to look for them the moment you write or change code. And what's the best way programmers can test their code? It's by stepping through it and taking a microscopic look at the intermediate results. I don't know many programmers who consistently write bug-free code, but the few I do know habitually step through all of their code.

As a project lead, I've instructed many programmers to walk through their code when they test it. Almost universally, they stare in shock—not because they disagree with the concept but because the process sounds so time consuming. They're usually barely staying on schedule as it is—when are they going to find time to step through their code?

Fortunately, that gut reaction is off. Yes, it does take time to step through your code, but only a fraction of the time it takes to write the code. Think about it. When you implement a new function, you must design the interface, figure out the algorithm, and physically type in the lines of program source. How much extra effort does it really take to set a breakpoint when you first run the code, and hit the "step" key as you check each line? Not much, especially once you make it a habit. It's like learning to drive a stick-shift car—it seems impossible at first, but after a few days of practice, you don't even notice when you shift; you just do it. Similarly, once you make it a habit to step through your code, you don't think much about setting a breakpoint and going through the process; you just do it. And you catch bugs.

———◆———

Don't wait until you have a bug to
step through your code.

———◆———

A FORK IN THE CODE

Of course, there are techniques you can use to make stepping through your code more effective. After all, it doesn't do much good if you step through your code but you don't step through all of the code. For example, every programmer knows that error handling code often has bugs in it because it is so rarely tested, and those bugs will stay there unless you make an effort

---

What About Sweeping Changes?

In the past, programmers have asked, "What if I add a feature that touches code in many places? Stepping through all that new code is going to be time consuming." Let me answer that question with another: Can you make such sweeping changes without introducing any bugs?

The habit of stepping through your code creates an interesting negative feedback loop. Programmers who step through their code soon learn to write small, easily-testable functions because stepping through large functions is so painful. Programmers also spend more time thinking about how they can localize the changes they need to make—again, so that they can more easily test their code. And isn't this exactly what you want? No project lead likes it when programmers touch a lot of code; it's too destabilizing. Nor do leads like large, unmanageable functions; they're often unmaintainable.

Try hard to localize your changes. If you find that you must make pervasive changes, think twice before you decide not to step through all the new code.

to test that code. Either you can create test cases that force the error conditions to occur, or you can simulate failures while you're stepping through the code. Simulating failures usually takes much less time. Take a look at this code extract, for example:

```
pbBlock = (byte *)malloc(32);
if (pbBlock == NULL)
{
    handle the error condition;
    .
    .
    .
}
```

Normally, when you step through this code, *malloc* will allocate a 32-byte block of memory and return a non-*NULL* pointer, which causes the code to bypass the error handling code. But instead of leaving the error code untested, step through the code a second time and use the debugger to set *pbBlock* to the *NULL* pointer right after you execute this line:

```
pbBlock = (byte *)malloc(32);
```

malloc may allocate the block, but if you set *pbBlock* to the *NULL* pointer, it will look to your code as if *malloc* failed, allowing you to step through the error handler. (For you detail-oriented readers: Yes, *malloc*'s block will be lost when you change *pbBlock*, but this is only a test.)

In addition to stepping through your error conditions, you should also step through every possible path in your code. The obvious cases in which you have more than one code path are the *if* and *switch* statements, but there are others: The *&&*, *//*, and *?:* operators also have two paths.

The idea is to step through every instruction of your code at least once to verify that it works correctly. After you've done that, you can be more confident that your code is bug-free—at least you'll know that the code definitely works for some inputs. And if you choose good test cases, stepping through your code can be invaluable.

———◆———

Step through every code path.

———◆———

DATA FLOW, THE LIFEBLOOD OF CODE

When I wrote the fast *memset* routine in Chapter 2, this is how my first version (stripped of assertions) looked:

```
void *memset(void *pv, byte b, size_t size)
{
    byte *pb = (byte *)pv;

    if (size >= sizeThreshold)
    {
        unsigned long l;

        /* Pack a long with 4 bytes. */
        l = (b<<24) | (b<<16) | (b<<8) | b;

        pb = (byte *)longfill((long *)pb, l, size / 4);
        size = size % 4;
    }

    while (size-- > 0)
        *pb++ = b;

    return (pv);
}
```

That code may look correct, but it contains a subtle bug. After I wrote the code, I ran it in an existing application. No problem—the code worked fine. But to be sure that the code worked, I set a breakpoint on the routine and reran the application. The moment the code debugger gave me control, I looked at the arguments: The pointer looked valid, so did the size, and the byte was *0*. Now I hate testing code using the value *0* because *0* makes it hard to see many types of data bugs, so I immediately changed the byte argument to a weird value like *0x4E*.

I first stepped through the case in which *size* was less than *sizeThreshold*. That path worked fine. Next I stepped through the case in which *size* was greater than or equal to *sizeThreshold*. I wasn't expecting to have any problems, but when I stepped over this line,

```
l = (b<<24) | (b<<16) | (b<<8) | b;
```

I saw that *l* was set to *0x00004E4E*, and not *0x4E4E4E4E*, the value I was expecting to see. A quick assembly language dump of the function showed me the bug—and explained why the application worked in spite of it.

You see, the compiler I was using had 16-bit integers, and what is the result of *b<<24* when you're using 16-bit integers? It is *0*. And what about *b<<16*? Again *0*. There wasn't anything wrong with the logic of the code, but the implementation was flawed. The code appeared to work with the application because it used *memset* to zero-fill blocks of memory, and *0<<24* is *0*, the correct answer—but for the wrong reason.

I was able to catch that bug almost immediately because I spent an extra minute to step through the code before setting it aside and moving on. True, the bug was serious enough that somebody would have spotted it eventually, but remember that the goal is to catch bugs at the earliest possible moment. Stepping through code helps to achieve that goal.

The real power in stepping through your code is that you see the data as it flows through your function. If you were to focus on data flow as you stepped through your code, how many of these bugs do you think it would help you catch?

◆ Overflow and underflow bugs

◆ Data conversion bugs

◆ Off-by-one bugs

◆ *NULL* pointer bugs

◆ Bugs using garbage memory (*0xA3* bugs)

◆ Assignment bugs in which you've used *=* instead of *==*

◆ Precedence bugs

◆ Logic bugs

Wouldn't you catch all of those bugs? The value in focusing on the data is that it gives you a second, very different view of your code. You may not notice the assignment bug in this code:

```
if (ch = '\t')
    ExpandTab();
```

but when you step through it focusing on data flow, it's easy to see *ch* getting clobbered.

———◆———

As you step through code, focus on data flow.

———◆———

Why Didn't the Compiler Issue a Warning?

Of the five compilers I used to test the code in this book, none warned me about my *b<<24* bug, even though each compiler was set at its maximum warning level. The code is legal ANSI C, but I can't imagine any scenario in which the code would actually be what the programmer intended, so why no warning?

As you run into bugs like this one, tell your compiler vendor about them so that future versions of the compiler will warn you about such mistakes. Don't underestimate the power you wield as a paying customer.

ARE YOU MISSING SOMETHING?

One problem with using a source level debugger is that stepping over a line of code can cause you to miss important details. Suppose that instead of typing *&&* in the code below, you had typed *&* by mistake:

```
/*  If the symbol exists and it has a textual
 *  name, then release the name.
 */
if (psym != NULL  &  psym->strName != NULL)
{
    FreeMemory(psym->strName);
    psym->strName = NULL;
}
```

This code is legal, but it's wrong. The intent of the *if* statement is to prevent a *NULL psym* pointer from being used to reference the *strName* field of a *symbol* structure, but the code doesn't do that. Instead, the code always references the *strName* field regardless of whether *psym* is *NULL*.

If you use a source level debugger to step through the code and hit the "step" key when you reach the *if* statement, the debugger will execute the entire test as one operation. But to spot the bug, you would have to see that the right-hand side of the expression is executed even when the left side is *FALSE*. (Or, if you're lucky, your system will fault when you dereference a *NULL* pointer, but not many desktop computers do that, at least not yet.)

Remember what I said earlier: The *&&*, *‖*, and *?:* operators have two code paths each, and to catch bugs, you must step through both paths. The problem with a source debugger is that it steps over both paths of the *&&*, *||*, and *?:* operators with a single step. There are two practical approaches to overcoming this problem.

First, anytime you step to a compound conditional that uses *&&* and *||* operators, scan the list to verify that they are "spelled" correctly. Next, use the debugger to display the result for each side of the expression. This will help you catch bugs in which the full expression evaluates correctly but for the wrong reason. For example, if you think the first part of an *||* expression is *TRUE* and the second part *FALSE* but just the opposite is so, the expression will incorrectly evaluate the correct result. Looking at the individual parts of the expression will alert you to such problems.

A second, more thorough approach is to step through compound conditionals and *?:* operations at the assembly language level. Yes, this takes

---

Turn Off Optimizations?

If you're using a good optimizing compiler, stepping through your code can be an interesting exercise because the compiler may intermix the machine code of adjacent source lines as it tries to generate optimal code. It's not at all uncommon for one "step" command to step over three lines of code; nor is it unusual to step across a source line that moves data from one spot to another and find that the data has not moved (yet).

To make it easier to step through your code, consider turning off unnecessary compiler optimizations in the debug version of the program; those optimizations do nothing but scramble your code.

I've heard programmers argue that by disabling optimizations, you introduce risk because you create unnecessary differences between the debug and ship versions of the code. There is truth in that reservation, especially if you're concerned about code-generation bugs in your compiler. But remember that the purpose of the debug version is to catch bugs, and if disabling optimizations helps you do that, it's worth considering.

The best approach is to try stepping through your optimized code to see how difficult it is. If you find that you must disable optimizations to step through the code effectively, then do it. You may miss the rare compiler generation bug, but you'll find many of your own bugs. The trade-off is worthwhile.

extra effort, but for critical code it is important that you actually step through the code to see the intermediate results. And as with stepping through your code in C, stepping through it in assembly language is quick once you're used to doing it; it just takes practice.

———◆———

*Source level debuggers can hide
execution details. Step through critical
code at the instruction level.*

———◆———

TRY IT—YOU'LL LIKE IT

I wish I knew a way to persuade programmers to step through their code, or at least to get them to try it for a month. But I've found that programmers in general can't get over thinking it will take too much time. That's one of the advantages of being a project lead; you can be a bit autocratic and insist that programmers on your project step through their code until they learn that it doesn't take much time and that it is worthwhile.

If you're not already stepping through your code, will you start to? Only you know the answer. But I'm guessing that you picked up this book and began reading because you're serious about reducing the number of bugs in your code or in the code of the programmers you lead. It really comes down to this choice: Would you rather spend a small amount of time up front verifying your code by stepping through it, or would you rather let bugs get into your master sources and hope that testers will notice them so that you can fix them later? The choice is yours.

QUICK REVIEW

◆   Bugs don't grow in code spontaneously; they are the result of a programmer's writing new code or changing existing code. If you want to find bugs in your code, there is no better method than stepping through every line of the code the moment it's compiled.

◆ Although your gut reaction might be that walking through your code will take a lot of time, your gut reaction would be wrong. Yes, initially it will take more time—until walking through your code becomes habitual. Once that happens, you'll zip right through your code.

◆ Be sure to step through every code path—especially in your error handling code—at least once. Don't forget that the *&&*, *||*, and *?:* operators have two code paths to test.

◆ In some cases, you may need to step through code at the assembly language level. While you don't need to do this often, don't avoid doing it when it's necessary.

PROJECT: If you take a look at the exercises in Chapter 1, you'll see that they talk about common bugs that a compiler could automatically detect for you. Review those exercises, but this time, ask yourself whether you would miss any of the bugs if you stepped through the code using your debugger.

PROJECT: Take a look at the bugs that have been reported against your code over the last six months. How many would you have caught had you stepped through the code when you wrote it?

5

CANDY-MACHINE INTERFACES

One of the perks that Microsoft gives its employees is free soft drinks, flavored seltzer water, milk (chocolate too!), and those little cartons of fruit juices. As much as you want. But, darn it, if you want candy, you have to pay for that yourself. Occasionally, I would get the munchies and stroll down to a vending machine. I'd plunk in my quarters, press 4 and then 5 on the selection keypad, and watch in horror as the machine spit out jalapeño-flavored bubble gum instead of the Grandma's Peanut Butter Cookie I thought I'd asked for. Of course, the machine was right and I was wrong—number 45 was the gum. A quick look at the little sign by the cookie would always verify my mistake: No. 21, 45¢.

That candy machine always infuriated me because if the engineers had spent an extra 30 seconds thinking about their design, they could have saved me, and I'm sure countless others, from getting something they didn't want. If one of the engineers had thought, "Hmm. People are going to be thinking '45¢' as they deposit their money—I'll bet some of them are going to turn to the keypad and mistakenly enter the price instead of the selection number. To prevent that from happening, we should use an alphabetic keypad instead of a numeric one."

The machine wouldn't have cost any more to make, and the improvement wouldn't have changed the design in any appreciable way, but every time I turned to the keypad to punch in 45¢, I would find I couldn't and so be reminded to punch in the letter code. The interface design would have led people to do the right thing.

When you design function interfaces, you face similar problems. Unfortunately, programmers aren't often trained to think about how other programmers will use their functions, but as with the candy machine, a trivial difference in design can either cause bugs or prevent them. It's not enough that your functions be bug-free; they must also be safe to use.

getchar GETS AN *int*, OF COURSE

Many of the standard C library functions, and thousands of functions patterned after them, have candy-machine interfaces that can trip you up. Think about the *getchar* function, for instance. The interface for *getchar* is risky for several reasons, but the most severe problem is that its design encourages programmers to write buggy code. Look at what Brian Kernighan and Dennis Ritchie have to say about it in *The C Programming Language*:

Consider the code

```
char c;

c = getchar();
if (c == EOF)
    ...
```

On a machine which does not do sign extension, c is always positive because it is a char, yet EOF is negative. As a result, the test always fails. To avoid this, we have been careful to use int instead of char for any variable which holds a value returned by getchar.

With a name such as *getchar* it's natural to define *c* to be a character, and that's why programmers get caught by this bug. But really, is there any reason *getchar* should be so hazardous? It's not doing anything complex; it's simply trying to read a character from a device and returning a possible error condition.

The code below shows another problem common in many function interfaces:

```
/* strdup -- allocate a duplicate of a string. */

char *strdup(char *str)
{
    char *strNew;

    strNew = (char *)malloc(strlen(str)+1);
    strcpy(strNew, str);

    return (strNew);
}
```

This code will work fine until you run out of memory and *malloc* fails, returning *NULL* instead of a pointer to memory. Who knows what *strcpy* will do when the destination pointer, *strNew*, is *NULL*, but whether *strcpy* crashes or quietly trashes memory, the result won't be what the programmer intended.

Programmers have trouble using *getchar* and *malloc* because they can write code that appears to work correctly even though it's flawed. It's not until weeks or months later that the code crashes unexpectedly because, as in the sinking of the *Titanic*, a precise series of improbable events takes place and leads to disaster. Neither *getchar* nor *malloc* leads programmers to write correct code; both lead programmers to ignore the error condition.

The problem with *getchar* and *malloc* is that their return values are imprecise. Sometimes they return the valid data that you expect, but other times they return magic error values.

If *getchar* didn't return the funny *EOF* value, declaring *c* to be a character would be correct and programmers wouldn't run into the bug that Kernighan and Ritchie talk about. Similarly, if *malloc* didn't return *NULL* as though it were a pointer to memory, programmers wouldn't forget to handle the error condition. The problem with these functions is not that they return errors, but that they bury those errors in normal return values where it's easy for programmers to overlook them.

What if you redesigned *getchar* so that it returned both outputs separately? It could return *TRUE* or *FALSE* depending upon whether it successfully read a new character, and the character itself could be returned in a variable that you pass by reference:

```
flag fGetChar(char *pch);      /* prototype */
```

With the interface above, it would be natural to write

```
char ch;

if (fGetChar(&ch))
    ch has the next character;
else
    hit EOF, ch is garbage;
```

The problem with *char* vs. *int* goes away, and it's unlikely that any programmer, no matter how green, would accidentally forget to test the error return value. Compare the return values for *getchar* and *fGetChar*. Do you see that *getchar* emphasizes the character being returned, whereas *fGetChar* emphasizes the error condition? Where do you think the emphasis should be if your goal is to write bug-free code?

True, you do lose the flexibility to write code such as

```
putchar(getchar());
```

but how often are you certain that *getchar* won't fail? In almost all cases, the code above would be wrong.

Some programmers might think, "Sure, *fGetChar* may be a safer interface, but you waste code because you have to pass an extra argument when you call it. And what if a programmer passes *ch* instead of &*ch*? After all, forgetting the & is an age-old source of bugs when programmers use the *scanf* function."

Good questions.

Whether the compiler will generate better or worse code is actually compiler dependent, but granted, most compilers will generate slightly more code at each call. Still, the minor difference in code size is probably not worth worrying about when you consider that the cost of disk and memory storage is plummeting while program complexity and associated bug rates are climbing. This gap will only get larger in the future.

The second concern—passing a character to *fGetChar* instead of a pointer to a character—shouldn't worry you if you're using function prototypes as suggested in Chapter 1. If you pass *fGetChar* anything but a pointer to a character, the compiler will automatically generate an error and show you your mistake.

The reality is that combining mutually exclusive outputs into a single return value is a carryover from assembly language, where you have a limited number of machine registers to manipulate and pass data. In that environment, using a single register to return two mutually exclusive values is not only efficient but often necessary. Coding in C is another matter—even though C lets you "get close to the machine," that doesn't mean you should write high-level assembly language.

When you design your function interfaces, choose designs that lead programmers to write correct code *the first time*. Don't use confusing dual-purpose return values—each output should represent exactly one data type. Make it hard to ignore important details by making them explicit in the design.

Make it hard to ignore error conditions.
Don't bury error codes in return values.

JUST A LITTLE EXTRA THOUGHT

Programmers know when they're combining multiple outputs into a single return value, so acting on the suggestion above is easy—they just stop doing it. In other cases, though, an interface can seem fine but, like the Trojan horse, contain hidden danger. Take a look at this code to change the size of a memory block:

```
pbBuf = (byte *)realloc(pbBuf, sizeNew);
if (pbBuf != NULL)
    use/initialize the larger buffer
```

Do you see what's wrong with this? If you don't, don't worry—the bug is serious, but it's subtle, and very few people spot it unless they're given a hint. So, here's a hint: If *pbBuf* is the only pointer to the block about to be resized, what happens if the call to *realloc* fails? The answer is that *NULL* is stuffed into *pbBuf* when *realloc* returns, destroying the only pointer to the original block. The code creates lost memory blocks.

Here's a question: How many times do you want to resize a block and store the pointer to the new block in a different variable? I'd imagine about as often as you'd want to drive to a restaurant in one car and leave in another. Sure, there are cases in which you want to store the new pointer in a different variable, but normally, if you change the size of a block, you want to update the original pointer. That's why programmers so often fall into *realloc*'s trap. *realloc* has a candy-machine interface.

Ideally, *realloc* would always return an error code and a pointer to the memory block regardless of whether the block was expanded. That's two separate outputs. Let's take another look at *fResizeMemory*, the cover function for *realloc* that I talked about in Chapter 3. Here it is again, stripped of all the debug code:

```
flag fResizeMemory(void **ppv, size_t sizeNew)
{
    byte **ppb = (byte **)ppv;
    byte *pbNew;

    pbNew = (byte *)realloc(*ppb, sizeNew);
    if (pbNew != NULL)
        *ppb = pbNew;
    return (pbNew != NULL);
}
```

Take a look at the *if* statement in the code above—it ensures that the original pointer is never destroyed. If you rewrote the *realloc* code at the start of this section using *fResizeMemory*, you would have

```
if (fResizeMemory(&pbBuf, sizeNew))
    use/initialize the larger buffer
```

In this case, if the attempt to resize the block fails, *pbBuf* is left untouched and continues to point to the original block; *pbBuf* is not set to *NULL*. That's exactly the behavior you want. So here's a question: "How likely is it that a programmer will lose a memory block using *fResizeMemory*?" Here's another: "How likely is it that a programmer will forget to handle *fResizeMemory*'s error condition?"

Another interesting point to note is that programmers who habitually follow the earlier suggestion in this chapter—"Don't bury error codes in return values"—would never design an interface such as *realloc*'s. Their first attempt would be more like *fResizeMemory*'s—and so wouldn't have *realloc*'s "lost block" problem. The recommendations in this book build on each other and interact in ways that you might not expect. This is an example of that happening.

But separating your outputs is not always going to save you from designing interfaces with hidden traps. I wish I could offer a better piece of advice, but the only sure way to catch such hidden traps is to stop and think about your design. The best approach is to examine every possible combination of inputs and outputs and look for side effects that can cause problems. I know this can sometimes be tedious, but remember, it's relatively cheap for you to take the extra time up front to think about this. The worst thing you can do is to skip this step and force who knows how many other programmers into tracking down and fixing bugs caused by a poorly designed interface.

Imagine how much total time has been wasted by programmers all over the world who have been forced to track down bugs caused by the interface traps of *getchar*, *malloc*, and *realloc*—to say nothing of all the functions that have been written using one of these three as a model. It's a sobering amount of time.

---◆---

Always look for, and eliminate,
flaws in your interfaces.

---◆---

THE ONE-FUNCTION MEMORY MANAGER

Although I spent a lot of time talking about the *realloc* function in Chapter 3, I didn't cover many of its more bizarre aspects. If you pull out your C library manual and look up the full description of *realloc*, you'll find something like this:

```
void *realloc(void *pv, size_t size);
```

realloc changes the size of a previously allocated memory block. The contents of the block are preserved up to the lesser of the new and old block sizes.

(continued)

continued

- ◆ If the new size of the block is smaller than the old size, *realloc* releases the unwanted memory at the tail end of the block and *pv* is returned unchanged.

- ◆ If the new size is larger than the old size, the expanded block may be allocated at a new address and the contents of the original block copied to the new location. A pointer to the expanded block is returned, and the extended part of the block is left uninitialized.

- ◆ If you attempt to expand a block and *realloc* cannot satisfy the request, *NULL* is returned. *realloc* will always succeed when you shrink a block.

- ◆ If *pv* is *NULL*, then *realloc* behaves as though you called *malloc(size)* and returns a pointer to a newly allocated block, or *NULL* if the request cannot be satisfied.

- ◆ If the new size is 0 and *pv* is not *NULL* , then *realloc* behaves as though you called *free(pv)* and *NULL* is always returned.

- ◆ If *pv* is *NULL* and *size* is *0*, the result is undefined.

Whew! *realloc* is a prime example of implementation overkill—it's a complete memory manager in just one function. Why do you need *malloc*? Why do you need *free*? *realloc* does it all.

There are several good reasons why you should not design functions this way. First, you can't expect programmers to use such a function safely. There are so many details that even experienced programmers don't know them all. If you doubt this, take a survey and tally how many programmers know that passing a *NULL* pointer to *realloc* simulates a call to *malloc*. Tally how many know that passing a *0* size is the same as calling *free*. True, this is fairly arcane behavior, so ask them a question they must know the answer to if they hope to avoid bugs. Ask them what happens when they call *realloc* to expand a block. Do they know that the block can move?

Here's another problem with *realloc*: You know it's possible to pass garbage to *realloc*, but because its definition is so general it's hard to guard against invalid arguments. If you pass a *NULL* pointer by mistake, that's legal. If you pass a *0* size by mistake, that's legal too. It's too bad if you *malloc* a new block or *free* the current one when your intent is to resize a block. How can you assert that *realloc*'s arguments are valid if practically everything is legal? No matter what you throw at it, *realloc* handles it, even to extremes. At one extreme it *frees* blocks; at the other it *mallocs* them. These are totally opposite behaviors.

To be fair, programmers don't usually sit down and think, "I'm going to design an entire subsystem in a single function." *realloc* and functions like it almost always arise for one of two reasons. Either they evolve into multi-purpose functions, or the extra behavior (such as *free* and *malloc*) falls out of the implementation and the programmer extends the formal description to include this "fortunate" behavior.

If, for whatever reason, you write a multipurpose function, break it down into its distinct behaviors. For *realloc* the breakdown would be expanding a block, shrinking a block, allocating a block, and freeing a block. By breaking *realloc* down into four distinct functions, you'll be able to do much better error checking. If you're shrinking memory, for instance, you'll know that the pointer must be to a valid block and you'll know that the new size must be less than (or possibly equal to) the current size. Anything else is an error. With a separate *ShrinkMemory* function, you could use assertions to validate those arguments.

In some cases, you may actually want a function to do more than one task. For example, when you call *realloc*, do you usually know whether the new size will be smaller or larger than the current one? Whether you know depends on your program, but I usually don't know (although I can often derive the information). I've found it better to have one function that both shrinks and expands blocks so that I don't have to write *if* constructs every time I need to resize memory. True, I give up some extra argument checking, but this is offset by the *if*s that I no longer need to write (and possibly mess up). I do always know when I'm allocating memory or freeing it, so I would rip those tasks out of *realloc* and make them separate functions. *fNewMemory*, *FreeMemory*, and *fResizeMemory* from Chapter 3 are the three well-defined functions.

If I were working on a program in which I normally knew whether I was expanding or shrinking the block, I would definitely break the expand and shrink functions out of *realloc* and create two additional functions:

```
flag fGrowMemory(void **ppv, size_t sizeLarger);

void ShrinkMemory(void *pv, size_t sizeSmaller);
```

This division of labor would allow me not only to thoroughly validate the pointers and sizes, but also to call *ShrinkMemory* with less risk since I would be guaranteed that the block would always be shrunk and that the block would never move. Instead of having to write

```
ASSERT(sizeNew <= sizeofBlock(pb));    /* Validate pb and sizeNew */
(void)realloc(pb, sizeNew);            /* Shrink can't fail */
```

I could write

```
ShrinkMemory(pb, sizeNew);
```

and be done with it. The simplest reason for using *ShrinkMemory* instead of *realloc* is that the code is so much clearer. With *ShrinkMemory*, you don't need the comment explaining that it can't fail, you don't need the *void* cast to drop an unused return value, and you don't need to verify that *pb* and *sizeNew* are valid—*ShrinkMemory* will do that for you.

———◆———

Don't write multipurpose functions.
Write separate functions to allow
stronger argument validation.

———◆———

WISHY-WASHY INPUTS

Earlier I said that your outputs should be separate and explicit to avoid confusing the programmers who use your functions. If you also apply that advice to the inputs of your functions, you naturally avoid writing all-encompassing functions such as *realloc*. *realloc* takes a pointer to a memory block, but sometimes it can be the magic *NULL* value that forces *realloc* to mimic *malloc*. *realloc* also takes a size value, but it allows the magic size of *0* that forces it to mimic *free*. These magic numbers may seem harmless enough, but they destroy comprehension. Quick, is the code below resizing, allocating, or releasing a memory block?

```
pbNew = realloc(pb, size);
```

You can't tell; it could be doing any one of those actions—it all depends on the values of *pb* and *size*. But if you knew that *pb* had to point to a valid block and that *size* had to be a legal block length, you'd know instantly that the code was resizing memory. Just as explicit outputs make it easier to decipher what's going on, so do explicit inputs, and that explicitness can be invaluable to maintenance programmers who have to read and understand code they didn't write.

Sometimes wishy-washy inputs aren't as easy to spot as *realloc*'s. For example, take a look at this specialized string copy routine that takes the first *size* characters of *strFrom* and turns them into a string stored at *strTo*:

```
char *CopySubStr(char *strTo, char *strFrom, size_t size)
{
    char *strStart = strTo;

    while (size-- > 0)
        *strTo++ = *strFrom++;
    *strTo = '\0';

    return (strStart);
}
```

CopySubStr is similar to the standard *strncpy* function, but unlike *strncpy*, it guarantees that the string at *strTo* is a true zero-terminated C string. You would typically use *CopySubStr* to extract a portion of a larger string—say, to pull the name of a day out of a packed string:

```
static char strDayNames[] = "SunMonTueWedThuFriSat";
    :
    :
ASSERT(day >= 0  &&  day <= 6);
CopySubStr(strDay, strDayNames + day*3, 3);
```

Now that you understand how *CopySubStr* works, do you see the questionable input? It's easy to spot if you try to write assertions to validate the arguments. The validation for *strTo* and *strFrom* would be

```
ASSERT(strTo != NULL  &&  strFrom != NULL);
```

but how do you validate the size argument? Is *0* a legal size? What if the size is larger than the length of *strFrom*? If you look at the code, you'll see that it handles both cases, sort of. The *while* loop quits if *size* is *0* on entry, so that works; and if *size* is larger than *strFrom*, the *while* loop will copy the entire string, including the null character terminating it. You just need to document the function to explain it, as in the example on the next page.

```
/*  CopySubStr -- extract a substring from a string.
 *
 *  Convert the first "size" characters of strFrom into
 *  a string stored at strTo. If there are fewer than
 *  "size" characters in strFrom, then the entire string
 *  is copied to strTo. If size is 0, strTo is set
 *  to the null string.
 */

char *CopySubStr(char *strTo, char *strFrom, size_t size)
{
    .
    .
    .
```

Sound familiar? Sure, because functions that behave that way are as common as dust on lightbulbs. Still, is this the best way to handle the size input? The answer is no, at least not when you view it in terms of writing bug-free code.

Suppose, for example, that a programmer mistyped 3 as 33 when he or she called *CopySubStr*:

```
CopySubStr(strDay, strDayNames + day*3, 33);
```

That's a realistic bug, but given its definition it's perfectly legal to call *CopySubStr* with a ridiculous value like 33. Oh sure, you would probably catch the bug before you released the code, but you wouldn't find it automatically; somebody would have to spot it. And don't forget that it's faster to track down an error starting from an assertion close to the bug than it is starting from faulty output.

From a "bug-free" point of view, if an argument is out of range or is meaningless, it should be illegal, because by silently accepting oddball values, you hide bugs rather than find them. In a way, allowing "loose" inputs is another form of defensive programming. Keep the defensive code for robustness, but disallow the questionable inputs:

```
/*  CopySubStr -- extract a substring from a string.
 *
 *  Convert the first "size" characters of strFrom into
 *  a string stored at strTo. There must be at least
 *  "size" characters in strFrom.
 */
```

```
char *CopySubStr(char *strTo, char *strFrom, size_t size)
{
    char *strStart = strTo;

    ASSERT(strTo != NULL  &&  strFrom != NULL);
    ASSERT(size <= strlen(strFrom));

    while (size-- > 0)
        *strTo++ = *strFrom++;
    *strTo = '\0';

    return (strStart);
}
```

Sometimes allowing a meaningless argument—such as a size of *0*—is worthwhile because it can eliminate unnecessary tests at the caller. For example, since *memset* allows its size argument to be *0*, you don't need the *if* statement in the code below:

```
if (strlen(str) != 0)          /* Fill str with spaces */
    memset(str, ' ', strlen(str));
```

But be careful when you allow *0* sizes. Programmers regularly handle sizes (or counts) of *0* because they can, not because they should. If you write a function that takes a size, you're not required to handle *0*. Instead, ask yourself, "How often will programmers call this routine with a size of *0*?" If the answer is never, or even rarely, don't handle *0*; assert instead. Remember that every time you ease a restriction, you eliminate a chance to catch a corresponding bug. A good rule is to initially choose strict definitions for your inputs to maximize the effectiveness of your assertions. If you later find that a restriction is overly harsh, you can remove it without affecting the rest of your program.

I used this philosophy in Chapter 3 when I included the *NULL* pointer check in *FreeMemory*. Since I would never call *FreeMemory* with a *NULL* pointer, it was more important to me to have the stronger error checking. Your views may be different—there is no right and wrong here. Just be sure that whatever you do is a conscious choice and not merely a habit you've picked up.

———◆———

*Don't be wishy-washy. Define explicit
function arguments.*

———◆———

DON'T FAIL ME NOW

Microsoft has a policy of asking potential employees technical questions during their interviews, and for programmers, that means being handed one or more coding problems. I used to start candidates off with the task of writing the standard *tolower* function. I would hand the candidate an ASCII table and ask, "How would you write a function that would convert an uppercase letter to its lowercase equivalent?" I would be deliberately vague about how to handle symbols and lowercase letters, primarily to see how the programmer would handle those cases. Would those characters remain unchanged? Would the programmer's code assert? Would symbols and lowercase letters be ignored? More than half the time, candidates would write something like this:

```
char tolower(char ch)
{
    return (ch + 'a' - 'A');
}
```

This code works if *ch* is an uppercase letter, but if *ch* is anything else, it breaks. When I would point this out to interviewees, sometimes they'd say, "I assumed that the character had to be uppercase. I could handle all characters by returning the character unchanged if it wasn't a capital letter." That's a reasonable solution; other solutions were less so. More often than not, candidates would say, "I didn't think of that. I can fix the problem by returning an error if *ch* isn't a capital letter." Sometimes they'd have *tolower* return *NULL*, at other times the null character, but the clear winner, for some reason, was *–1*:

```
char tolower(char ch)
{
    if (ch >= 'A'  &&  ch <= 'Z')
        return (ch + 'a' - 'A');
    else
        return (-1);
}
```

Returning *–1* violates the interface suggestion I made earlier because it mixes an error value with a real piece of data. But the problem is not that the candidates failed to heed a suggestion they'd probably never heard of, but rather that they were generating an error when they didn't need to.

This brings up another observation: If a function returns an error, every single caller must handle that error. If *tolower* were to return *–1*, instead of writing the simple

```
ch = tolower(ch);
```

you would have to write something like this:

```
int chNew;        /* This *must* be an int in order to hold -1. */

if ((chNew = tolower(ch)) != -1)
    ch = chNew;
```

If you consider how you'd have to use *tolower* at every call, you can see that returning an error may not be the best way to define the function.

If you find yourself designing a function so that it returns an error, stop and ask yourself whether there's any way you can redefine the function to eliminate the error condition. Instead of defining *tolower* to "return the lowercase equivalent of an uppercase letter," have *tolower* "return the lowercase equivalent of *ch* if one exists; otherwise, return the character unchanged."

If you find that you can't eliminate an error condition, consider disallowing the problematic cases altogether. For example, you could require that the argument to *tolower* be a capital letter and say that any other character is illegal. You would then use an assertion to verify the argument:

```
char tolower(char ch)
{
    ASSERT(ch >= 'A'  &&  ch <= 'Z');

    return (ch + 'a' - 'A');
}
```

Whether you redefine a function or eliminate the problematic cases, you remove the need for callers to do runtime error checking, which results in smaller code and fewer bugs.

———◆———

Write functions that, given valid
inputs, cannot fail.

———◆———

READ BETWEEN THE LINES

I can't emphasize enough how important it is to examine your interfaces from the point of view of the caller. When you consider that you define a function just once but you call it from many places, it seems foolish not to examine how it will be called. The *getchar*, *realloc*, and *tolower* examples we've seen bring this point home—all complicate code at the point of call. But fusing outputs and returning needless error codes aren't the only ways in which you can complicate code. Sometimes all it takes is a careless disregard for how the function will "read" when you call it.

Suppose you were trying to improve the disk handling portion of your application and you ran into a file seek call written this way:

```
if (fseek(fpDocument, offset, 1) == 0)
    :
    :
```

You can tell that some sort of seek is happening, and you can see that the error is being handled, but how readable is the call? What kind of seek is happening—from the beginning of the file, from the current file position, or from the end-of-file? If the return value is *0*, does that indicate success or failure?

Suppose, instead, that the programmer had written the call using predefined names:

```
#include <stdio.h>          /* Pull in SEEK_CUR. */
#define ERR_NONE 0
    :
    :
if (fseek(fpDocument, offset, SEEK_CUR) == ERR_NONE)
    :
    :
```

Does this clarify the call? Sure it does. But this isn't a surprising new revelation—programmers have known for decades that they should avoid using magic numbers in their code. What I would like to point out is that *NULL*, *TRUE*, and *FALSE* are not named constants the way they're often used, but rather are textual representations of magic numbers. For instance, what do the calls below do?

```
UnsignedToStr(u, str, TRUE);

UnsignedToStr(u, str, FALSE);
```

You can probably guess that these calls convert an unsigned value to its textual representation, but how does the boolean argument affect that conversion? Would it be clearer if I instead wrote the calls as

```
#define BASE10 1
#define BASE16 0
  :
  :
UnsignedToStr(u, str, BASE10);
UnsignedToStr(u, str, BASE16);
```

When a programmer sits down to write such functions, the boolean values may seem perfectly clear. First the programmer launches into a description and then into the implementation:

```
/*  UnsignedToStr
 *
 *  This function converts an unsigned value to its
 *  textual representation. If fDecimal is TRUE, u is
 *  converted to a decimal representation; otherwise,
 *  u is converted to a hexadecimal representation.
 */

void UnsignedToStr(unsigned u, char *strResult, flag fDecimal)
{
    :
    :
```

What could be clearer than that?

The reality is that boolean arguments often indicate that the designer didn't put much thought into what he or she was doing. Either the function is doing two different things and the boolean argument selects which of the two behaviors you want, or the function is generally flexible but the programmer used a boolean to specify the only two cases he or she was interested in. Often both are true.

If you view *UnsignedToStr* as a function that is doing two different things, you could drop the boolean argument and and split *UnsignedToStr* into two specific functions:

```
void UnsignedToDecStr(unsigned u, char *str);

void UnsignedToHexStr(unsigned u, char *str);
```

But a better solution—in this case—would be to make *UnsignedToStr* more flexible by changing the boolean argument to a general-purpose one. Instead of passing in *TRUE* or *FALSE,* have programmers pass in the conversion base:

```
void UnsignedToStr(unsigned u, char *str, unsigned base);
```

This solution gives you a clean, flexible design that makes the calling code understandable and that at the same time increases the usefulness of the function.

This advice may seem to contradict what I said earlier about defining your arguments rigidly—we went from a concrete *TRUE* or *FALSE* input to a general one in which most of the possible values aren't useful. But remember, *base* may be general, but you can always include an assertion to verify that it is either *10* or *16.* If you later decide that you also need binary or octal conversions, you can relax the assertion to allow programmers to pass in *2* and *8.*

That's far better than some functions I've seen that have an argument with the values *TRUE, FALSE, 2,* and *–1!* Because boolean arguments don't extend easily, you either end up with such nonsense or have to update every preexisting call.

———◆———

Make the code intelligible at the
point of call.

Avoid boolean arguments.

———◆———

WARN PEOPLE OF THE HAZARDS

As a final guard against bugs, write your documentation so that it both emphasizes the hazards and shows how you expect people to use the code. Instead of documenting *getchar* this way,

```
/* getchar -- this is the same as getc(stdin). */

int getchar(void)
    :
    :
```

which doesn't really help programmers much, you could write something
like this:

```
/*  getchar -- equivalent to getc(stdin).
 *
 *  getchar returns the next character from stdin. When
 *  an error occurs, it returns the *int* EOF. A typical
 *  use is
 *
 *      int ch;         // ch *must* be an int in order to hold EOF.
 *
 *      if ((ch = getchar()) != EOF)
 *          // success -- ch has the next character
 *      else
 *          // failure -- ferror(stdin) gives error type
 */

int getchar(void)
    ⋮
    ⋮
```

If you were to hand both of these descriptions to a programmer just
learning the C library, which one do you think would leave stronger im-
pressions about the hazards of using *getchar*? And what about when that
programmer uses *getchar* for the first time? Do you think she's going to
make up new code, or do you think she will simply copy the "typical use"
example from your documentation and adapt it to her needs?

Another positive side effect of documenting functions this way is that
it forces less-careful programmers to stop and think about how other programmers have to use their functions. If a programmer writes a function
with a clunky interface, he should notice that the interface is bad when he
tries to write the "typical use" example. But even if he doesn't notice the
problems with the interface, it won't matter as long as the example is thorough and correct. What if the documentation for *realloc* provided an example such as the one on the next page?

```
/*  realloc(pv, size)
 *  ...
 *  A typical use is
 *
 *    void *pvNew;        // used to protect pv if realloc fails
 *
 *    pvNew = realloc(pv, sizeNew);
 *    if (pvNew != NULL)
 *    {
 *        // success -- update pv
 *        pv = pvNew;
 *    }
 *    else
 *        // failure -- don't destroy pv with the NULL pvNew
 */

void *realloc(void *pv, size_t size)
  :
  :
```

By copying such an example, less-cautious programmers are more likely to avoid the lost memory problem I talked about earlier in this chapter. Your examples won't protect all programmers, but like the warnings on medicine bottles, they will influence some people, and every bit helps.

But don't use examples as a substitute for designing good interfaces. *getchar* and *realloc* both have bug-prone interfaces—their hazards should be eliminated, not merely documented.

———◆———

Write comments that emphasize
potential hazards.

———◆———

THE DEVIL IS IN THE DETAILS

Designing bug-resistant interfaces is not difficult, but it does take some extra thought and a willingness to abandon ingrained coding habits. The suggestions in this chapter show how, with simple changes to your interfaces, you can lead programmers to write correct code without much thought on their part. The key concept running through this chapter is "Make everything as clear and as obvious as possible." If programmers understood and remembered every detail, they might not make mistakes; but programmers do make mistakes, in part because they forget about or never learned about the important details. Make it hard for programmers to unwittingly ignore details; design bug-resistant interfaces.

QUICK REVIEW

◆ Create function interfaces that are easy to use and understand: Ensure that input and output represent exactly one type of data. Mixing error and other special-purpose values into your inputs and outputs does nothing but clutter your interfaces.

◆ Design your function interfaces in such a way that programmers are forced to think about all the important details, such as handling error conditions. Don't make it easy for them to ignore or forget the details.

◆ Consider how programmers must call your functions. Look for flaws in your function interfaces that can cause programmers to unwittingly introduce bugs. Of particular importance: Strive to write functions that always succeed so that callers don't need to do any error handling.

◆ Increase comprehension and thus reduce bugs by making sure that the calls to your functions are understandable to programmers who have to read those calls. Magic numbers and boolean arguments work against this goal.

◆ Break apart multipurpose functions. Not only do the more specific function names increase comprehension (for example, *ShrinkMemory* instead of *realloc*), but you can use more rigid assertions to automatically detect bad arguments.

◆ Document your interfaces to show programmers how to properly call your functions. Emphasize the danger zones.

THINGS TO THINK ABOUT

1. The *strdup* function at the beginning of the chapter allocates a duplicate string but returns *NULL* if it fails. What would be a more bug-resistant interface for *strdup*?

2. I said that the presence of boolean inputs often indicates that there could be a better interface for the function. But what about boolean outputs? For example, if *fGetChar* fails, it returns *FALSE* and requires programmers to call *ferror(stdin)* to determine the cause of the error. What would be an even better interface for *getchar*?

3. Why is the ANSI *strncpy* function bound to trip up the unwary programmer?

4. If you're familiar with C++'s *inline* function specifier, describe its contribution to the writing of bug-resistant interfaces.

5. C++ introduced & reference arguments similar to Pascal's *VAR* arguments. Instead of writing

```
flag fGetChar(char *pch);    /* prototype */
    :
    :
if (fGetChar(&ch))
    ch has the new character...
```

you could write

```
flag fGetChar(char &ch);     /* prototype */
    :
    :
if (fGetChar(ch))               /* &ch is actually passed. */
    ch has the new character...
```

On the surface, this appears to be a good addition since programmers can't "forget" the explicit & required in regular C. But why would using this feature result in bug-prone rather than bug-resistant interfaces?

6.   The standard *strcmp* function takes two strings and compares them, character by character. If the two strings are equal, *strcmp* returns *0*; if the first is less than the second, it returns a negative number; and if the first is greater than the second, it returns a positive number. So, when you call *strcmp*, the code usually looks like this:

```
if (strcmp(str1, str2)  rel_op  0)
     .
     .
     .
```

where *rel_op* is one of ==, !=, >, >=, <, or <=. This works, but the code is meaningless unless you're familiar with the *strcmp* function. Describe at least two other function interfaces for string comparisons. The interfaces should be both more bug-resistant and more readable than *strcmp*'s interface.

PROJECT: Review the functions in the standard C library and redesign the interfaces so that they will be more bug-resistant. What are the pros and cons of renaming the functions so that they are more intelligible?

PROJECT: Search a large body of code for all occurrences of *memset*, *memmove*, *memcpy*, and the set of *strn-* functions (*strncpy*, etc.). How many of those calls require that the function accept a *0* count? Does your organization use the convenience enough to justify allowing it?

6

RISKY BUSINESS

If you were to put a programmer at the top of a cliff and give him a rope and a hang glider, how do you think he'd get to the bottom? Would he climb down the rope, or would he glide to the bottom? I have no idea whether he'd use the rope or the hang glider, but I'll bet you anything that he wouldn't jump to the bottom—it's too risky. But for some reason, when programmers can choose among several possible implementations, they often consider only size and speed and completely ignore risk. What if the programmer on that cliff ignored risk and instead just took the most efficient route to the bottom? Geronimoooooooooooo. . .

There are at least two reasons why programmers ignore risk.

Programmers ignore risk, in part, because they blindly assume that no matter how they implement their code, they're going to implement it without bugs. Nobody says, "Guess what, I'm going to write a quicksort routine and I plan to have three bugs in it." Programmers don't plan to have bugs; they're just not very surprised when bugs show up later.

But the major reason, I believe, that programmers ignore risk is that they have never been taught to ask questions such as, "How risky is this design?" "How risky is this implementation?" "Is there a safer way to write this expression?" "Is it even possible to test this design?" To ask questions like these, you must let go of the belief that regardless of your choices you'll end up with bug-free code. That might even be a well-founded belief, but the question in that case is When will you have bug-free code? Will it be hours or days from now because you use safe coding practices, or will it be weeks or months from now because you ignore risk and have lots of bugs to track down and fix?

Throughout this chapter I will talk about the risks inherent in some common coding practices and about what you can do to reduce, or even eliminate, those risks.

How Long Is a *long*?

When the ANSI committee looked at the various flavors of C running on numerous platforms, they saw that C wasn't the truly portable language everybody thought it was. Not only were the standard libraries different on every system, but even the preprocessor and the language itself differed in important ways. The ANSI committee standardized most of these problem areas, giving programmers a real shot at writing portable code, but one important area that the ANSI standard largely ignores is the definitions of the intrinsic data types. Rather than concretely defining *char*, *int*, and *long*, the ANSI standard leaves important implementation details up to the compiler writer.

Thus, one ANSI standard compiler can have 32-bit *int*s and signed *char*s, while another ANSI compiler can have 16-bit *int*s and unsigned *char*s. Yet even with such profound differences, it's possible for both compilers to strictly adhere to the ANSI standard.

Take a look at this code:

```
char ch;          /* Declare ch. */
  :
  :
ch = 0xFF;
if (ch == 0xFF)
    :
    :
```

My question is Will the expression in the *if* statement evaluate to *TRUE* or to *FALSE*?

Of *course* the expression will evaluate to *TRUE*—or will it? The correct answer is that you don't know; the result is completely compiler dependent. If your characters are unsigned by default, the expression will indeed be *TRUE*. But on compilers in which *char* is signed, as is often the case for 80x86 and 680x0 compilers, the test will fail every time. The reason has to do with C's promotion rules.

In the code above, the character *ch* is being compared to the integer *0xFF*. According to C's promotion rules, the compiler must first promote *ch* to an *int* so that it can compare compatible types. The catch is that if *ch* is signed, promoting it sign-extends the value from *0xFF* to *0xFFFF* (assuming you have 16-bit *int*s). That's why the test can fail, despite the fact that it looks as if it should always succeed.

I realize that the code above is just a contrived example to demonstrate my point, and you could claim that it's an unrealistic piece of code, but you'd run into exactly the same problem with this common code extract:

```
char *pch;               /* Declare pch. */
  :
  :
if (*pch == 0xFF)
    :
    :
```

The *char* type isn't alone in this kind of ill-defined behavior; bit fields are just as bad. What's the numerical range for the bit field below?

```
int reg : 3;
```

Again, you don't know. Even though *reg* is defined to be an *int*, which implies that it's signed, *reg* can be either signed or unsigned, depending upon your compiler. You must use *signed int* or *unsigned int* if you definitely want *reg* to be one or the other.

And how big is a *short*? An *int*? A *long*? The ANSI standard doesn't say, preferring to leave it up to the compiler writer to decide.

I don't want to leave you with the impression that the members of the ANSI committee were blind to the problems of ill-defined data types. That's far from the truth. In fact, they looked at numerous C implementations and concluded that, because the types varied so widely across compilers, defining a strict standard would invalidate too much preexisting code. That violated one of the committee's guiding principles: *Existing code is important.* Their goal was not to create a better language but to standardize an existing one, and whenever possible, they weren't going to break large bodies of existing code.

Nailing down the types would also have violated another of the committee's guiding principles, which is *Keep the spirit of C: Make it fast, even if it is not guaranteed to be portable.* If an implementor feels that signed characters are more efficient for a given machine, that's what you'll get. This attention to speed also means that implementors get to choose whether *int*s will be 16 bits, 32 bits, or some other "natural" size dictated by the hardware. And it means that you have no idea whether you'll have signed or unsigned bit fields by default.

The point I'm making here is that the intrinsic types have gaping holes in their specifications, holes you can fall into the next time you upgrade or switch compilers, move to a new target environment, share your code with another group or company, or even switch jobs and find yourself using a compiler in which all the rules have changed.

None of this means that you can't safely use the intrinsic types. You can. But to reduce risk you shouldn't assume that the types have any properties that the ANSI standard doesn't explicitly specify.

For instance, you can use the fickle *char* data type provided that you stick to the values *0* through *127*, the intersection of the guaranteed ranges of signed and unsigned characters. So, while the code below works with any compiler because it doesn't make range assumptions,

```c
char *strcpy(char *pchTo, char *pchFrom)
{
    char *pchStart = pchTo;

    while ((*pchTo++ = *pchFrom++) != '\0')
        NULL;

    return (pchStart);
}
```

the code below will not:

```
/*   strcmp -- compare two strings.
 *
 *   Returns a negative # if strLeft < strRight,
 *   0 if strLeft == strRight, and a positive #
 *   if strLeft > strRight.
 */

int strcmp(const char *strLeft, const char *strRight)
{
    for (NULL; *strLeft == *strRight; strLeft++, strRight++)
    {
        if (*strLeft == '\0')          /* Match to the end? */
            return (0);
    }

    return ((*strLeft < *strRight) ? -1 : 1);
}
```

The code above isn't portable because of the comparison in the last line. The moment you use <, or any other operator that uses sign information, you force the compiler to generate nonportable code. It's easy to fix *strcmp*. Either declare *strLeft* and *strRight* to be unsigned character pointers, or cast them in the comparison:

```
(*(unsigned char *)strLeft < *(unsigned char *)strRight)
```

A good rule to remember, one worth taping to your wall, is *Don't use "plain" chars in expressions*. A similar rule for bit fields, since they suffer from the same problems, is *Never use "plain" bit fields*. I say "never" because of the misleading nature of the *int* keyword when applied to bit fields.

If you read the ANSI standard and interpret it conservatively, you can derive a well-defined set of portable types that work across compilers and across the three most common numbering systems—one's complement, two's complement, and signed magnitude:

`char`	0 through 127
`signed char`	−127 (not −128) through 127
`unsigned char`	0 through 255
	Unknown size, but no smaller than 8 bits

(continued)

continued

short	–32767 (not –32768) through 32767
signed short	–32767 through 32767
unsigned short	0 through 65535
	Unknown size, but no smaller than 16 bits
int	–32767 (not –32768) through 32767
signed int	–32767 through 32767
unsigned int	0 through 65535
	Unknown size, but no smaller than 16 bits
long	–2147483647 (not –2147483648) through 2147483647
signed long	–2147483647 through 2147483647
unsigned long	0 through 4294967295
	Unknown size, but no smaller than 32 bits
int i:n	0 through $2^{n-1}-1$
signed int i:n	$-(2^{n-1}-1)$ through $2^{n-1}-1$
unsigned int i:n	0 through 2^n-1
	Unknown size, but at least n bits

Using the Portable Data Types

Some programmers may be concerned that using the portable types is less efficient than using "natural" types. For instance, the *int* type is supposed to be whatever size is optimally efficient for the target hardware. That means its "natural" size could well be larger than 16 bits and hold values greater than *32767*.

Suppose your compiler uses 32-bit *int*s and you have a value with the range *0* through *40000*. Do you use an *int* because your machine can efficiently handle *40000* in an *int*, or do you stick to the portable types and use a *long* instead?

Here's a nice weasely answer: If your machine uses 32-bit *int*s, it probably also uses 32-bit *long*s and will generate similar if not identical code for the two (historically, that has been true), so use a *long*. If you're worried that a *long* may be inefficient on some future machine you have to support, you should be using portable types anyway.

OK, so maybe you don't need to worry about writing portable code. But treat the issue the way you would choose new tile for your kitchen counter. If you're like most people, you would pick tile that you like and that you think future home buyers will at least tolerate. That way, you get a pattern you want, but also one you don't have to rip out and replace in order to sell your house. View portable code the same way because in many cases it's just as easy to write portable code as it is to write nonportable code. Protect yourself from a future reconstruction job—write portable code whenever possible.

Use well-defined data types.

DOTH YOUR DATA RUN OVER?

Some of the most sinister bugs are those in which the code appears to be obviously correct yet fails because of a subtle implementation problem. The "plain *char*" bug has that property, and so does the code below, which initializes a lookup table for the standard *tolower* macro:

```
#include <limits.h>              /* Pull in UCHAR_MAX. */
   :
   :
char chToLower[UCHAR_MAX+1];

void BuildToLowerTable(void)     /* ASCII version */
{
    unsigned char ch;

    /* First set every character to itself. */
    for (ch = 0; ch <= UCHAR_MAX; ch++)
        chToLower[ch] = ch;

    /* Now poke lowercase letters into the uppercase slots. */
    for (ch = 'A'; ch <= 'Z'; ch++)
        chToLower[ch] = ch + 'a'-'A';
}
   :
   :
#define tolower(ch) (chToLower[(unsigned char)(ch)])
```

Despite how solid the code looks, *BuildToLowerTable* will probably hang your system. Take a look at the test in the first loop. When will *ch* be greater than *UCHAR_MAX*? If you guessed Never, you're right. If you didn't guess that way, let me explain.

Suppose *ch* is equal to *UCHAR_MAX* and the loop executes for what you expect is the last time. Then, just before the final test, *ch* is incremented to *UCHAR_MAX+1*, causing it to overflow and wrap to *0*. The machine hangs in an infinite loop because *ch* will always be less than or equal to *UCHAR_MAX*.

How obvious is that problem when you look at the code?

You can underflow a variable and find yourself in a similar predicament. Below is an implementation for the *memchr* function, which searches a block of memory for the first occurrence of a character. If it finds the character in the block, it returns a pointer to the character's location; otherwise, it returns the *NULL* pointer. And like *BuildToLowerTable* above, the code for *memchr* seems correct when you read it but fails nevertheless.

```
void *memchr(void *pv, unsigned char ch, size_t size)
{
    unsigned char *pch = (unsigned char *)pv;

    while (--size >= 0)
    {
        if (*pch == ch)
            return (pch);
        pch++;
    }

    return (NULL);
}
```

When will the loop terminate? When *size* is less than *0*, of course, but will that ever be true? No, because *size* is an unsigned value—when it reaches *0*, the expression --*size* will cause it to underflow and wrap to the largest unsigned value defined by the type *size_t*.

This underflow bug is worse than the bug in *BuildToLowerTable* because *memchr* will work correctly as long as it finds *ch* in the memory run. Even if it doesn't find the character, it probably won't hang your system—it'll just keep searching memory until it finds *ch* somewhere, and return a pointer to that character. This could be a hard bug to spot.

I'd like to think that your compiler would warn you of the "plain *char*" bug, and of the other two bugs above, but I've found very few compilers that do warn of these problems, although there is no technical reason why they couldn't. Until compiler vendors learn that there's more to a compiler than good code generation, you'll have to spot such overflow and underflow bugs yourself.

The good news is that if you step through your code as I suggested in Chapter 4, you'll pounce on all three bugs. You'll see that *pch* is promoted to *0xFFFF* before it's compared to *0xFF*, you'll see that *ch* overflows and wraps to *0*, and you'll see that *size* underflows to *0xFFFF*. You could read your code for hours and never spot overflow bugs because they are so subtle, but if you look at the data flow in a debugger, such bugs will become obvious.

————◆————

Always ask, "Can this variable or
expression over- or underflow?"

————◆————

CLOSE COUNTS ONLY IN HORSESHOES

You can see another often-used overflow example in the code below, which converts an integer to its ASCII representation:

```
void IntToStr(int i, char *str)
{
    char *strDigits;

    if (i < 0)
    {
        *str++ = '-';
        i = -i;                     /* Strip i's negative sign. */
    }

    /* Derive the digits in reverse order. */
    strDigits = str;
    do
        *str++ = (i % 10) + '0';
    while ((i /= 10) > 0);
    *str = '\0';

    ReverseStr(strDigits);      /* Unreverse the digits. */
}
```

This code breaks on two's-complement machines for the single case in which *i* is equal to the smallest negative number (*–32768* on a 16-bit machine, for instance). The reason usually given is that the *–i* in the expression *i* = *–i*; overflows the range of the *int* type, and that's perfectly true. But the real bug lies in the way the programmer implemented the code: He didn't implement his design; he implemented something almost the same.

The design says, "If *i* is negative, stuff in a minus sign, and convert *i's* unsigned counterpart to ASCII." But that's not what the code does. The code actually implements, "If *i* is negative, stuff in a minus sign, and convert *i's* positive but signed counterpart to ASCII." It's the signed math that causes all the trouble. If you follow the original design and use unsigned math, the code works fine, plus you can break the code into two, more useful, functions:

```
void IntToStr(int i, char *str)
{
    if (i < 0)
    {
        *str++ = '-';
        i = -i;
    }
    UnsToStr((unsigned)i, str);
}


void UnsToStr(unsigned u, char *str)
{
    char *strStart = str;

    do
        *str++ = (u % 10) + '0';
    while ((u /= 10) > 0);
    *str = '\0';

    ReverseStr(strStart);
}
```

You might be wondering why this code works, given that it negates *i* just as the previous example did. It works because if *i* is the smallest negative number, *0x8000*, and you negate it by "flipping all the bits and adding 1," you still get *0x8000*, which looks like *–32768* as a signed number, but like *32768* as an unsigned number. It's all in how you interpret the bits. By definition, flipping the bits and adding 1 must give you the negative value of any two's-complement number, but it's up to you to correctly interpret the bit-pattern. In this case, interpreting the bit-pattern as a signed value is wrong.

Still, being right is not always being smart. The code above feels wrong. It also assumes that *–32768* is a valid *int*, which it isn't—at least not if you're sticking to the portable types. If you agree that *–32768* is a nonportable *int*, you can cast aside the whole mess with one well-placed assertion in *IntToStr*:

```
void IntToStr(int i, char *str)
{
    /* i out of range?  Use LongToStr... */
    ASSERT(i >= -32767  &&  i <= 32767);
    :
    :
```

By using such assertions you not only avoid oddball problems related to one particular numbering system, but you also nudge other programmers into writing more portable code.

———◆———

Implement your designs as accurately as possible. Being kinda close is being kinda buggy.

———◆———

FUNCTIONS JUST "DOING THEIR THING"

I once thoroughly reviewed the code for Character Windows—a Windows-like library designed for Microsoft's character-based DOS applications—because the two primary groups using the library, the Word and Works groups, felt that the code was bulky, sluggish, and unstable. I had just begun reviewing the code when I ran across an example of programmers not quite implementing what they had designed—and of the violation of another guiding principle for writing bug-free code.

But first, some background.

The basic design for Character Windows was simple: The user views the video display as a set of windows, each of which can have its own subwindows. In the design, a root window represents the entire display, and this window has subwindows: a menu bar, pull-down menus, application document windows, dialogs, and so on. Each of these windows may have its own subwindows. A dialog might have subwindows for OK and Cancel buttons, and it might have a listbox window that has its own subwindows for scrollbars. You get the idea.

To represent the hierarchical window structure, Character Windows used a binary tree in which one branch pointed to subwindows, called "children," and the other branch pointed to windows with the same parent, called "siblings":

```
typedef struct WINDOW
{
    struct WINDOW *pwndChild;       /* NULL if no children */
    struct WINDOW *pwndSibling;     /* NULL if no brothers/sisters */
    char *strWndTitle;
        .
        .
        .
} window;                           /* Naming: wnd, *pwnd */
```

You can turn to any algorithm book and find efficient routines to manipulate binary trees, so I was a bit shocked when I reviewed the Character Windows code for inserting a child window into the tree. The code looked like this:

```
/*  pwndRootChildren is the pointer to the list of top-level
 *  windows, such as the menu bar and the main document windows.
 */
static window *pwndRootChildren = NULL;
```

Why a Hierarchy of Windows?

If you're wondering why it's worthwhile having a hierarchy of windows, consider this: The hierarchical arrangement simplifies operations such as moving, hiding, and deleting windows. What if you moved a dialog window and the OK and Cancel buttons stayed where they were? Or what if you hid a window and its subwindows remained visible? That's not what you want. By supporting subwindows, you can say "move this window" and know that all of its associated windows will tag along.

```
void AddChild(window *pwndParent, window *pwndNewBorn)
{
    /* New windows may have children but not siblings... */
    ASSERT(pwndNewBorn->pwndSibling == NULL);

    if (pwndParent == NULL)
    {
        /* Add window to the top-level root list. */
        pwndNewBorn->pwndSibling = pwndRootChildren;
        pwndRootChildren = pwndNewBorn;
    }
    else
    {

        /*  If Parent's first child, start a new sibling chain;
         *  otherwise, add child to the end of the existing
         *  sibling chain.
         */
        if (pwndParent->pwndChild == NULL)
            pwndParent->pwndChild = pwndNewBorn;
        else
        {
            window *pwnd = pwndParent->pwndChild;

            while (pwnd->pwndSibling != NULL)
                pwnd = pwnd->pwndSibling;
            pwnd->pwndSibling = pwndNewBorn;
        }
    }
}
```

Despite the fact that the windowing structure was designed to be a binary tree, it hadn't been implemented that way. Since the root window (the one representing the entire display) never has siblings and never has a title and since you can't move, hide, or delete it, the only field in the *window* structure that ever has any meaning is *pwndChild*—it points to the menu bar and application subwindows. That led somebody to decide that declaring an entire window structure was wasteful, and the *wndRoot* structure was replaced with *pwndRootChildren*, a simple pointer to the top-level windows.

Replacing *wndRoot* with a pointer may have saved a few bytes of data space, but the cost in code space was enormous. Instead of working with a simple binary tree, routines such as *AddChild* had to handle two different data structures: a linked list of window trees at the root level, and the window trees themselves. Worse, every routine that took a window pointer as an argument—and there were many—had to check for the special *NULL* pointer that represented the display "window." No wonder the Word and Works groups were concerned about code bloat.

I didn't bring up the problems with *AddChild* so that I could talk about design issues, but rather to point out that its implementation violated at least three guiding principles for writing bug-free code. You've seen two of these principles already: *Don't accept special purpose arguments* such as the *NULL* pointer, and *Implement your design, not something that approximates it.* The third principle is new: *Strive to make every function perform its task exactly one time.*

What do I mean by that? If you think about it, *AddChild* has one task, to add a child to an existing window, but the code has three separate insertion routines. Common sense tells you that if you have three pieces of code instead of one, you're more likely to have bugs. If you find yourself writing a function in which you do "the task" more than once, stop and ask yourself whether you can do the same job with one piece of code.

You may sometimes want to write a function so that it does whatever it does more than once. The fast version of *memset* in Chapter 2 is an example of that—recall that it has two separate fill loops, a fast one and a slow one. You can break the rules; just be sure you have a good reason to.

The first step in improving *AddChild* is easy enough: Rip out the "optimization" and implement the original design. To do that, you replace *pwndRootChildren* with *pwndDisplay*, a pointer to a *window* structure representing the display. And instead of passing *NULL* to *AddChild* to insert root-level windows, you pass *pwndDisplay*. That eliminates the need for any special code to handle root windows.

```
/*  pwndDisplay points to the root-level window, which is
 *  allocated during program initialization.
 */
window *pwndDisplay = NULL;
```

```
void AddChild(window *pwndParent, window *pwndNewBorn)
{
    /* New windows may have children but not siblings... */
    ASSERT(pwndNewBorn->pwndSibling == NULL);

    /*  If Parent's first child, start a new sibling chain;
     *  otherwise, add child to the end of the existing sibling
     *  chain.
     */
    if (pwndParent->pwndChild == NULL)
        pwndParent->pwndChild = pwndNewBorn;
    else
    {
        window *pwnd = pwndParent->pwndChild;

        while (pwnd->pwndSibling != NULL)
            pwnd = pwnd->pwndSibling;
        pwnd->pwndSibling = pwndNewBorn;
    }
}
```

The code above not only improves *AddChild* (and every other function that had to accommodate the oddball tree structure) but also fixes a bug in the original version whereby root windows were inserted backwards. Interestingly enough, that bug had been "fixed" in Character Windows by the expedient of handling root-level windows in reverse order everywhere it mattered—adding to the code bloat.

———◆———

Implement "the task" just once.

———◆———

NO *if*S, *&&*S, OR BUTS

That last version of *AddChild* is better than its predecessor, but it's still doing twice the work it needs to do. The trip wire that should set off alarms in your head is the *if* statement, a sure sign that you're probably doing the same work twice, although in different ways. True, there are cases in which you legitimately need an *if* statement in order to take some conditional action, but many times an *if* statement is the result of a sloppy implementation or design—it's a lot easier to whip together a design filled with exceptions than it is to stop and derive a model without them.

For example, to traverse the sibling chain, you work with *window* structures and the pointers to the "next window," but you can traverse the sibling chain in two ways: You can enter the loop pointing to the *window* structure and step from window to window as you loop, or you can enter the loop pointing to the "next window" pointer and step from pointer to pointer. You use either a window-centric algorithm or a pointer-centric one. The current implementation for *AddChild* uses a window-centric algorithm.

But if you use the pointer-centric model, you're always pointing at the "next window" pointer, and it doesn't matter whether that "next window" pointer is the parent's child pointer or merely a sibling pointer. This lets you eliminate the *if* statement required in the window-centric algorithm because there is no special case. It may be easier to understand this point if you compare the code below with the previous implementation:

```
void AddChild(window *pwndParent, window *pwndNewBorn)
{
    window **ppwndNext;

    /* New windows may have children but not siblings... */
    ASSERT(pwndNewBorn->pwndSibling == NULL);

    /*  Traverse the sibling chain using a pointer-centric
     *  algorithm. We set ppwndNext to point at
     *  pwndParent->pwndChild since the latter pointer
     *  is the first "next sibling pointer" of the list.
     */
    ppwndNext = &pwndParent->pwndChild;

    while (*ppwndNext != NULL)
        ppwndNext = &(*ppwndNext)->pwndSibling;

    *ppwndNext = pwndNewBorn;
}
```

Don't be surprised if the code above seems familiar. It should. After all, it's a minor variant of the classic "dummy header" linked-list insertion algorithm famous for handling empty lists without any special-case code.

If you're concerned that this version of *AddChild* violates my earlier advice about implementing your design and not something that approximates it, you needn't be. The code may not implement the design the way you normally think about a linked list, but it does implement it truthfully. It's like looking at a lens in a pair of glasses—is the lens concave or convex?

It could be either, depending upon how you view it. For *AddChild*, using a pointer-centric algorithm lets you write code without special cases.

   And if you're worried about code efficiency, think about this: This final version of *AddChild* will generate much less code than any of the previous versions. Even the code for the loop will be comparable to—and possibly better than—the code generated for previous versions. Don't let those extra **s and &s trick you into thinking the loop is doing more than before—it's not. Compile the two to see for yourself.

———◆———

Get rid of extraneous if *statements.*

———◆———

THE *?:* OPERATOR IS AN *if* STATEMENT TOO

C programmers must regularly forget that the *?:* operator is nothing but an *if-else* statement in disguise; nothing else adequately explains why programmers write code using *?:* that they would never write using explicit *if-else* statements. I ran across a good example of this in Excel's dialog handling code. The code contained the function below, which determines the "next state" for a checkbox:

```
/*  uCycleCheckBox -- return the next state for a checkbox.
 *
 *  Given the current setting, uCur, return what the next
 *  checkbox state should be. This function handles both
 *  two-state checkboxes that toggle between 0 and 1, and
 *  three-state checkboxes that cycle through 2, 3, 4, 2,...
 */

unsigned uCycleCheckBox(unsigned uCur)
{
    return ((uCur<=1) ? (uCur?0:1) : (uCur==4)?2:(uCur+1));
}
```

   I've worked with programmers who wouldn't think twice about writing *uCycleCheckBox* using the nested *?:* above, but these same programmers would switch to COBOL before putting their name on the version below that uses explicit *if*s, even though the code generated by all but the best compilers would be nearly, if not actually, identical for the two versions.

```
unsigned uCycleCheckBox(unsigned uCur)
{
    unsigned uRet;

    if (uCur <= 1)
    {
        if (uCur != 0)      /* Handle the 0, 1, 0,... cycle. */
            uRet = 0;
        else
            uRet = 1;
    }
    else
    {
        if (uCur == 4)      /* Handle the 2, 3, 4, 2,... cycle. */
            uRet = 2;
        else
            uRet = uCur+1;
    }
    return (uRet);
}
```

And the code of those compilers that do generate better code for the nested ?: version isn't that much better. If you have a good compiler that's efficient for your target machine, you would get code comparable to this:

```
unsigned uCycleCheckBox(unsigned uCur)
{
    unsigned uRet;

    if (uCur <= 1)
    {
        uRet = 0;           /* Handle the 0, 1, 0,... cycle. */
        if (uCur == 0)
            uRet = 1;
    }
    else
    {
        uRet = 2;           /* Handle the 2, 3, 4, 2,... cycle. */
        if (uCur != 4)
            uRet = uCur+1;
    }
    return (uRet);
}
```

Take a good look at the three versions of *uCycleCheckBox*. Even though you know exactly what they're supposed to be doing, how obvious is it from the implementations? If I asked you what the return value would be if I passed in 3, could you easily see that the answer is 4? I couldn't. For functions that maintain two simple cycles, these implementations are about as clear as the used oil in your car, and about as hard to grasp.

The problem with the *?:* operator is that it's concise and easy to use; it appears ideal for producing efficient code, so programmers don't look for better solutions. Even worse, programmers will collapse the *if* version into the *?:* version to get a "better" solution that isn't better at all. It makes about as much sense as exchanging a $100 bill for 10,000 pennies so that you'll have more money. If these programmers would take the time to derive an alternative algorithm instead of expressing the same one in a slightly different way, they might come up with this straightforward implementation:

```
unsigned uCycleCheckBox(unsigned uCur)
{
    ASSERT(uCur >= 0  &&  uCur <= 4);

    if (uCur == 1)       /* Time to restart the first cycle? */
        return (0);

    if (uCur == 4)       /* What about the second one? */
        return (2);

    return (uCur+1);     /* Nope, nothing special this time. */
}
```

Or they might come up with this table solution:

```
unsigned uCycleCheckBox(unsigned uCur)
{
    static const unsigned uNextState[] = { 1, 0,  3, 4, 2 };

    ASSERT(uCur >= 0  &&  uCur <= 4);
    return (uNextState[uCur]);
}
```

By avoiding the nested *?:*, you can derive better algorithms instead of algorithms that just look better. Compare the table implementation with any of the previous implementations. Which is the easiest to understand?

Which generates the best code? And which is most likely to be correct the very first time? That should tell you something.

———◆———

Avoid using nested ?: operators.

———◆———

RID YOUR CODE OF REDUNDANCY

Here's an obvious point: If you find that you must support a special case, at least try to isolate the code so that the details aren't sprinkled throughout the function where a maintenance programmer might later miss them and unwittingly introduce bugs.

Earlier I showed you two implementations for *IntToStr*. What I didn't show you is the way *IntToStr* is often shown in C programming books—although there it's called *itoa*. The code usually looks something like this:

```
void IntToStr(int i, char *str)
{
    int iOriginal = i;
    char *pch;

    if (iOriginal < 0)
        i = -i;                     /* Strip i's negative sign. */

    /* Derive the string in reverse order. */
    pch = str;
    do
        *pch++ = i % 10 + '0';
    while ((i /= 10) > 0);

    if (iOriginal < 0)              /* Don't forget the '-' sign. */
        *pch++ = '-';
    *pch = '\0';

    ReverseStr(str);               /* Unreverse the string. */
}
```

Notice that the two *if* statements in the code are testing for the same special case. My question is why, when, as we saw on page 119, it's so easy to wrap the two bodies of code under a single *if* statement.

Sometimes repeated tests don't appear in *if* statements, but in the conditions of *for* or *while* statements, as in this other possible implementation of the *memchr* function:

```
void *memchr(void *pv, unsigned char ch, size_t size)
{
    unsigned char *pch = (unsigned char *)pv;
    unsigned char *pchEnd = pch + size;

    while (pch < pchEnd  &&  *pch != ch)
        pch++;

    return ((pch < pchEnd) ? pch : NULL);
}
```

But compare that version to this one:

```
void *memchr(void *pv, unsigned char ch, size_t size)
{
    unsigned char *pch = (unsigned char *)pv;
    unsigned char *pchEnd = pch + size;

    while (pch < pchEnd)
    {
        if (*pch == ch)
            return (pch);
        pch++;
    }

    return (NULL);
}
```

Which looks better to you, the first one, which compares *pch* to *pchEnd* twice, or the second one, which compares *pch* to *pchEnd* only once? Which is easier to figure out? And the crucial question: Which is more likely to be correct the first time you execute the code?

By localizing the block range check in the *while* condition, the second version is easier to understand and does exactly what it needs to do, and no more.

Handle your special cases just once.

HIGH RISK, NO RETURN

If those last two versions of *memchr* look correct to you, look again—they share the same subtle bug. Do you see it? Here's a hint: What range of memory would *memchr* search when *pv* points to the last 72 bytes of memory and *size* is also *72*? If you said "all of memory, over and over and over," you're right. Those versions of *memchr* go into an infinite loop because they use a risky language idiom—and Risk wins.

A risky language idiom is any phrase or expression that appears to work correctly but in fact fails for some specific cases. C is loaded with such phrases, and you need to avoid them whenever possible. Here's the risky idiom in *memchr*:

```
pchEnd = pch + size;

while (pch < pchEnd)
    :
    :
```

So that *pchEnd* can be used in the *while* expression, it is set to point to the memory location right after the last character to be searched. While this may be convenient for programmers, it works only if such a memory location exists, and if you're searching right up to the end of memory, of course the location does not exist. (The one exception to this—if you're using ANSI C—is that you can always compute the address of the first element beyond the end of a named array. ANSI C requires implementations to support this capability.)

As a first attempt to fix the bug, you might rewrite the code so that it tests against the last legal memory location:

```
pchEnd = pch + size - 1;

while (pch <= pchEnd)
    :
    :
```

but that doesn't work either. Remember the *UCHAR_MAX* overflow bug we saw earlier in *BuildToLowerTable*? You have the same bug here. *pchEnd* may now point to a legal memory location, but the loop will never end because every time *pch* is bumped to *pchEnd+1*, it overflows.

The safe way to cover a range when you have both a pointer and a counter is to use the *counter* as the control expression:

```
void *memchr(void *pv, unsigned char ch, size_t size)
{
    unsigned char *pch = (unsigned char *)pv;

    while (size-- > 0)
    {
        if (*pch == ch)
            return (pch);
        pch++;
    }

    return (NULL);
}
```

The code above is not only correct, but may also generate better code than the previous versions since it does not have to initialize *pchEnd*. A common belief is that the *size--* version will be larger and slower than the *pchEnd* version because *size* must be duplicated (for the imminent test against *0*) before it can be decremented. The reality, though, is that the *size--* version is actually slightly faster and smaller for many compilers; the code you get depends on how the compiler allocates the machine registers, and in the case of 80*x*86 compilers, on which memory model you use. But either way, the difference in size and speed is so small as to be unnoticeable.

This brings up another language idiom I touched upon earlier. Some programmers would urge you to rewrite the loop expression using *--size* instead of *size--*:

```
while (--size >= 0)
    .
    .
    .
```

The rationale for the change is that writing the expression above should never generate worse code than before but may in some cases generate slightly better code. The only problem with that advice is that if you blindly follow it, bugs will swoop down on your code like vultures to a carcass.

Why?

Well, for starters, the expression never works if *size* is an unsigned value (as it is in *memchr*) because unsigned values, by definition, will always be greater than or equal to *0*. The loop will execute forever. Oops.

The expression doesn't work properly for signed values either. What happens if *size* is an *int* and enters the loop with the most negative value possible, *INT_MIN*? *size* will be predecremented and will underflow, causing the loop to execute a large number of times instead of not at all. Oops again.

Using *size* -- > *0* works correctly no matter how you declare *size*—a subtle but important distinction.

The only reason programmers use --*size* >= *0* is to gain some efficiency, but let's take a look at that rationale for a moment. If you really have a speed problem, making such a minuscule improvement would be about as effective as cutting your lawn with nail clippers—you can do it, but one snip isn't going to show. And if you don't have a speed problem, why take the risk? Just as it's not important for every blade of grass to be exactly the same length, it's not important that every line of code be optimally efficient. What is important is the overall effect.

For some programmers, the idea of tossing aside any possible efficiency gain seems almost criminal. But, as you've seen throughout this book, the idea is to systematically reduce risk by using safer designs and implementations even though they might be slightly less efficient. Users won't notice if you slip in a few extra cycles here and there, but they will notice the occasional bug you introduce as you try to save those cycles. In investment terms, the return doesn't justify the risk.

Another risky idiom that falls into the category of "wasted efficiency" is using bitwise operators to multiply, divide, and mod values by a power of *2*. For example, the fast version of *memset* I showed you in Chapter 2 had these lines:

```
pb = (byte *)longfill((long *)pb, 1, size / 4);
size = size % 4;
```

I'm sure some programmers read that code and thought, "How inefficient." Those are the same programmers who would have written the division and the modulo operations using bitwise operators:

```
pb = (byte *)longfill((long *)pb, 1, size >> 2);
size = size & 3;
```

Using the bitwise operators is much faster than dividing or mod'ing on many machines, but it's also true that dividing or mod'ing an unsigned value (such as *size*) by a perfect power of *2* is such a basic inefficiency— along with adding *0*, and multiplying by *1*—that even the stupidest commercial compilers will routinely optimize the expressions for you if that will be more efficient for your target machine. There is no reason to hand-optimize these unsigned expressions.

But what about signed expressions? Are the explicit optimizations worthwhile for those? Well, they are and they aren't.

Suppose you have a signed expression such as this one:

```
midpoint = (upper + lower) / 2;
```

A two's-complement compiler would not optimize the division to a shift because shifting a negative value would give you a different result than a signed division would. But if you knew that *upper+lower* was always positive, you could rewrite the expression using a shift to get faster code:

```
midpoint = (upper + lower) >> 1;
```

So, yes, explicitly optimizing a signed expression is worthwhile. The question, though, is whether shifting is the best way to do it. And the answer is No. Casting works just as well and is far safer than shifting. Try this with your compiler:

```
midpoint = (unsigned)(upper + lower) / 2;
```

The idea is not to tell the compiler what to do, but rather to give it the information it needs to do optimization for you. By telling the compiler that the sum is unsigned, you grant it permission to shift. Compare the cast with the shift. Which is easier to understand? Which is more portable?

Over the years, I have tracked down bugs in which programmers used shifts to divide signed values that weren't guaranteed to be positive. I've tracked down bugs in which programmers shifted in the wrong direction. I've tracked down bugs in which programmers used the wrong shift count. I've even tracked down bugs in which programmers introduced precedence errors by carelessly converting expressions such as $a=b+c/4$ to $a=b+c>>2$. I don't recall ever tracking down a bug in which a programmer meant to divide by 4 and made a mistake typing the characters / and 4.

There are many other risky language idioms in C. The best way for you to find those that you use is to look at every bug you have and ask yourself the question I've given you before: "How could I have prevented this bug?" You'll soon develop your personal list of risky idioms to avoid.

———◆———

Avoid risky language idioms.

———◆———

Don't Overestimate the Cost

Microsoft was one of the few companies ready with Macintosh applications when Apple introduced the Macintosh in 1984. For obvious reasons, being the first out the door with products was good for Microsoft, but there were also drawbacks. To release products at the time the Macintosh was introduced meant that Microsoft had to develop the products while the Macintosh itself was still under development. As a result, Microsoft programmers sometimes had to use work-arounds to get the software to function correctly on the evolving Macintosh. That wasn't a problem until Apple tried to do their first major upgrade to the Macintosh operating system and found that their seemingly innocent changes broke Microsoft products. To make a long story short: Apple asked Microsoft to remove the outdated work-arounds and conform to the final operating system as described in their *Inside Macintosh* volumes.

Removing one of the work-arounds in Microsoft Excel meant rewriting a critical hand-optimized assembly language routine, and the rewrite added 12 cycles to the code. Since the routine was critical, a drawn-out debate went on about whether the function should be updated. It was a battle between those who wanted to conform and help Apple out and those who wanted to keep the speed.

Finally, one of the programmers put a temporary counter into the function and ran Excel's three-hour torture test to see how many times the function was actually called. The number was high: about 76,000 times. But even with that large number of calls, rewriting the function and executing the 12 extra cycles 76,000 times would have extended the three-hour test by a mere tenth (0.1) of a second, and that was assuming that you ran the test on Apple's slowest Macintosh. With these findings, the code was changed.

This is just another example which demonstrates that worrying about local efficiency is rarely worthwhile. If you're concerned about efficiency, focus on global and algorithmic efficiency, where you might see significant results for your efforts.

INCONSISTENCY, THE GREMLIN OF CODE

Take a look at the code below, which contains one of the easiest kinds of bugs to keep out of your code: a precedence bug.

```
word = high<<8 + low;
```

The code is supposed to pack two 8-bit bytes into a 16-bit word, but because the *+* operator has a higher precedence than the shift operator, that's not what the code does—it shifts *high* by *8+low*. The bug is understandable because programmers don't normally mix the bitwise and arithmetic operators. But why mix bitwise and arithmetic operators when it's just as easy to stick with one type or the other?

```
word = high<<8 | low;       /* bitwise solution */

word = high*256 + low;      /* arithmetic solution */
```

Are these examples any harder to understand than the first? Are they any less efficient than the first? Of course not. But there's one big difference: Both of these solutions are correct.

When programmers write expressions that contain just one kind of operator, they have a better chance of writing bug-free code because intuitively they know the precedence order within each group of operators. Sure, there are exceptions, but as a rule it's true. How many programmers do you know who would write

```
midpoint = upper + lower / 2;
```

and expect the addition to happen before the division?

Programmers don't seem to have much trouble remembering the precedence order of the bitwise operators either—I suspect because memories of their Logic 101 courses linger on, where they played with functions like $f(A,B,C)=\overline{A}B+C$. Most programmers know that the order from high to low is ~, &, and then /, and it doesn't take much extra thought to squeeze the shift operators between ~ and &.

Programmers tend to know the precedence order within groups of operator types, and it's not until they start mixing operator types that they run into trouble. So the first guideline is *Don't mix operator types if you don't have to.* The second guideline is *If you must mix operator types, use parentheses to isolate those operations.*

You've already seen how the first guideline can protect you from bugs. You can see how the second guideline protects you by taking another look at the *while* loop we saw in the first exercise in Chapter 1:

```
while (ch=getchar() != EOF)
    :
    :
```

The loop mixes an assignment operator with a comparison operator and introduces a precedence bug. You could fix the bug by rewriting the loop without mixing operators, but the result looks terrible:

```
do
{
    ch = getchar();
    if (ch == EOF)
        break;
    :
    :
} while (TRUE);
```

In this case, it's better to ignore the first guideline and instead apply the second by separating the operations with parentheses:

```
while ((ch=getchar()) != EOF)
    :
    :
```

———◆———

Don't needlessly mix operator types. If you must mix operators, use parentheses to isolate the operations.

———◆———

> ### Don't Look It Up!
>
> When it comes to inserting parentheses, some programmers will turn to a precedence table to see whether they're necessary, and if not, they'll leave them out. If you're one of those programmers, tape this message to your monitor: *If you have to look it up, the code is not obvious; make it obvious.* If that means inserting parentheses where technically they may not be needed, so what? Don't just be right—be obviously right so that nobody has to look it up. This guideline is good for more than parentheses. It's worth thinking about anytime you have to look up a nit-picky detail.

DON'T ASSOCIATE WITH FAILURES

In Chapter 5, I pointed out that if your functions return errors it's easier for programmers to mishandle or ignore those error conditions. I suggested that you simply design your functions so that they don't return errors. In this chapter, I'm going to turn that around and say, *Don't call functions that return errors.* That way, you won't mishandle or ignore an error condition returned by somebody else's function. Sometimes you have no choice, and in those cases, be sure to walk through your error handling code in a debugger to be sure it works.

There is one bit of advice I want to stress: *If you repeatedly handle the same error condition throughout your program, isolate that error handling.* The simplest approach, the one every programmer already knows about, is to localize error handling in a subroutine. That works fine, but in some cases you can do even better.

Suppose that Character Windows had code to rename a window in half a dozen spots. The code below changes the window title if it can grab enough memory to hold the new title; otherwise, it keeps the current title and tries to handle the error condition somehow.

```
if (fResizeMemory(&pwnd->strWndTitle, strlen(strNewTitle)+1))
    strcpy(pwnd->strWndTitle, strNewTitle);
else
    /* Unable to allocate space for the window title... */
```

But the question is How do you handle the error? Do you alert the user? Ignore the request and silently keep the old title? Copy a truncated version of the new title on top of the current one? Hmm. None of those solutions is ideal, particularly if the code is part of a general subroutine.

This is one of those cases in which you just don't want the code to fail—ever. You always want to be able to rename a window. And you can.

The problem with the code above is that you're not guaranteed to have enough memory for the new window title. But that's easy to guarantee if you're willing to over-allocate the title memory. For instance, in a typical Character Windows application, there are only a handful of windows that you would ever rename, and none of those windows' titles takes much memory, even at maximum length. Instead of allocating just the memory you need for the current title string, allocate enough memory to hold the longest possible title. Renaming a window then becomes as simple as a string copy:

```
strcpy(pwnd->strWndTitle, strNewTitle);
```

Better still, you could hide the implementation in a *RenameWindow* function and use assertions to verify that the allocated title memory is large enough to hold any possible title:

```
void RenameWindow(window *pwnd, char *strNewTitle)
{
    ASSERT(fValidWindow(pwnd));
    ASSERT(strNewTitle != NULL);

    ASSERT(fValidPointer(pwnd->strWndTitle, sizeMaxWndTitle));
    strcpy(pwnd->strWndTitle, strNewTitle);
}
```

The obvious drawback to this approach is that you waste memory. But at the same time, you regain code space because you don't need any error handling code. Your job is to weigh data-space against code-space and decide which is more important in each case you run across.

———◆———

Avoid calling functions that return errors.

———◆———

A SLAP ON THE RISK

By now, you should have a good idea of what I meant when I said that programming is "risky business." All of the points in this chapter focus on trading in a risky coding practice for one that produces results comparable in size and speed but less error-prone.

But don't stop with these points. Pull out your listings and take a hard look at the way you code. Did you think through all your coding habits, or did you adopt them because you saw other programmers using them? Entry level programmers often think shifting to divide is a "trick," and experienced programmers think it's perfectly obvious and have no qualms about doing it. But should they? Who is really right here?

QUICK REVIEW

- Choose your data types carefully. Even though the ANSI standard requires all implementations to support *chars*, *ints*, *longs*, and so on, it does not concretely define those types. Protect yourself from bugs by relying only on what the ANSI standard specifically guarantees.

- Remember that it's possible for your algorithm to be correct but still have bugs because of less-than-ideal characteristics of the hardware it runs on. In particular, always check that your calculations and tests don't overflow or underflow your data types.

- Be faithful to your design. The easiest way to introduce subtle bugs is to cheat on the implementation.

- Every function should have one well-defined task, but more than that, it should have only one way to accomplish that task. If the same code executes regardless of the inputs, you decrease the odds of having undetected bugs.

- An *if* statement is a particularly good warning sign that you may be doing more work than necessary. Strive to eliminate every unnecessary *if* statement in your code by asking yourself, "How can I change my design to remove this special case?" Sometimes you may have to alter your data structures, and at other times you may have to alter the way you view them. Remember, is the lens concave or convex?

◆   Don't forget that *if* statements are sometimes disguised as control expressions in *while* and *for* loops. The *?:* operator is another type of *if* statement.

◆   Be wary of risky language idioms—always keep an eye out for comparable but safer idioms. Pay particular attention to coding tweaks that supposedly give you better performance. Since it's rare for an implementation tweak to have any noticeable effect on overall efficiency, the extra risk is rarely worth the trade-off.

◆   When you write expressions, try not to mix different types of operators. If you must mix operators, use parentheses to separate the operations.

◆   The special case of special cases is error handling. If possible, avoid calling functions that can fail. But if you must call a function that can return an error, try to localize the error handling—this will increase your chances of finding bugs in the error handling code.

◆   In some cases, it's possible to eliminate general error handling by guaranteeing that what you want to do can't fail. That may mean handling the error once during initialization, or it may mean changing your design.

THINGS TO THINK ABOUT

1.   What is the portable range of a "plain" 1-bit bit field?

2.   How are functions that return boolean values like "plain" 1-bit bit fields?

3.   At one point I changed *AddChild* to use *pwndDisplay* instead of *pwndRootChildren*. Instead of using *pwndDisplay*, which points to an allocated *window* structure, I could have declared a global *window* structure, *wndDisplay*. Although that would have worked, why do you think I didn't take that approach?

4.   Occasionally a programmer will ask whether, for efficiency, he or she should take a loop like

```
while (expression)
{
    A;
    if (f)        /* f is a constant expression. */
        B;
    else
        C;
    D;
}
```

and rewrite it as

```
if (f)
    while (expression)
    {
        A;
        B;
        D;
    }
else
    while (expression)
    {
        A;
        C;
        D;
    }
```

where *A* and *D* represent collections of statements. The second version will be faster, but how risky is it compared to the first version?

5. If you read the ANSI standard, you'll find functions that have several nearly identical arguments—for example,

```
int strcmp(const char *s1, const char *s2);
```

Why is using such similar names risky? How could you eliminate the risk?

6. I've shown why it's risky to use loop conditions such as

```
while (pch++ <= pchEnd)
```

But why is it risky to use similar countdown loops?

```
while (pch-- >= pchStart)
```

7. For efficiency or brevity, some programmers take the shortcuts below. Why should you avoid them?

   a. Using *printf(str);* instead of *printf("%s", str);*

   b. Using *f = 1-f;* instead of *f = !f;*

   c. Using multiple assignments as in

   ```
   int ch;                 /* ch *must* be an int. */
   :
   :
   ch = *str++ = getchar();
   :
   :
   ```

   instead of using two separate assignment statements.

8. *tolower*, *uCycleCheckBox*, and the disassembler in Chapter 2 use table-driven algorithms. What are the pros and cons of using such tables?

9. Assuming that your compiler does not automatically use bitwise operators for unsigned power-of-2 math, why, besides the risk and nonportability issues, should you still avoid using shifts and *&*s in explicit optimizations?

10. One of the golden rules in programming is *Never lose the user's data.* Suppose that in order to save a user's file, you had to successfully allocate a temporary data buffer. How could you ensure that it would be possible to save the user's data even in low memory situations?

PROJECT: Make a list of all the risky language features you can think of—falling through *switch* cases, arbitrary *goto*s, evaluating the same macro argument more than once, and so on—and write down the pros and cons of using the feature. Next, for each item on your list, decide under what conditions you're willing to accept the risk and use the feature.

7

*T*REACHERIES OF THE *T*RADE

When you write a mystery novel, you want every page to grip the reader. You want to evoke surprise, fear, suspense in the reader. If you wrote, "Someone walked up and stabbed Joe," you'd put your reader to sleep. For the reader to remain interested, you'd have to make her feel Joe's fear with each footstep behind him. You'd have to make her experience Joe's pounding heart as the steps got slowly closer. You'd have to raise in the reader a feeling of panic, like Joe's, as the pace of the footsteps picked up. Most important, you'd have to keep the reader wondering: Will Joe get away?

Using surprise and suspense in a mystery novel is critical, but using them in code is terrible. When you write code, the "plot" should be so obvious and boring that other programmers know well in advance what's going

145

to happen. If your code has to have someone walk up and stab Joe, then "So and So walked up and stabbed Joe" is exactly what you want. It's short, it's clear, and it tells you everything you need to know.

But for some reason, programmers resist writing code that is obvious and boring. The urge to use tricks, to be clever, to do things out of the ordinary, seems to be overpowering.

In this chapter we'll look at a few coding styles that don't result in straightforward, boring code. The examples are clever, tricky, and anything but obvious. And, of course, they all cause subtle bugs.

THE NEED FOR SPEED

Here's the bug-free version of *memchr* we saw in the last chapter:

```
void *memchr(void *pv, unsigned char ch, size_t size)
{
    unsigned char *pch = (unsigned char *)pv;

    while (size-- > 0)
    {
        if (*pch == ch)
            return (pch);
        pch++;
    }

    return (NULL);
}
```

One of the games most programmers play is the "How can I make this code even faster?" game. That's not a bad game to play, but, as we've seen throughout this book, it can have unexpected results if you take it to extremes.

If you played that game with the *memchr* code above, you'd ask yourself, "How can I speed up the loop?" There are only three possibilities: Remove the size check, remove the character test, or remove the pointer increment. It may seem impossible to remove any of those steps, but you can—if you're willing to chuck traditional coding practices and try something daring.

Take a look at the size check. You need that check only so that you can return *NULL* if you don't find *ch* in the first *size* bytes of memory. To remove the check, you simply guarantee that you can always find *ch*, and you can guarantee that by storing *ch* at the tail of the memory run, where you know it will be found in the "not found" case:

```
void *memchr(void *pv, unsigned char ch, size_t size)
{
    unsigned char *pch = (unsigned char *)pv;
    unsigned char *pchPlant;
    unsigned char chSave;

    /*  pchPlant points to the first character following
     *  the memory run that memchr is searching. Plant
     *  ch at that location so that memchr is guaranteed
     *  to find ch even if it is not in the run.
     */
    pchPlant = pch + size;

    chSave = *pchPlant;        /* Save the original char. */
    *pchPlant = ch;

    while (*pch != ch)
        pch++;

    *pchPlant = chSave;        /* Now put the original back. */

    return ((pch == pchPlant) ? NULL : pch);
}
```

Clever, right? By blotting out the character that *pchPlant* points to, you guarantee that *memchr* will find *ch*, and that allows you to remove the size check, doubling the speed of the loop.

But is it robust? Is it solid?

memchr may look robust in this new incarnation, particularly since it meticulously preserves the character that it changes, but this version of *memchr* has more problems than Batman has gadgets. For starters, think about these points:

◆　If *pchPlant* points to read-only memory, storing *ch* at **pchPlant* will have no effect and the function will return an invalid pointer if it can't find *ch* in the first *size+1* characters.

◆　If *pchPlant* points to memory-mapped I/O, storing *ch* at **pchPlant* could cause any weird interaction, from making floppy disks stop (or start) spinning to making factory robots go berserk with their welding torches.

◆   If *pch* points to the last *size* bytes of RAM, both *pch* and *size* will
    be legal, but *pchPlant* will point to nonexistent or write-protected
    memory. Storing *ch* at **pchPlant* could cause a memory fault, or
    it could quietly do nothing and the function would fail if *ch*
    weren't in the first *size+1* characters.

◆   If *pchPlant* points to data shared by concurrent processes, one
    process storing *ch* at **pchPlant* could garble memory that an-
    other process might need to reference when it switches into
    context.

The last possibility is particularly troublesome because there are so
many ways in which you can crash your system if you have concurrent processes. What if you call *memchr* to search a block of memory that you've
allocated and it garbles one of your memory manager's data structures? If a
concurrent process—a code thread or an interrupt routine, say—then
switches into context, it had better not invoke the memory manager because
the system may crash. What if you call *memchr* to scan a global array and it
steps on an adjacent variable used by another task? Or what if two instances
of your program try to search shared data in parallel? Any number of scenarios can kill your program.

Of course, you probably won't realize that the optimized *memchr*
causes subtle bugs, because unless it modifies critical memory, it will appear to work fine. But when functions such as the optimized *memchr* do
cause bugs, isolating those bugs is about as easy as finding your contact lens
in the middle of a sandstorm: After all, the process executing *memchr* will
work fine; it's the other process—the one with mangled memory—that will
crash. And you'll have no reason to suspect that *memchr* is the culprit.

If you've ever wondered what those $50,000 in-circuit emulators are
for, now you know—they keep a record of every cycle, every instruction,
and every piece of data the computer references up to the point of a crash. It
may take you days to wade through an emulator's output, but if you're per-
sistent and you don't go blind staring at the reams of output, you should
find the bug.

But why go through all that pain and effort? The alternative is so
much easier: *Don't reference memory that you don't own.* And note: "Reference" means reading as well as writing. Reading unknown memory may
not cause weird interactions with other processes, but such references can

stop your program in its tracks if you reference protected memory, nonexistent memory, or memory-mapped I/O.

———◆———

Don't reference memory
that you don't own.

———◆———

A Thief with a Key Is Still a Thief

Curiously enough, I know programmers who would never reference memory they didn't own but who would feel just fine writing code like the *FreeWindowTree* routine below:

```
void FreeWindowTree(window *pwndRoot)
{
    if (pwndRoot != NULL)
    {
        window *pwnd;

        /* Release pwndRoot's children... */
        pwnd = pwndRoot->pwndChild;
        while (pwnd != NULL)
        {
            FreeWindowTree(pwnd);
            pwnd = pwnd->pwndSibling;
        }

        if (pwndRoot->strWndTitle != NULL)
            FreeMemory(pwndRoot->strWndTitle);
        FreeMemory(pwndRoot);
    }
}
```

Take a look at the *while* loop. Do you see the problem with it? As *FreeWindowTree* releases each child window in the linked list of siblings, it first frees *pwnd* and then references the freed block in the line:

```
pwnd = pwnd->pwndSibling
```

But what is the value of *pwnd -> pwndSibling* once *pwnd* has been freed? It's garbage, of course, but some programmers don't accept that. The memory wasn't garbage a moment ago, and they haven't done anything to affect it; therefore, they think, it should still be valid. They haven't done anything, that is, but release it.

I've never understood why some programmers believe it's permissible to reference memory they have released. How is that different from using a spare key to enter an apartment you once lived in, or to drive off in a car you once owned? You can't safely reference freed memory because as I pointed out in Chapter 3, the memory manager may use that storage for free chains or for other private information.

The Privileges of Data

You may not see it in any programming manuals, but every piece of data in your code has implied read and write privileges associated with it. The privileges aren't blatantly announced; they're not emblazoned across the front of every variable you declare. Rather they're implied by the designs of your subsystems and your function interfaces.

For example, there is an implicit covenant between a programmer who calls a function and a programmer who writes a function that in effect declares,

> If I, the Caller, pass you, the Callee, a pointer to an input, you agree to treat that input as if it were constant and promise not to write to it. Furthermore, if I pass you a pointer to an output, you agree to treat the output as a write-only object and promise never to read from it. Finally, whether the pointer is to an input or to an output, you agree to restrict your references to the memory required to hold that input or output.

> In return, I, the Caller, agree to treat read-only outputs as if they were constant and promise never to write to them. I further agree to restrict references to those outputs to the memory required to hold them.

In other words, "Don't mess with my stuff, and I won't mess with yours." Remember this: Any time you violate an implied read or write privilege, you risk breaking code written by programmers who believed that every programmer would honor the agreement. A programmer who calls a function such as *memchr* should not have to worry that *memchr* may behave erratically in uncommon scenarios.

---

*Don't reference memory
that you have freed.*

TAKE ONLY WHAT YOU NEED

In the last chapter, I presented an implementation for the *UnsToStr* function. It looked like this:

```
/* UnsToStr -- convert an unsigned value to a string. */

void UnsToStr(unsigned u, char *str)
{
    char *strStart = str;

    do
        *str++ = (u % 10) + '0';
    while ((u /= 10) > 0);
    *str = '\0';

    ReverseStr(strStart);
}
```

The code above is a straightforward implementation of *UnsToStr*, but no doubt there are programmers who feel uncomfortable with it because the code derives digits in reverse order, requiring a call to *ReverseStr* to reorder the digits. That seems wasteful. If you're going to derive the digits in reverse order, why not build the string backwards and eliminate the need for *ReverseStr*? Why not, indeed:

```
void UnsToStr(unsigned u, char *str)
{
    char *pch;

    /* u out of range?  Use UlongToStr... */
    ASSERT(u <= 65535);

    /*  Store the digits in str from back to front. Start
     *  storing the digits deep enough into the string to
     *  hold the largest possible value for u.
     */
```

(continued)

```
    pch = &str[5];
    *pch = '\0';
    do
        *--pch = (u % 10) + '0';
    while ((u /= 10) > 0);

    strcpy(str, pch);
}
```

Some programmers feel more comfortable with this code because it's more efficient and easier to understand. *UnsToStr* becomes more efficient because *strcpy* (which you still need) is faster than *ReverseStr*, particularly for compilers that can generate the "call" as a few inline instructions. The code is easier to understand because C programmers are familiar with *strcpy*. When programmers see *ReverseStr*, they stumble for a moment much the way people do when they hear that their friend in the hospital is "ambulatory."

What's the catch? Why am I telling you this if *UnsToStr* is now so perfect? Well, it's not perfect. In fact, the new *UnsToStr* has a serious flaw.

Tell me, how much memory does the *str* parameter point to? You don't know. But that's not unusual for C interfaces. The unspoken rule between the caller and the implementor is that *str* will point to enough memory to hold the textual representation for *u*. But this optimized *UnsToStr* assumes that *str* points to enough memory to convert the largest possible value for *u* when that may not be the case. What if the caller wrote

```
DisplayScore()
{
    char strScore[3];      /* UserScore is from 0 through 25. */

    UnsToStr(UserScore, strScore);
    :
    :
```

Since *UserScore* will never generate a string longer than three characters (two digits plus the null character), it's perfectly reasonable for a programmer to define *strScore* as a 3-character array. *UnsToStr*, however, will assume that *strScore* is a 6-character array and destroy the 3 bytes of memory following *strScore*. In the *DisplayScore* example above, *UnsToStr* would typically—if you're using a machine with a down-growing stack—destroy the frame back-pointer or the return address to *DisplayScore*'s caller or maybe both. You'd notice that problem since your machine would likely crash. But if *strScore* weren't the only local variable, you might not notice that *UnsToStr* was mangling the variable that follows *strScore* in memory.

I'm sure there are programmers who will argue that it's risky declaring *strScore* to be "just big enough" to hold the longest string that it needs. This is risky, but only because of programmers who write code like this last version of *UnsToStr*. It's not necessary to be this tricky when you can implement *UnsToStr* efficiently and safely by building the string in a local buffer and then copying the finished product to *str*:

```
void UnsToStr(unsigned u, char *str)
{
    char strDigits[6];                   /* conversion buffer */
    char *pch;

    /* u out of range?  Use UlongToStr... */
    ASSERT(u <= 65535);

    /* Store the digits in strDigits from back to front. */
    pch = &strDigits[5];
    *pch = '\0';
    do
        *--pch = (u % 10) + '0';
    while ((u /= 10) > 0);

    strcpy(str, pch);
}
```

You need to remember that, unless they are defined otherwise, pointers such as *str* don't point to memory you can use as workspace buffers. Pointers such as *str* are outputs that for efficiency's sake are passed by reference instead of by value.

———◆———

Don't use output memory as
workspace buffers.

———◆———

KEEP PRIVATE THINGS TO YOURSELF

Of course, some programmers think that even calling *strcpy* in *UnsToStr* is too inefficient. After all, *UnsToStr* just created the output string. Why copy it to another buffer when you can save cycles by returning a pointer to the string you already have?

```
char *strFromUns(unsigned u)
{
    static char *strDigits = "?????";     /* 5 chars + '\0' */
    char *pch;

    /* u out of range?  Use UlongToStr... */
    ASSERT(u <= 65535);

    /* Store the digits in strDigits from back to front. */
    pch = &strDigits[5];
    ASSERT(*pch == '\0');
    do
        *--pch = (u % 10) + '0';
    while ((u /= 10) > 0);

    return (pch);
}
```

This code is nearly identical to the version of *UnsToStr* we saw in the last section, except that *strDigits* is declared to be *static* so that it will remain allocated even after *strFromUns* returns.

But imagine this: You have to implement a function in which you need to convert two unsigned values to strings, and you write

```
strHighScore = strFromUns(HighScore);
.
.
.
strThisScore = strFromUns(Score);
```

What's wrong with that? Well, by calling *strFromUns* to convert *Score*, you destroy the string that *strHighScore* points to.

You could argue that the bug is in the code that calls *strFromUns* and not in *strFromUns* itself, but remember what we talked about in Chapter 5: It's not enough that functions work correctly; they must also prevent programmers from making obvious mistakes. I would argue that at the very least *strFromUns* has an interface bug because you and I both know that some programmers will make the mistake above.

Even if programmers are aware of the fragile existence of *strFromUns*'s strings, they can still introduce bugs without realizing they're doing it. Suppose a programmer calls *strFromUns* and then calls another function which, unbeknownst to her, also calls *strFromUns* and destroys her string. Or suppose there are multiple code threads and one code thread calls *strFromUns*, wiping out a string still in use by another thread.

But even those threats are minor compared to the bomb ticking in *strFromUns*, a bomb that will surely explode as your project evolves. If you decide to insert a call to *strFromUns* into one of your functions:

◆ You must ensure that none of your callers (and callers to your callers, and so on) is still using a string that *strFromUns* returned to it. In other words, you must verify that no function in any of the possible call chains to your function assumes that *strFromUns*'s private buffer is preserved.

◆ You must also ensure that you don't call any functions that call *strFromUns*, destroying a string that you still need. Of course, that means that you can't call a function that calls a function (and so on) that calls *strFromUns*.

A Global Problem

The *strFromUns* example illustrates the dangers you face when you return data through a pointer to static memory. What the example doesn't show is that the same hazards exist any time you pass data in a nonlocal buffer. You could rewrite *strFromUns* so that it builds the numeric string in a global buffer, or even in a permanent buffer that you allocate at program startup using *malloc*, but that wouldn't defuse *strFromUns* because programmers could still call the function twice in a row and the second call would destroy the string returned by the first call.

The rule of thumb is *Never pass data in global buffers unless you absolutely have to*. You can avoid the entire problem if you force the calling function to provide a pointer to the output buffer.

If you insert a call to *strFromUns* into one of your functions without performing these two checks, you risk introducing a bug. That's bad enough. Imagine how much more difficult it is to adhere to those two conditions as programmers fix bugs and add new features. Every time they change a call chain to your function, or modify functions that your code calls, maintenance programmers must reverify the two conditions. But do you think they will? Hardly. Those programmers won't even realize that they should be verifying those conditions. After all, they're just fixing bugs, rearranging code, and adding features; what does that have to do with *strFromUns*, a function they may never have used or even seen?

Functions such as *strFromUns* cause bugs again and again because their very design makes it easy to introduce bugs as programs are maintained. And of course, when programmers isolate a *strFromUns* class of bug, the bug is not in *strFromUns* but in code that uses *strFromUns* incorrectly. Instead of fixing the true problem by rewriting *strFromUns*, programmers fix the specific bug and leave *strFromUns* in the program, ticking away. . . .

———◆———

Don't pass data in static (or global)
memory.

———◆———

FUNCTIONAL LEECHES

Passing data in public buffers is risky, but you can get away with it if you're careful and a bit lucky. But writing parasitic functions that rely on the internal workings of other functions is not only risky, but also irresponsible: If you change the host function, you kill the parasite.

The best example I know of a parasitic function is from, of all places, a widely ported, widely promoted standard implementation of the FORTH programming language. In the late 1970s and early 1980s, the FORTH Interest Group tried to stimulate interest in the FORTH language by providing public domain implementations of the FORTH-77 standard. Those FORTH implementations defined three standard functions: *FILL*, which filled a block of memory with a byte; *CMOVE*, which copied memory using a head-to-head algorithm; and *<CMOVE*, which copied memory using a tail-to-tail algorithm. *CMOVE* and *<CMOVE* were specifically defined as "head-to-

head" and "tail-to-tail" moves so that programmers would know which function to use when they needed to copy overlapping memory blocks.

In the FORTH implementations, *CMOVE* was written in optimized assembly language, but for portability, *FILL* was written in FORTH itself. The code for *CMOVE* (translated into C here) was what you would expect:

```
/* CMOVE -- move memory using a head-to-head move. */

void CMOVE(byte *pbFrom, byte *pbTo, size_t size)
{
    while (size-- > 0)
        *pbTo++ = *pbFrom++;
}
```

But the implementation for *FILL* was surprising:

```
/* FILL -- fill a range of memory. */

void FILL(byte *pb, size_t size, byte b)
{
    if (size > 0)
    {
        *pb = b;
        CMOVE(pb, pb+1, size-1);
    }
}
```

FILL calls *CMOVE* to do its job, which is surprising until you figure out how it works. Then the implementation is either "clever" or "gross," depending upon your point of view. If you think that *FILL* is clever, consider this: FORTH may require that you implement *CMOVE* as a head-to-head move, but what if, for efficiency, you rewrite *CMOVE* so that it moves memory using *long*s instead of *byte*s? The answer, of course, is that you could write a bug-free, blazing version of *CMOVE* and break every function that calls *FILL*. To me, that's not clever; that's gross.

But let's suppose you know that *CMOVE* absolutely won't change. You've even placed an ominous comment in *CMOVE* warning other programmers that *FILL* relies on its internal workings. That fixes only half the problems with *CMOVE*.

Suppose you're working on the control code for a simple four-axis factory robot, where each axis has 256 positions. A simple design for such a robot would be to use 4 bytes of memory-mapped I/O such that each memory location would control a separate axis. To reposition an axis, you would write a value from *0* through *255* into its corresponding memory location. To retrieve the current position of an axis (which is especially useful while the axis is moving to a new position), you would read a byte from the corresponding memory location.

If you wanted to "home" all four axes to the *(0,0,0,0)* position, you could, in theory, write

```
FILL(pbRobotArm, 4, 0);     /* Put robot to bed. */
```

Of course, that code doesn't work given the way *FILL* is defined—*FILL* would write a *0* to the first axis and garbage to the other three axes, causing the robot to go wild. Why? If you look at *FILL*'s design, you can see that it fills memory by copying the previously stored byte to the current byte. But when *FILL* reads the first byte—expecting it to be *0*—it reads instead the first axis's current location, which is probably not *0* since the axis won't have moved to position *0* in the fraction of a second between storing the *0* and trying to read it back. That location could be any value, sending the second axis to some indeterminate spot. Of course, the third and fourth axes will be sent to similarly strange positions.

For *FILL* to work correctly, you would have to guarantee that it could read the same value from memory that it just wrote to memory. And you can't guarantee that for memory-mapped I/O.

Assertions Keep Programmers Honest

If *CMOVE* had used an assertion to verify that its arguments were valid (that is, that the source memory would not be destroyed before being copied to the destination), the programmer who wrote *FILL* would have gotten an assertion the first time he tested his code. That would have left the programmer with two choices: Rewrite *FILL* using a reasonable algorithm, or remove the assertion from *CMOVE*. Fortunately, very few programmers would remove *CMOVE*'s assertion just so that *FILL*'s slimy implementation would work.

But my point is that *FILL* is wrong because it peeks at the private details of another function and abuses that knowledge. That *FILL* doesn't work correctly with anything but RAM is a secondary problem, but it again demonstrates that you ask for trouble any time you stray from straightforward, boring code.

———◆———

Don't write parasitic functions.

———◆———

THE OLD PAINT-STIRRER TRICK

One of the oldest tricks in home maintenance is to pick up a screwdriver to pry the lid off a can of paint and then use the screwdriver as a stir-stick. I should know; I have a collection of multicolored screwdrivers. Why do people use screwdrivers to stir paint when they know darn well they shouldn't? I'll tell you why: because at that moment the screwdriver is convenient, and it works. There are programming tricks that are convenient and guaranteed to work and, like those screwdrivers, are not used for their intended purpose.

Take a look at the code below, which uses the result of a comparison as part of a computational expression:

```
unsigned atou(char *str);    /* unsigned version of atoi */


/* atoi -- convert an ASCII string to an integer value. */

int atoi(char *str)
{
    /* str has the format "[white space][+/-]digits". */

    while (isspace(*str))
        str++;

    if (*str == '-')
        return (-(int)atou(str + 1));

    /* Skip the optional '+' sign if there is one. */
    return ((int)atou(str + (*str == '+')));
}
```

The code skips an optional leading + sign by adding the result of the test *(*str == '+')* to the string pointer. You can write such code because the ANSI standard states that the result of any relational operation will be either 0 or 1. But what some programmers fail to recognize is that the ANSI standard is not a rulebook that tells you what you can and can't do any more than a tax guide tells you how to do your taxes. In both cases, you can adhere to the letter of the code but violate the intent.

The real problem in this example is not so much in the code as in the programmer's attitude. If a programmer feels comfortable using logical evaluations in computational expressions, what other shortcuts is he or she willing to take? How safe are those?

———◆———

*Don't abuse your programming
language.*

———◆———

Standards Change

When the FORTH-83 standard was released, some FORTH programmers found that their code broke. Boolean results that had been defined as *0* and *1* in the FORTH-77 standard were, for a variety of reasons, changed to *0* and *–1* in the FORTH-83 standard. Of course, that change broke code that relied on "true" being *1*.

FORTH programmers weren't alone.

UCSD Pascal was quite popular in the late 1970s and early 1980s. If you used Pascal on a microcomputer, the odds were good that it was a UCSD implementation. Then one day, UCSD Pascal programmers received a compiler update, and many found that their code stopped working. The compiler writers, for whatever reason, had changed the value for "true."

Who can say that in some future standard, C won't change? If not C, what about C++ or some other derivative language that you may have migrated to?

APL SYNDROME

Programmers who aren't aware of how C code translates into machine code will often try to improve the quality of the machine code by using terse C. Their idea is that if you use a minimal amount of C, you should get a minimal amount of machine code. There is a correlation between the size of your C code and the size of the corresponding machine code, but that correlation breaks down when you apply it to individual lines of code.

Do you remember the *uCycleCheckBox* function from Chapter 6?

```
unsigned uCycleCheckBox(unsigned uCur)
{
    return ((uCur<=1) ? (uCur?0:1) : (uCur==4)?2:(uCur+1));
}
```

uCycleCheckBox may be terse C code, but as I've already pointed out, it generates terrible machine code. And what about the return statement we saw in the last section?

```
return ((int)atou(str + (*str == '+')));
```

Adding the result of a comparison to a pointer may generate decent code if you use a good optimizing compiler *and* your target machine can generate a *0/1* test result without using any branches. If that doesn't describe your setup, more likely than not your compiler will internally expand the comparison to a *?:* operation and generate machine code as though you had written the C code below:

```
return ((int)atou(str + ((*str == '+') ? 1 : 0)));
```

Since a *?:* operation is nothing but an *if-else* statement in disguise, you would get worse code than if you had written the obvious, boring, and straightforward version:

```
if (*str == '+')          /* Skip the optional '+' sign. */
    str++;
return ((int)atou(str));
```

Of course, there are other ways to optimize the code. I've seen cases in which a programmer took a two-line *if* statement and "improved" it by replacing the *if* statement with an *||* operator:

```
(*str != '+')  ||  str++;        /* Skip the optional '+' sign. */
return ((int)atou(str));
```

Such code works because of C's rules for short-circuit evaluation, but fitting the code onto a single line doesn't guarantee that you'll get better machine code than if you used an *if* statement; you could even get worse code using *||* if your compiler generated a 0 or a 1 result as a side effect.

A simple guideline is *Use || for logical expressions, use ?: for conditional expressions, and use if for conditional statements.* Following this guideline may be downright boring, but your code will be more likely to be efficient and maintainable.

If you suffer from the dread "one-line-itis" disease (also known as "APL syndrome") in which you constantly use bizarre expressions so that your C code will fit on one source line, get into your best yoga position, take a deep breath, and start repeating, "It *is* possible for efficient code to span multiple lines. It *is* possible for efficient code to span multiple lines. . . ."

——————◆——————

Tight C does not guarantee efficient machine code.

——————◆——————

NO HOITY-TOITY PROGRAMMING

Some computer experts can't bring themselves to use plain, everyday English in their documentation and technical papers. Instead of saying, "That bug may hang or crash your system," one of these experts would say, "Such a software defect may cause a loss of system control or cause system termination." These experts throw around terms like "axiomatic program verification" and "defect taxonomies" as though they were part of a programmer's everyday vocabulary. Rather than helping readers, such experts confuse readers by burying their message in obscure terminology.

Technical writers aren't alone in this tendency to obfuscate; some programmers actually strive to write obscure code, thinking that it is impressive when it is merely unclear. For example, how does this function work?

```
void *memmove(void *pvTo, void *pvFrom, size_t size)
{
    byte *pbTo   = (byte *)pvTo;
    byte *pbFrom = (byte *)pvFrom;

    ((pbTo > pbFrom) ? tailmove : headmove)(pbTo, pbFrom, size);

    return (pvTo);
}
```

Would you understand the function better if I rewrote it like this?

```
void *memmove(void *pvTo, void *pvFrom, size_t size)
{
    byte *pbTo   = (byte *)pvTo;
    byte *pbFrom = (byte *)pvFrom;

    if (pbTo > pbFrom)
        tailmove(pbTo, pbFrom, size);
    else
        headmove(pbTo, pbFrom, size);

    return (pvTo);
}
```

The first example may not look like legal C, but it is. And the odds are good that your compiler will generate much smaller code for the first example than for the second one. But how many programmers will grasp how that first function works? What if they have to maintain that code? You're not doing anybody a favor if you write correct, small code that nobody can understand. You might as well write the code in hand-optimized assembly language.

Here's another example that confuses many programmers:

```
while (expression)
{
    int i = 33;          /* Declare locals. */
    char str[20];

    :                    /* code... */
    :

}
```

Quick! Is *i* initialized each time through the loop, or only the first time the loop is entered? Do you know the correct answer without thinking

about it? If you're not sure, you're in good company—even expert C programmers usually pause for a few moments as they mentally scan C's
initializer rules.

What if I tweaked the code slightly?

```
while (expression)
{
    int i;              /* Declare locals. */
    char str[20];

    i = 33;             /* code... */
    :
    :
}
```

Who Does Maintenance Programming?

At Microsoft, the amount of new code you write is directly proportional to
how well you understand the internal workings of the product you're
working on; the more you know, the more new code you write and the less
maintenance programming you do. And, of course, if you're at the other
end of the spectrum and know very little about your project, you spend
most of your time reading other people's code, fixing other people's bugs,
and adding small localized enhancements to existing features. That arrangement makes sense. After all, you can't very well add major features to
a project unless you already know something about how it is written.

The downside to that arrangement is that, as a general rule, experienced programmers write new code and novice programmers maintain
code. This is a practical arrangement, and it works. But it works only if the
experienced programmers understand that they have a responsibility to
write code that maintenance (novice) programmers can maintain.

Don't misunderstand me. I'm not saying that you should write in
baby-C so that any novice programmer can understand your code; that
would be silly. I'm saying that you should avoid writing difficult or arcane
C when you can use common, everyday language. If you make your code
easy to understand, novices should be able to maintain it without introducing bugs. You also won't have to keep explaining how the code works.

Do you have any doubt that *i* is set to *33* each time through the loop? Would any programmer on your team doubt it? Of course not.

Programmers frequently forget that they have two audiences: the customers who use the code and the maintenance programmers who have to update the code. I don't know many programmers who forget about the customer, but judging from the code I've read over the years, I get the impression that programmers do tend to forget about their second audience, the maintenance programmers.

The idea that you should be writing maintainable code is nothing new. Programmers know they should be writing such code. Programmers don't always realize, though, that if they use language that only C experts will understand, their code is not actually maintainable. After all, maintainable code is, by definition, code that maintenance programmers can easily understand and modify without introducing bugs. And regardless of whether they should be, the maintenance programmers tend to be the newcomers to a project, not the experts who have been there awhile.

Keep those maintenance programmers in mind as you code.

---◆---

Write code for the "average"
programmer.

---◆---

WASTE THAT BAG OF TRICKS

We've looked at a number of questionable coding practices, many of which may look fine at first glance. But as we've seen, the second, or even fifth, glance may not alert you to the subtle side effects that tag along with clever code. If you find yourself writing code that feels tricky to you, stop and find another solution. If your code feels tricky, that's your gut telling you that something isn't right. Listen to your gut. If you find yourself thinking of a piece of your code as a neat trick, you're really saying to yourself that an algorithm produces correct results even though it's not apparent that it should. The bugs won't be apparent to you either.

Be truly clever; write boring code. You'll have fewer bugs, and the maintenance programmers will love you for it.

QUICK REVIEW

- If you're working with data you don't own, don't write to it, even temporarily. And though you might think that reading from data is always safe, remember that reading from memory-mapped I/O may be hazardous to your hardware.

- Don't reference memory once you have released it. There are too many ways in which referencing free memory can cause bugs.

- It may be tempting, for efficiency, to pass data in global or static buffers, but that's a shortcut fraught with dangers. If you write a function that creates data useful only to the caller, return the data to the caller, or guarantee that you won't unexpectedly change that data.

- Don't write functions that rely on the specific implementations of other functions. That *FILL* routine we saw had no business calling *CMOVE* the way it did. Such nonsense is suitable only as an example of bad programming.

- When you program, write clear, accurate code by using your programming language as it was intended to be used. Avoid questionable programming idioms even though the language standard happens to guarantee that they will work. Remember, standards can change.

- Logically, it would seem that the efficient expression of a concept in C would result in similarly efficient machine code. It doesn't work that way. Before you take a clean multiline piece of C code and squash it into something that fits on one line, be sure that you're getting better machine code for your trouble. Even then, remember that local efficiency gains are rarely noticeable and are not usually worth mucking up your code.

- Finally, don't write code the way lawyers write contracts. If an average programmer can't read and understand your code, it's too complicated; use simpler language.

THINGS TO THINK ABOUT

1. C programmers regularly modify the arguments passed to functions. Why doesn't this practice violate the write privilege for input data?

2. I've already talked about the major flaw with the *strFromUns* function below—recall that it returns data in an unprotected buffer. That major problem aside, what specifically is risky about the declaration of *strDigits*?

```c
char *strFromUns(unsigned u)
{
    static char *strDigits = "?????";   /* 5 chars + '\0' */
    char *pch;

    /* u out of range?  Use UlongToStr... */
    ASSERT(u <= 65535);

    /* Store the digits in strDigits from back to front. */
    pch = &strDigits[5];
    ASSERT(*pch == '\0');
    do
        *--pch = (u % 10) + '0';
    while ((u /= 10) > 0);

    return (pch);
}
```

3. I was once reading some code in a journal when I noticed a function that set three local variables to *0* using, of all things, the *memset* function:

```c
void DoSomething(...)
{
    int i;
    int j;
    int k;

    memset(&k, 0, 3*sizeof(int)); /* Set i, j, and k to 0. */
        :
        :
```

Such code may work with some compilers, but why should you avoid using this trick?

4. Although your computer may have parts of its operating system
    stored in read-only memory, why would you be taking a risk if,
    to avoid unnecessary overhead, you bypassed the system inter-
    faces and called the ROM routines directly?

5. C has traditionally allowed programmers to pass fewer argu-
    ments to a function than the function expects to receive. Some
    programmers use that feature to optimize calls that don't require
    all the arguments. For instance,

```
    .
    .
    .
DoOperation(opNegAcc);      /* No need to pass val. */
    .
    .
    .

void DoOperation(operation op, int val)
{
    switch (op)
    {
    case opNegAcc:
        accumulator = -accumulator;
        break;

    case opAddVal:
        accumulator += val;
        break;
    .
    .
    .
```

    Although the optimization works, why should you avoid it?

6. The following assertion is correct. Why should it be rewritten?

```
ASSERT((f & 1) == f);
```

7. Take another look at the version of *memmove* that used the code
    below:

```
((pbTo > pbFrom) ? tailmove : headmove)(pbTo, pbFrom, size);
```

    How could you rewrite *memmove* so that it retains the efficiency
    of the code above but is easier to understand?

8. The assembly language code below shows a common shortcut to calling a function. Why are you asking for trouble if you use this practice?

```
            move    r0,#PRINTER
            call    Print+4
            .
            .
            .
Print:  move    r0,#DISPLAY   ; (4-byte instruction)
            .                     ; r0 == device ID
            .
            .
```

9. The assembly language code below shows another trick that pops up every once in a while. The code suffers from the same problems as the code in the previous exercise, relying as it does on the internal implementation of the *Print* code, but why else should you avoid this trick?

```
instClearR0 = 0x36A2          ; hex for "clear r0" instruction
            .
            .
            .
        call    Print+2           ; output to the PRINTER
            .
            .
            .
Print:  move    r0,#instClearR0 ; (4-byte instruction)
        comp    r0,#0             ; 0==PRINTER, non-0==DISPLAY
            .
            .
            .
```

8

THE REST IS ATTITUDE

Throughout this book, I've talked about techniques you can use to detect and to prevent bugs. Using these techniques won't guarantee that you'll write bug-free code any more than having a team of skillful ball players will guarantee that you'll have a winning team. The other necessary ingredient is a set of good habits and attitudes.

Would you expect those ball players to have a winning season if they grumbled all day about having to practice? What if they were constantly angry because their salary was a meager $1.2 million per year or were always worried about being traded or cut? These concerns have nothing to do with playing ball, but they have everything to do with how well the players perform.

You can use all of the suggestions in this book to help eliminate bugs, but if you have "buggy" attitudes or coding habits that cause bugs, you're going to have a tough time writing bug-free code.

In this chapter, I'll talk about some of the most common barriers to writing bug-free code. All are easily correctable; often all you need to do is become aware of them.

FOR MY NEXT TRICK, DISAPPEARING BUGS

How many times have you asked somebody about a bug they were fixing and heard in response, "Oh, that bug went away"? I said that once, many years ago, to my very first manager. He asked me if I'd managed to track down a bug in the Apple II database product we were wrapping up, and I said, "Oh, that bug went away." The manager paused for a moment and then asked me to follow him into his office, where we both sat down.

"Steve, what do you mean when you say 'the bug went away'?"

"Well, you know, I went through the steps in the bug report, and the bug didn't show up."

My manager leaned back in his chair. "So what do you suppose happened to that bug?"

"I don't know," I said. "I guess it already got fixed."

"But you don't know that, do you?"

"No, I guess I don't," I admitted.

"Well don't you think you had better find out what really happened? After all, you're working with a computer; bugs don't fix themselves."

That manager went on to explain the three reasons bugs disappear: The bug report was wrong, the bug has been fixed by another programmer, or the bug still exists but isn't apparent. His final words on the subject were to remind me that, as a professional programmer, it was my job to determine which of the three cases described my disappearing bug and to act accordingly. In no case was I to simply ignore the bug because it had disappeared.

That advice was valuable in the days of CP/M and Apple IIs when I first heard it, it was valuable in the decades before that, and it's still valuable today. I didn't realize how valuable the advice was until I became a project lead myself and found that it was common for programmers to happily assume that the testers were wrong or that somebody had already fixed the bug in question.

Bugs will often disappear simply because you and the tester are using different versions of the program. If a bug doesn't show up in the code you're using, dig up the version the tester was using. If the bug still doesn't show up, notify the testing team. If the bug does show up, track it down in those earlier sources, decide how to fix it, and then look at the current sources to see why the bug disappeared. Very often, the bug still exists but surrounding changes have hidden it. You need to understand why the bug disappeared so that you can take appropriate steps to correct it.

---◆---

Bugs don't just "go away."

---◆---

Too Much Effort?

Programmers sometimes grumble when I ask them to drag out older sources to look for a reported bug; it seems like a waste of time. If it seems that way to you, consider that you're not reverting to earlier sources on a whim. You're looking at those sources because there is an excellent chance that there is a bug and looking at those older sources is the most efficient way to track it down.

Suppose you isolate the bug in those earlier sources and find that the bug has indeed been fixed in the current sources. Have you wasted your time? Hardly. After all, which is better, closing the bug as "fixed" or labeling it as "nonreproducible" and sending it back to the testing group? What will the testers do then? They certainly can't assume that the bug has been fixed—their only two options are to spend additional time trying to reproduce the bug or to leave it marked as nonreproducible and hope that it was fixed. Both options are a lot worse than tracking down the bug in earlier sources and closing the bug as "fixed."

A FIX IN TIME SAVES NINE

When I first joined the Microsoft Excel group, the practice was to postpone all bug-fixes to the end of the project. It's not that the group had a cast-iron scroll staked to a wall that read, "Thou shalt not fix bugs until all features have been implemented," but there was always pressure to keep to the schedule and knock out features. At the same time, there was very little pressure to fix bugs. I was once told, "Unless a bug crashes the system or holds up the testing group, don't worry about fixing it. We'll have plenty of time to fix bugs later, after we complete the scheduled features." In short, fixing bugs was not a high priority.

I'm sure that sounds backwards to current Microsoft programmers because projects aren't run that way anymore; there were too many problems with that approach, and the worst was that it was impossible to predict when you would finish the product. How do you estimate the time it takes to fix 1742 bugs? And of course, there aren't just 1742 bugs to fix—programmers will introduce new bugs as they fix old ones. And (closely related) fixing one bug can expose other, latent, bugs that the testing group was unable to find because the first bug was getting in the way.

And those weren't the only problems.

By finishing the features before fixing the bugs, the developers made the product look like it was much further along than it actually was. Important people in the company would use the internal releases, see that they worked except for the occasional bug, and wonder why it was taking Development six months to finish a nearly final product. They wouldn't see out-of-memory bugs or the bugs in features they never tried. They just knew that the code was "feature complete" and that it basically appeared to work.

Fixing bugs for months on end didn't do much for morale either. Programmers like to program, not to fix bugs, but at the end of every project they would spends months doing nothing but fixing bugs, often under much pressure because it was obvious to everybody outside Development that the product was nearly finished. Why couldn't it be ready in time for COMDEX, MacWorld Expo, or the local computer club meeting?

What a mess.

Then a run of buggy products, starting with Macintosh Excel 1.03 and ending with the cancellation—because of a runaway bug list—of an unannounced Windows product, forced Microsoft to take a hard look at the way it developed products. The findings were not too surprising:

◆ You don't save time by fixing bugs late in the product cycle. In fact, you lose time because it's often harder to fix bugs in code you wrote a year ago than in code you wrote days ago.

◆ Fixing bugs "as you go" provides damage control because the earlier you learn of your mistakes, the less likely you are to repeat those mistakes.

- Bugs are a form of negative feedback that keep fast but sloppy programmers in check. If you don't allow programmers to work on new features until they have fixed all their bugs, you prevent sloppy programmers from spreading half-implemented features throughout the product—they're too busy fixing bugs. If you allow programmers to ignore their bugs, you lose that regulation.

- By keeping the bug count near zero, you have a much easier time predicting when you'll finish the product. Instead of trying to guess how long it will take to finish 32 features and 1742 bug-fixes, you just have to guess how long it will take to finish the 32 features. Even better, you're often in a position to drop the unfinished features and ship what you have.

None of these points is uniquely suited to Microsoft development; they are general points that apply to any software development. If you are not already fixing bugs as you find them, let Microsoft's negative experience be a lesson to you. You can learn through your own hard experience, or you can learn from the costly mistakes of others.

---◆---

Don't fix bugs later; fix them now.

---◆---

BUG-DOCTOR TO THE RESCUE!

In his book *Awaken the Giant Within*, Anthony Robbins tells the story of a doctor who is standing beside a raging river when she hears the cry of a drowning man. The doctor looks around and seeing nobody else to help, jumps into the water. She swims out, brings the drowning man to shore, and gives him mouth-to-mouth resuscitation. She no sooner has the man breathing again than she hears two more cries from the river. She dives in and brings those two ashore. Just as she stabilizes those people, the doctor hears four cries for help. Then she hears eight cries for help. . . . Unfortunately, the doctor is so busy saving people that she has no time to go upstream to find out who is throwing them in.

Like that doctor, programmers are sometimes so busy "healing" bugs that they never stop to figure out what's causing them. The *strFromUns* function we talked about in Chapter 7 is an example of this problem. The *strFromUns* routine causes bugs because it forces programmers to pass data in static memory. But when bugs show up, they're downstream in the callers to *strFromUns*, not in *strFromUns* itself. Which buggy routine do you think gets fixed, *strFromUns*—the true source of the bugs—or the functions that call *strFromUns* and wipe out the results of a previous call?

Another example of this problem occurred when I was porting a Windows Excel feature to Macintosh Excel. (They were still two independent bodies of source code at the time.) After I ported the feature, I began testing the code and found a function that was getting an unexpected *NULL* pointer. I looked at the code, but it wasn't clear whether the bug was in the caller (passing *NULL*) or in the function (not handling *NULL*). I went to the original programmer and explained the problem to him. He promptly loaded the function into an editor and said, "Oh, that function can't take a *NULL* pointer." Then, as I stood there watching, he fixed the bug by inserting a "quick escape" if the pointer was *NULL*:

```
if (pb == NULL)
    return (FALSE);
```

I pointed out that if the function shouldn't be getting a *NULL* pointer, the bug was in the caller, not in the function, to which he replied, "I know the code; this will fix it." And it did. But to me the solution felt as if we'd fixed a symptom of the bug and not the cause of it, so I went back to my office and spent 10 minutes tracking down the source of the *NULL* pointer. Not only was the *NULL* pointer the true bug, but it also accounted for two other known bugs.

Other times, I've tracked a bug to its source and then thought, "Wait, this can't be right; if it is, this function over here would be broken too, and it's not." I'm sure you can guess why that other function worked. It worked because somebody had used a local fix for a more general bug.

———◆———

Fix the cause, not the symptom.

———◆———

ARE YOU A CODE MEDDLER?

"If it ain't broke, fix it anyway" seems to be the battle cry of some programmers. No matter how well a piece of code works, some programmers feel compelled to put their mark on it. If you've ever worked with a programmer who reformats entire files to suit his or her tastes, you know what I'm talking about. Most programmers are much more conservative than that about "cleaning up" code, but all programmers seem to clean up code to some degree.

The trouble with cleaning up code is that programmers don't always treat their improved version of the code as if it were new code. There are programmers who, while scrolling through a file, might see the code below and feel compelled to change the test against *0* to a test against '\0'; others might feel compelled to remove the test altogether.

```
char *strcpy(char *pchTo, char *pchFrom)
{
    char *pchStart = pchTo;

    while ((*pchTo++ = *pchFrom++) != 0)
        NULL;

    return (pchStart);
}
```

The problem with changing the *0* to a null character is that it's easy to mistakenly type '0' instead of '\0', but how many programmers would bother to test *strcpy* after making such a simple change? Here's a better question: When you make such simple changes, do you thoroughly test the code as though it were freshly written? If you don't, you risk introducing bugs with those unnecessary changes.

You might think that some changes couldn't possibly be wrong as long as the code still compiles. How could changing the name of a local variable, for example, cause problems? Well, it can. I once tracked a bug to a function which had a local variable named *hPrint* that was conflicting with a global variable of the same name. Since the function had worked until recently, I looked at the older sources to see what had changed and to verify that my fix would not reintroduce an earlier bug. What I found was a clean-up. The earlier version had a local variable named *hPrint1*, but no *hPrint2* or *hPrint3* to justify the '1' in the name. Whoever removed the '1' probably assumed that *hPrint1* was an artifact from earlier days and cleaned it up, causing the name conflict and a bug.

To keep yourself from making the same kind of clean-up mistake, tape yet another message to your monitor: *The programmers I work with are not bozos.* That message should remind you that if you see code that is obviously wrong, or clearly unnecessary, you should proceed with utmost caution. If the code is that obviously questionable, there is probably a good, but nonobvious, reason it's there. I've seen ridiculous code whose only purpose was to work around a compiler code-generation bug. Clean up the code, and you reintroduce the bug. Of course, such code should have a comment to explain what's going on, but not all programmers are that thoughtful.

If you find code like

```c
char chGetNext(void)
{
    int ch;        /* ch *must* be an int. */

    ch = getchar();
    return (chRemapChar(ch));
}
```

don't clean up the function by removing the obviously "unnecessary" *ch*:

```c
char chGetNext(void)
{
    return (chRemapChar(getchar()));
}
```

If you remove *ch*, you could introduce a bug if *chRemapChar* is a macro that evaluates its argument more than once. Keep the "unnecessary" local and prevent the unnecessary bug.

———◆———

Don't clean up code unless the clean-up is critical to the product's success.

———◆———

Put "Cool" Features into Cold Storage

Refraining from code clean-ups is a specific case of a more general principle that results in fewer bugs: *Don't write (or change) code if you don't have to.* That may seem like strange advice, but you'd be surprised by how often you can drop a feature by asking, "How important is this feature to the success of the product?"

Some features add no value to the product and exist merely to fill out feature sets; others exist because large corporate customers ask for them; and still others exist because a competitor's product has them and a reviewer somewhere decided to put them on a feature-list chart. If you have a good marketing and product planning team, you shouldn't run into any of these useless features. But as a programmer, you may run into or even originate unnecessary features.

Have you ever heard a programmer say something like "It would be so cool if WordSmasher could do. . ."? The question, though, is whether the feature is "cool" because it would improve the product or because implementing it would be technically challenging. If the feature will improve the product, postpone consideration of it until the next version of your program so that it can be properly evaluated and scheduled. If it is merely challenging, kill it. I don't suggest this to stifle creativity; I suggest it to stifle needless feature growth and associated bugs.

Sometimes technically challenging features improve the product; sometimes they don't. Choose carefully.

---◆---

*Don't implement nonstrategic
features.*

---◆---

There Are No Free Lunches

"Free" features are another source of unnecessary bugs. On the surface, free features seem worthwhile because they fall out of existing designs with little or no effort. What could be better than that? But there's one big fat problem with free features—they're almost never critical to the success of the product. And of course, any noncritical feature is a potential source of bugs. Programmers add free features to a program because they can, not because they should. After all, why shouldn't you add a feature if it doesn't cost you anything?

There's the fallacy. Free features may not cost the programmer much, but there is more to a feature than code. Somebody has to write documentation for the feature. Somebody has to test the feature. And of course somebody has to fix any bugs that show up with the feature.

When I hear a programmer say that a feature is free, that tells me he or she has not spent much time thinking about the true costs involved.

———◆———

There are no free features.

———◆———

FLEXIBILITY BREEDS BUGS

Another strategy you can use to prevent bugs is to strip unnecessary flexibility from your designs. You've seen me use this principle throughout the book. In Chapter 1, I used optional compiler warnings to disallow redundant and risky C language idioms. In Chapter 2, I defined *ASSERT* as a statement to prevent the macro from being mistakenly used in expressions. In Chapter 3, I used an assertion to catch *NULL* pointers passed to *FreeMemory* even though it's quite legal to call the *free* function with a *NULL* pointer. From every chapter I could list examples in which I reduced flexibility in order to prevent bugs.

The trouble with flexible designs is that the more flexible they are, the harder it is to detect bugs. Do you remember the points I made about *realloc* in Chapter 5? You can throw almost any set of inputs at *realloc* and it will do something, even though that something may not be at all what you expect. Worse, it's hard to detect *realloc* bugs because the function is so flexible that you can't insert meaningful assertions into it to validate the inputs. But if you break *realloc* into four specific functions that expand, shrink, allocate, and release memory blocks, you make it much easier to validate function arguments.

In addition to watching out for unduly flexible functions, you should keep a wary eye open for unduly flexible features. Flexible features are troublesome because they can lead to unexpected "legal" situations that you didn't think to test for or even realize were legal.

When I was adding color support to Microsoft Excel for Apple's then new Macintosh II machines, I ported code from Windows Excel that would allow users to specify the color of the text displayed in a spreadsheet cell. To add color to a cell, the user would take an existing cell format like the one below

```
$#,##0.00            /* Print 1234.5678 as $1,234.57. */
```

and tack a color specification onto the front of it. To display a number in blue, the user would change the format to

```
[blue]$#,##0.00
```

If the user typed *[red]*, the number would be drawn in red, and so on.

Excel's product specification was quite clear—the color specification should preface the number format—but after I ported the feature and began testing the code, I found that the formats below would work as well:

```
$#,##0.00[blue]
$#,##[blue]0.00
$[blue]#,##0.00
```

The user could put the *[blue]* anywhere. When I asked the original programmer whether this was a bug or a feature, he said that the arbitrary placement of the color specification "just fell out of the parsing loop." He didn't see anything wrong with allowing a bit of extra flexibility—nor did I at the time—so the code remained that way. In retrospect, I see that we should never have allowed that extra flexibility.

It didn't take the testing group long to find half a dozen subtle bugs, all ultimately traceable to the format parser, which did not expect to find color specifications in the middle of a format.

Unfortunately, instead of fixing the problem by removing the unnecessary flexibility—a fix that would have taken one simple *if* statement—the other programmer and I kept fixing the specific bugs—fixing symptoms—in order to retain a flexibility that nobody needed. To this day, Microsoft Excel lets you put color specifications anywhere you want.

When you implement features in your own projects, make them easy to use; don't make them unnecessarily flexible. There is a difference.

———◆———

Don't allow unnecessary flexibility.

———◆———

Ported Code Is **New** *Code*

One lesson I learned from porting so much Windows Excel code to Macintosh Excel was that there is a temptation to skimp on testing such code. After all, you reason, it was tested in the original product. I should have caught all of the bugs in the Excel number formatting code before the code ever reached the testing group, but I didn't. Instead, I copied the code to Macintosh Excel, made the necessary changes to hook the code into the project, and then casually tested the code to verify that I had hooked it in correctly. I didn't thoroughly test the feature itself since I thought it had already been tested. That was a mistake, especially since Windows Excel was under development itself and this was still in the days when Microsoft groups postponed fixing bugs to the end of the product cycle.

It doesn't matter how you implement your features—whether you design and implement them from scratch or leverage existing code—you are still responsible for keeping bugs out of the code that you add to your project. The fact that Windows Excel had the same bugs didn't make the bugs any less severe in Macintosh Excel. I got lazy, and it showed.

"TRY" IS A FOUR-LETTER WORD

How many times have you said something like "I can't figure out how to . . ." and another programmer has answered, "Have you tried . . ."? You'll see that dialogue in one form another in almost every programmers' news group on the Internet. One programmer will post a message asking "How do I hide the cursor so that it doesn't obscure the display?" and somebody will respond, "Try moving the cursor to an off-screen coordinate." Another will suggest, "Try setting the cursor mask to zeros to indi-cate that none of the cursor pixels should be visible." Still a third might say, "The cursor is just a bitmap, so try setting its width and height to zero."

Try. Try. Try.

Admittedly, this is a silly example, but I'm sure you've seen such dia-logues take place, whether in a news group on the Internet or in front of the office coffee maker. And more often than not, none of the things you're sup-posed to "try" is the proper course to pursue. When somebody tells you to try something, they're giving you an educated guess, not the officially documented solution.

Well, what's wrong with trying different approaches to solving a problem? There's nothing wrong with it provided that everything you try is clearly defined by the system you're using. But more often than not, when programmers start trying things, it means that they've gone beyond the sys-tem as they understand it and have entered the realm of looking for any-thing that works, even though what works may rely on an unintended side effect that can change in the future. How do you think those programmers who intentionally read from free memory got into that bad habit? *free* cer-tainly doesn't define what happens to the contents of free memory, but at some point those programmers felt they needed to reference free memory. They tried it, it worked, and now they rely on *free* to allow that behavior.

Listen carefully to the suggestions that follow "Have you tried . . ." I think you'll probably find that most of those suggestions exploit undefined or ill-defined side effects of code. If the programmers making the sugges-tions knew the proper solution, they wouldn't tell you to "try" something. They'd tell you to "Just use the *SetCursorState(INVISIBLE)* system call."

———◆———

Don't keep "trying" solutions until
you find one that works. Take the
time to find the correct solution.

———◆———

Don't "Try." Read.

For years the Macintosh programmers at Microsoft received read-only compilations of the Macintosh news groups on the Internet. Those compilations were interesting, but it was frustrating not being able to respond to the questions other programmers posed. Programmers were always asking questions that were clearly answered in Apple's *Inside Macintosh* manuals, but it seemed as if the programmers responding would outline every possible solution but the one that was clearly documented. Fortunately, there were always a few *Inside Macintosh* experts who would post precise answers if nobody else would: "See Inside Macintosh IV, page 32. It says there that you should. . . ."

If you find yourself testing possible solutions to a problem, stop yourself, pull out your manuals, and read. No, it's not as much fun as playing around with code, or as easy as asking everybody for something to try, but you'll learn more about your operating system and about how to write programs for it.

THE SACRED SCHEDULE

There are programmers who, when given a sizable feature to implement, will spend two weeks hunched over a keyboard writing code, never bothering to test their work. Other programmers will implement a dozen small features before stopping to check things out. There's nothing wrong with those approaches provided that the programmers thoroughly test their code. But do they?

Think about the case in which a programmer has five days in which to implement five features. Suppose that the programmer has two choices: to implement and test the features one at a time or to implement all five features and then test all five. Which approach, in practice, do you think will result in sturdier code? I've seen both coding styles over the years, and with rare exceptions, programmers who test code as they go have fewer bugs. I can even tell you why that's true.

Suppose the programmer uses all five days to implement the five features but then realizes that he doesn't have much, if any, scheduled time remaining to thoroughly test the code. Do you think the programmer will take an extra day or two to thoroughly test his code, or do you think he'll merely play with the code and verify that it seems to work? The answer will depend to an extent upon the programmer and the work environment. But it comes down to slipping the schedule, which is frowned upon at most companies, or cutting back on testing, which often results in no negative feedback whatsoever; the programmer will probably be praised for staying on schedule. It takes only one difficult feature per batch to suck up the testing time for all of the features.

A drawback to using a schedule is that programmers will give it higher priority than testing, which essentially means that the schedule gets higher priority than writing correct code does. My experience has been that if a programmer can write the code for a feature in the scheduled amount of time, he will "finish" the feature on schedule, even if that means cutting back on testing. "Besides," he'll think, "if there are any unknown bugs in the code, the testing group will let me know about them."

To counteract this tendency, programmers should write and test each feature before moving on to the next. Then if it takes five days to implement the first three features, the programmers are forced into taking extra time to implement the remaining two features. They might still skip testing on the final two features to incur as little schedule slip as possible, but at least the first three features will have been tested, which is better than none at all.

———◆———

Write and test code in small chunks.

Always test your code, even if that means your schedule will slip.

———◆———

WHAT'S IN A NAME?

In Chapter 5, I explained how *getchar*'s name often tricks programmers into thinking that the function returns a character when it actually returns an *int*. In the same way, programmers often believe that the testing group is responsible for testing their code. What else would a testing group be for? But despite what many programmers believe, the testing group's job is not to test programmers' code; the group is there to protect the company and ultimately the customer from shoddy workmanship.

It might be easier to understand the role testing plays if you look at the same process in another field: house construction. There, contractors do the work, and inspectors verify it. But inspectors don't test the work. An electrician would never wire up a house and then leave without first turning on the power, testing the circuit breakers, and checking every outlet using a receptacle tester. The electrician would never think "I don't need to make these tests. If there's a problem, the inspector will let me know about it." Any electrician who thought that way would soon find it hard to get work.

The good reason that testers, like inspectors, are not responsible for testing the work is that they rarely have the necessary access, tools, or skills. Despite computer folklore to the contrary, testers cannot test your code better than you can. Can testers add assertions to catch bad data flow? Can they incorporate subsystem tests like the ones in Chapter 3 for the memory manager? Can they use a debugger to step through the code one instruction at a time to check that every code path is executed and works as expected? The sad truth is that programmers, who actually can test their code more effectively than testers, often don't.

The testing group plays a valuable part in the development process; it's just not the part that many programmers think it is. When testers examine a product, they look for flaws and holes in features, they verify that the product is backwards compatible with previous releases, they alert the development team to quirks and rough edges that, if smoothed, would improve the product, and they use the product in "real world" scenarios to make sure that the features are truly useful. And testers report any bugs they notice.

Even if your testers do nothing but look for bugs, you still cannot assume that they will test your code for you. Remember what I said in Chapter 1: Testers hurl inputs at programs and hope that lurking bugs will somehow show themselves. Of course, nobody really thinks of it that way, because with modern testing tools it seems as if the approach is more scientific than that. But in fact, modern testing tools simply make the approach more efficient. The strongest statement a tester can make is "The code *appears* to work." To me, that's not nearly as reassuring as knowing that the programmer has stepped through and observed every path in his or her code, verifying that legal inputs generate the correct outputs.

Besides, from a practical viewpoint, what if some members of the testing team aren't very experienced? Or what if you don't even have a testing team because they've been pulled off your project to work on something more pressing? This happens all the time at Microsoft; I'm sure it happens elsewhere too.

Duplication of Effort?

If programmers are responsible for thoroughly testing their code, the question naturally arises, "Aren't programmers and testers duplicating each other's efforts?" Perhaps they do here and there, but when programmers test code, they test it from the inside and move out. Testers start from the outside and move in.

Programmers start by testing each function, stepping through every code path one instruction (or line) at a time, verifying code and data flow. From there, they move one step outward to verify that each function works correctly with the other functions in its subsystem. Finally programmers use unit tests to verify that the subsystems interact properly. The unit tests may, as extra verification, regularly check the state of internal data structures throughout the tests.

Testers view code as a black box and write global tests that throw all possible inputs at the program as a way of looking for flaws. The testers may also use regression tests to verify that all reported bugs have been fixed and have stayed fixed. From there, testers move steadily inward, using code coverage tools to give them an idea of how much internal code their global tests are executing. The testers use that information to create new tests that try to execute the untouched code.

This is a grand example of using two separate "algorithms" to test the program. The combination of approaches works because programmers focus on code while testers focus on features. With the two working from opposite directions, the chances of finding unknown bugs are increased.

You simply cannot rely on the testing group to test your code for you—at least not if you want to consistently write bug-free code.

————◆————

*Don't rely on the testing group to find
your bugs.*

————◆————

TESTERS WEAR WHITE HATS

Have you ever noticed how some programmers heave a sigh of relief when the testing group finds a bug? "Whew!" they say, "I'm sure glad Testing found that bug before we shipped." Other programmers resent it when a tester reports a bug, especially if the tester reports many bugs against the same piece of code. I've seen programmers bristle with anger: "Why won't that tester leave me alone?" I've heard project leads (who should know better) say, "It's Testing's fault that we've slipped this beta date." Once, I even had to prevent a project lead and a testing lead from throwing punches at each other.

Does that sound silly? It's easy for us to sit back and see how ridiculous such behavior is when we're not the ones under pressure to ship a product and under attack. But when you're months past your ship date and buried in bugs, it's easy to view the testers as the Bad Guys.

When I see programmers getting upset with testers, I pull them aside and ask them why they're holding the testers responsible for bugs that programmers created. It makes no sense to get angry at testers; they're just the messengers.

When a tester reports a bug in your code, your first reaction should be shock and disbelief—you should never expect testers to find bugs in your code. Your second reaction should be gratitude because that tester has saved you from shipping a bug.

————◆————

Don't blame testers for finding your bugs.

————◆————

> ### *There Are No Silly Bugs*
>
> Sometimes you'll hear a programmer complain that a particular bug is ridiculous, or that certain testers regularly report silly bugs. If you hear a programmer grumbling about silly bugs, stop and remind him or her that it's not up to testers to judge how serious bugs are or whether they're worth fixing. Testers must report all bugs, silly or not, because for all they know, those silly bugs may be the side effects of serious problems.
>
> The real question isn't whether the bug is silly but why the programmer who tested the code didn't catch the bug. Even if the bug is minor and not worth fixing, it's still important to determine its cause so that you can prevent similar bugs in the future.
>
> A bug may be minor; that it exists is serious.

ESTABLISH YOUR PRIORITIES

If you flip back through the pages of this book and look at all of the Quick Review points, you might be surprised to find that some of them appear to contradict others. Then again, maybe you won't be surprised. After all, programmers have long dealt with the sometimes contradictory goals of writing fast code and writing tight code.

When you're faced with a choice between two possible implementations, which do you choose? I doubt you would have trouble choosing between a fast algorithm and a small one—you make that choice all the time—but what about choosing between a fast algorithm and a maintainable one, or between a small-but-risky algorithm and a larger-but-easily-tested one? Some programmers could answer those questions without much thought, but others would be unsure, and if you asked them the same questions weeks apart, you might get different answers.

Those programmers would be unsure about such trade-offs because they don't know what their priorities are beyond the common ones such as size and speed. Programming without a clear set of priorities is like going on a trip without knowing your destination. At every corner you have to stop and ask, "What do I do now?" and you're bound to take wrong turns.

Then there are programmers who know quite clearly what their priorities are but who, because their priorities are wrong or conflicting, don't ponder at corners and instead take wrong turns consistently. For example, many experienced programmers are still locked into the priorities of the late 1970s, when memory was scarce and microcomputers were so slow that a pong game taxed them. To write a usable program then, you had to trade maintainability for size and speed. But today, RAM is plentiful and computers are fast enough to accomplish most tasks without delay even if you use a poor algorithm. The priorities have reversed. It simply doesn't make sense to consistently trade maintainability for size and speed because in most cases you end up with an unnoticeably faster program that you can't maintain. Still, some programmers contrive to make Size and Speed the gods that rule all of their code. These programmers consistently make the wrong implementation choices because their priorities are outdated.

Whether you've never thought about your priorities or haven't reviewed them lately, you need to sit down and consciously create a roadmap for yourself (or for your team if you're a project lead) so that you can consistently make the best choices to accomplish the goals of your project. Notice what I said there: "the goals of your project." Your priority list should reflect not what you want to do, but what you should do. If a programmer listed "personal expression" as a high priority, would that benefit the programmer or the product? Would that programmer accept a naming standard or agree to use a { }-placement style other than his or her own?

There is no one "right" way to order your priorities, but the order you choose will dictate the style and quality of your code. Take a look at the priorities of two programmers, Jack and Jill:

Jack's Priority List	Jill's Priority List
Correctness	Correctness
Global efficiency	Testability
Size	Global efficiency
Local efficiency	Maintainability/clarity
Personal convenience	Consistency
Maintainability/clarity	Size
Personal expression	Local efficiency
Testability	Personal expression
Consistency	Personal convenience

How will these priorities affect Jack's and Jill's code? Both programmers focus on writing correct code above all else, but that's the end of their agreement on priorities. You can see that Jack emphasizes size and speed, is only marginally concerned about writing clear code, and doesn't appear to think much at all about how easy it will be to test the code.

Jill puts an emphasis on writing correct code too, both now and for the future, when the code will have to be maintained. She worries about size and speed only if it's vital to the success of the product. She has "testability" high on her list because she believes that unless you can easily test the code, you can't easily verify that it is correct (which is, of course, her highest priority).

Given these two programmers, who is more likely

◆ To enable all optional compiler warnings to automatically catch bugs, even though it requires some extra work to use the safe work-arounds?

◆ To use assertions and subsystem debug checks?

◆ To walk through every code path, microscopically verifying all new code the moment it is written?

◆ To use safe function interfaces over risky ones even though they may generate an extra instruction or two at every call site?

◆ To use portable types, and to divide or multiply when using a shift would work (for example, using /4 instead of >>2)?

◆ To avoid the efficiency tricks described in Chapter 7?

Is that a list of loaded questions? I don't think so. I could just as easily have asked, "Which of the two programmers do you think will read this book and act on the suggestions it contains?" "Which programmer would read *The Elements of Programming Style*, or any other how-to book, and act on those suggestions?"

Because of his priorities, Jack would focus on code to the detriment of the product. He would waste time trying to make every line of code as fast and as small as possible, and he would give little thought to the long-term health of the product. Jill is just the opposite. With her priorities, she would focus on the product, not the code, and she wouldn't concern herself with size or speed unless there were a demonstrated (or obvious) need.

Ask yourself which is more important to your company, the code or the product. Where do you think your priorities should be?

————◆————

Establish your priorities and stick to them.

————◆————

Gee, I Don't Know

Have you ever looked at somebody's code and wondered why they wrote it the way they did? When you asked them about the code, have they said something like, "Gee, I don't know why I wrote it that way. I guess it just felt right at the time"?

I'm always reviewing code, looking for ways to help programmers improve their skills, and I've found the "Gee, I don't know" response to be pretty common. I've also found that the programmers who respond with "Gee, I don't know" don't have clear priorities; they make their decisions based, it sometimes seems, on what they had for lunch that day. Programmers with clear priorities know exactly why they chose a specific implementation and will rattle off the reasons if you ask.

If you find that you often don't know why you wrote a piece of code the way you did, that's a good indication that you need to stop and create a priority list for yourself.

YOU DON'T GET WHAT YOU DON'T ASK FOR

One important point I haven't yet mentioned in this chapter is that you must develop the habit of asking questions about how you code. This entire book is the result of consistently asking a few simple questions over a long period of time:

◆   How could I have automatically detected this bug?

◆   How could I have prevented this bug?

And in this last chapter:

◆   Does this belief help or hinder my ability to write bug-free code?

It is important to question your beliefs because they are reflected in your personal priority list. If you believe that the testing group exists to test your code, you're going to have trouble writing bug-free code because you'll think, at some level, that it's okay to skimp on testing. Consider this: What are your chances of writing bug-free code if you don't believe that it's possible? If you don't believe it's possible, will you even try?

If you want to write bug-free code, you need to weed out the beliefs that prevent you from achieving that goal. The way to start weeding is to ask whether this or that belief helps or hinders your ability to write bug-free code.

QUICK REVIEW

◆   Bugs don't create themselves; nor do they fix themselves. If you have a bug report but you can't reproduce the bug, don't assume that the tester was seeing things. Make the effort to find the bug, even if that means reverting to an older version of the program.

◆   Don't fix bugs "later." It's becoming alarmingly common to read of major products being canceled because of runaway bug lists. Your project won't suffer that fate if you fix bugs as you find them. You can't have a runaway bug list if the project is always near zero bugs.

◆   When you track down a bug, always ask yourself whether the bug is a symptom of a larger bug. Yes, it's easier to fix the symptom you've tracked down, but you should always make the effort to find the true cause.

◆   Don't write unnecessary code or make unnecessary fixes. Let your competitors implement cool but worthless features, clean up code, and slip their ship dates because of "free" features that aren't. Let your competitors waste time fixing the unnecessary bugs that come with all that useless code.

◆   Remember that being flexible is not the same as being easy to
    use. When you design functions and features, focus on making
    them easy to use; if they're merely flexible—as the *realloc* func-
    tion and that color formatting feature in Microsoft Excel are—
    you're not making them more useful; you're making it more
    difficult to find the bugs.

◆   Resist the urge to "try" things to achieve a desired effect. Use the
    time you would have spent trying things to do some research to
    find the correct solution. If you have to, call the company respon-
    sible for your operating system and talk to their developer sup-
    port group. That's better than coming up with oddball
    implementations that may break in the future.

◆   Write your code in chunks small enough to thoroughly test, and
    don't skimp on your testing. Remember, if you don't test your
    code, it's possible that nobody will. Whatever you do, don't ex-
    pect the testing group to test your code for you.

◆   Determine what the priorities are for your group and follow
    them. If you're a Jack but your project requires a Jill, you're go-
    ing to have to change your habits, at least at work.

PROJECT: Persuade your programming team to create and adopt a
    priorities list that they agree to work by. If your company recog-
    nizes different skill levels (entry level programmer, regular old
    programmer, senior-level programmer, awesome programmer, for
    example), you might want to consider using different priority lists
    for the different levels. Why?

Epilogue

WHERE DO YOU GO FROM HERE?

We've reached the end. And you're probably wondering if I really believe it's possible to write bug-free programs. The answer is no, I don't, not absolutely. But I do believe you can come very close to writing bug-free programs, much closer than the current norm; you just have to decide to do it. You can paint a room in your house without getting paint where you don't want it, but you have to put down drop cloths, tape up the baseboards, and use care. Painting without getting splotches everywhere doesn't just happen—it takes effort, effort you must decide to make. In the same way, it takes effort to keep bugs out of your code. And the only way you're going to make that effort is to decide that it's necessary.

Even if you make writing bug-free code a priority, using the techniques in this book isn't enough. Nobody's list of guidelines will protect you from bugs. The key is to continue to build the list by asking yourself how you could have detected or prevented every bug you find in the future. Some of your findings may surprise you. Mine have surprised me.

I once introduced a nasty but subtle bug into Microsoft Excel's recalculation engine when I accidentally deleted a line while I scrolled though a file. I didn't detect the mistake, and I merged that change into the master sources along with a feature I had just implemented. Eventually somebody noticed the bug and tracked it to my deletion. When I asked my-self how I could have detected or prevented the bug, the answer was clear: Use the source code control manager to list my changes before merging them into the master sources. That extra step takes practically no time, and in the five years that I've been doing it, it has caught three serious bugs and a number of minor changes I intentionally made but thought I had re-moved. Is three bugs in five years worth the effort? Yes, to me it's worth the effort because it takes almost no time and I know if I do it that no unex-pected changes will make it into the master sources. Again, you have to decide that keeping bugs out of your code is a priority.

You may find that code reviews help solve your problems, or that pro-viding better documentation for the internal workings of the product will help. If you're not using unit tests, maybe you should start. You may even find it worthwhile to add *DEBUG* code specifically to help your testers.

The reality is that you will never completely eliminate bugs, but you *can* increase the time between occurrences by constantly striving to abolish every class of bug you encounter. To help you in this endeavor, I've pro-vided a task-oriented programmer's checklist in Appendix A that covers the most important guidelines in this book.

The final key to successfully writing bug-free code can be summed up with one last guideline:

———◆———

Never allow the same bug to bite you twice.

———◆———

A

CODING CHECKLISTS

To remind you of the most important points in the book, I've created several checklists you can review during the primary development steps: design, implementation, *DEBUG* support, testing, and debugging. I haven't listed the points that have to do with development overall—I assume that you're using your optional compiler warnings, maintaining *DEBUG* versions of your program, fixing bugs as they are reported, and so on.

To make effective use of these checklists, review them each time you add new code to your project. From a practical standpoint, "each time" really means the "next few times" you write new code. After that, you should have developed a sixth sense for code that bends or breaks the guidelines.

DESIGN

When you consider different designs for a feature, don't stop with the design that gives you the fastest or the smallest result. Consider the risks involved in implementing, maintaining, and using the code that will result from your design. For each possible design, review these points.

◆ Does this design include undefined or meaningless behavior? What about random or rare behavior? Does the design allow unnecessary flexibility or make unnecessary assumptions? Are there arbitrary details in the design?

◆ Do you pass any data in static or global buffers? Do any functions rely on the internal workings of other functions? Do any functions do more than one task?

◆ Does your design have to handle any special cases? Have you isolated the code that handles those special cases?

◆ Look at the inputs and outputs of your functions. Does each of the inputs and outputs represent exactly one type of data, or do some of them contain error values or other hard-to-notice values? Robust interfaces make every input and output explicit so that programmers can't miss important details such as the *NULL* error value returned by *malloc*, or the fact that *realloc* can release a memory block if you pass in a size of *0*.

◆ Anticipate how programmers will call your functions. Does the "obvious" approach work correctly? Recall that in *realloc*'s case, the obvious approach creates lost memory blocks.

◆ On the maintenance side, are your functions readable at the point of call? Each function should perform one task, and its arguments should make the meaning of the call clear. The presence of *TRUE* and *FALSE* arguments often indicates that a function is doing more than one task, or that it is not well designed.

◆ Do any of your functions return error values? Is it possible to redefine those functions to eliminate the error conditions? Remember that when a function returns an error, that error must be handled—or mishandled—at every point of call.

◆ Most important, is it possible to automatically and thoroughly validate the design using a unit test? If not, you should consider using an alternative design that can be tested.

IMPLEMENTATION

After implementing your design, you should review these points to ensure that your implementation is robust and error resistant.

◆ Compare your implementation to your design. Have you accurately implemented the design? Be careful. Minor differences between your design and your implementation can trip you up. Remember the *UnsToStr* example that broke because it used non-negative integers when the design called for integers that were unsigned.

◆ Do you make unnecessary assumptions in the code? Have you used nonportable data types when portable data types would work? Are there any arbitrary aspects of the implementation?

◆ Examine the expressions in your code. Can any of them overflow or underflow? What about your variables?

◆ Have you used nested *?:* operators or other risky C language idioms such as shifting to divide? Have you mixed bitwise operators and arithmetic operators without good cause? Have you used any C idioms in a questionable way? For example, using the 0/1 result of a logical expression in an arithmetic context? Rewrite risky expressions using comparable yet safer expressions.

◆ Take a close look at your code. Have you used any arcane C that the average programmer on your team wouldn't understand? Consider rewriting the code using mainstream C.

◆ Each of your functions probably does a single task, but is that task implemented using a single code path, or is the task actually achieved using different code to implement various special cases? If the task is implemented using special-case code, can you eliminate those special cases by using an alternative algorithm? Try to eliminate every *if* statement in your code.

♦ Do you call any functions that return errors? Can you alter your design so that the call is unnecessary and thus eliminate the need to do error handling?

♦ Do you reference memory you have no right to touch? Specifically, do you reference memory you have released? Do you peek at private data structures owned by other subsystems?

♦ If your functions take pointers to inputs or to outputs, does your code restrict its references to only the memory required to hold those inputs and outputs? If not, your code may be making an erroneous assumption about how much memory the caller has allocated for that data.

ADDING DEBUG SUPPORT

Adding assertions and other debugging code to your implementations can reduce the time required to find any bugs hiding in your code. This checklist points out worthwhile assertions and debugging code you should consider using.

♦ Have you used assertions to validate your function arguments? If you find that you can't validate a particular argument because you don't have enough information, would maintaining extra debug information help? Recall how the debug-only *sizeofBlock* function was useful in validating pointers to allocated memory.

♦ Have you used assertions to validate your assumptions, or to detect illegal uses of undefined behavior? Asserting for undefined behavior prevents programmers from abusing unspecified details of your implementations.

♦ Defensive programming "fixes" internal bugs when they occur, making such bugs hard to spot. Have you used assertions to detect these bugs in the *DEBUG* version of your program? (Of course, this view of defensive programming doesn't apply to defensive programming used to correct bad end-user inputs.)

♦ Are your assertions clear? If not, be sure to include comments to explain the tests. Unfortunately, when programmers get an assertion failure and don't understand the purpose of the test, they will often assume that the assertion is invalid and remove it. Comments help preserve your assertions.

◆ If your code allocates memory, have you used debug-only code to set the uninitialized contents to a known but obviously garbage state? Setting memory to a consistent value will make it easier to find and reliably reproduce bugs that use uninitialized memory.

◆ If your code releases memory, does it first destroy the contents so that you don't have valid-looking garbage hanging around?

◆ Are any of your algorithms critical enough that you should use a second, but different, debug-only algorithm to verify the primary one?

◆ Are there any debug checks you can make at program startup to detect bugs at the earliest possible moment? In particular, are there any data tables you could validate at program startup?

TESTING

It is vitally important that programmers test their code, even if it means slipping the schedule. The questions in this section point out the most beneficial testing steps to take.

◆ Does the code compile without generating any warnings, including all optional compiler warnings? If you're using *lint*, or a similar diagnostic tool, does the code pass all tests? Does the code pass your unit tests? If you've skipped any of these steps, you're missing an opportunity to easily detect bugs.

◆ Have you stepped through all new code using a debugger, focusing not only on the code, but also on the data flowing through that code? This is perhaps the best approach to catching bugs in your implementations.

◆ Have you "cleaned up" any code? If so, have you tested the code? Have you stepped through the code in a debugger? Remember, code that has been cleaned up is actually new code that must be thoroughly tested.

◆ Should you write a unit test for the new code?

DEBUGGING

You should review the questions below each time you have to track down
a reported bug.

♦   Were you able to find the reported bug? If not, remember that
    bugs don't just go away; either they're hiding, or they have been
    fixed already. To determine which is true, you should look for
    the bug in the same version of the code in which the bug was
    reported.

♦   Have you found the true cause of the bug or merely a symptom
    of the bug? Be sure to track down the cause of the bug.

♦   How could this bug have been prevented? Come up with a pre-
    cise guideline that could prevent this bug in the future.

♦   How could this bug have been detected automatically? Would
    an assertion catch it? What about some *DEBUG* code? What
    changes in your coding practices or process would help?

B

MEMORY LOGGING ROUTINES

The code in this appendix implements a simple linked-list version of the memory logging routines that are discussed in Chapter 3. The code is intentionally simple so that it can be easily understood—it is not meant to be used in any application that makes heavy use of the memory manager. But before you spend time rewriting the routines to use an AVL-tree, a B-tree, or any other data structure that provides fast searches, first try the code to verify that it is indeed too slow for practical use in your application. You may find that the code works well for you as is, particularly if you don't maintain many globally allocated memory blocks.

The implementation in this file is straightforward: For every allocated memory block, these routines allocate an extra bit of memory to hold a *blockinfo* structure that contains the log information. See its definition below. When a new *blockinfo* structure is created, it is filled in and placed at the head of the linked-list structure—there is no attempt to maintain any particular ordering for the list. Again, this implementation was chosen because it is simple and easy to understand.

block.h

```
#ifdef DEBUG


/*---------------------------------------------------------------
 *  blockinfo is a structure that contains the memory log
 *  information for one allocated memory block.  Every
 *  allocated memory block has a corresponding blockinfo
 *  structure in the memory log.
 */

typedef struct BLOCKINFO
{
    struct BLOCKINFO *pbiNext;
    byte    *pb;                    /* Start of block     */
    size_t  size;                   /* Length of block    */
    flag    fReferenced;            /* Ever referenced?   */
} blockinfo;                        /* Naming:  bi, *pbi  */


flag fCreateBlockInfo(byte *pbNew, size_t sizeNew);
void FreeBlockInfo(byte *pbToFree);
void UpdateBlockInfo(byte *pbOld, byte *pbNew, size_t sizeNew);
size_t sizeofBlock(byte *pb);

void ClearMemoryRefs(void);
void NoteMemoryRef(void *pv);
void CheckMemoryRefs(void);
flag fValidPointer(void *pv, size_t size);

#endif
```

block.c

```
#ifdef DEBUG

/*-----------------------------------------------------------
 *  The functions in this file must compare arbitrary pointers,
 *  an operation that the ANSI standard does not guarantee to
 *  be portable.
 *
 *  The macros below isolate the pointer comparisons needed in
 *  this file. The implementations assume "flat" pointers, for
 *  which straightforward comparisons will always work. The
 *  definitions below will *not* work for some of the common
 *  80x86 memory models.
 */

#define fPtrLess(pLeft, pRight)    ((pLeft) <  (pRight))
#define fPtrGrtr(pLeft, pRight)    ((pLeft) >  (pRight))
#define fPtrEqual(pLeft, pRight)   ((pLeft) == (pRight))
#define fPtrLessEq(pLeft, pRight)  ((pLeft) <= (pRight))
#define fPtrGrtrEq(pLeft, pRight)  ((pLeft) >= (pRight))

/*------------------------------------------------------------*/
/*          * * * * *  Private data/functions  * * * * *      */
/*------------------------------------------------------------*/




/*-----------------------------------------------------------
 *  pbiHead points to a singly linked list of
 *  debugging information for the memory manager.
 */

static blockinfo *pbiHead = NULL;


/*-----------------------------------------------------------
 *  pbiGetBlockInfo(pb)
 *
 *  pbiGetBlockInfo searches the memory log to find the
 *  block that pb points into and returns a pointer to the
 *  corresponding blockinfo structure of the memory log.
 *  Note: pb *must* point into an allocated block or you
 *  will get an assertion failure; the function either asserts
 *  or succeeds -- it never returns an error.
 *
```

(continued)

```
 *      blockinfo *pbi;
 *
 *      ...
 *      pbi = pbiGetBlockInfo(pb);
 *      // pbi->pb points to the start of pb's block
 *      // pbi->size is the size of the block that pb points into
 */

static blockinfo *pbiGetBlockInfo(byte *pb)
{
    blockinfo *pbi;

    for (pbi = pbiHead; pbi != NULL; pbi = pbi->pbiNext)
    {
        byte *pbStart = pbi->pb;            /* for readability */
        byte *pbEnd   = pbi->pb + pbi->size - 1;

        if (fPtrGrtrEq(pb, pbStart)  &&  fPtrLessEq(pb, pbEnd))
            break;
    }

    /*  Couldn't find pointer?  Is it (a) garbage? (b) pointing
     *  to a block that was freed? or (c) pointing to a block
     *  that moved when it was resized by fResizeMemory?
     */
    ASSERT(pbi != NULL);

    return (pbi);
}


/*-------------------------------------------------------------*/
/*          * * * * *  Public functions  * * * * *           */
/*-------------------------------------------------------------*/



/*-------------------------------------------------------------
 *  fCreateBlockInfo(pbNew, sizeNew)
 *
 *  This function creates a log entry for the memory block
 *  defined by pbNew:sizeNew.  The function returns TRUE if it
 *  successfully creates the log information; FALSE otherwise.
 *
 *      if (fCreateBlockInfo(pbNew, sizeNew))
 *          // success -- the memory log has an entry.
 *      else
 *          // failure -- no entry, so release pbNew
 */
```

```
flag fCreateBlockInfo(byte *pbNew, size_t sizeNew)
{
    blockinfo *pbi;

    ASSERT(pbNew != NULL  &&  sizeNew != 0);

    pbi = (blockinfo *)malloc(sizeof(blockinfo));
    if (pbi != NULL)
    {
        pbi->pb = pbNew;
        pbi->size = sizeNew;
        pbi->pbiNext = pbiHead;
        pbiHead = pbi;
    }

    return (flag)(pbi != NULL);
}




/*-------------------------------------------------------------
 *  FreeBlockInfo(pbToFree)
 *
 *  This function destroys the log entry for the memory block
 *  that pbToFree points to.  pbToFree *must* point to the
 *  start of an allocated block; otherwise, you will get an
 *  assertion failure.
 */

void FreeBlockInfo(byte *pbToFree)
{
    blockinfo *pbi, *pbiPrev;

    pbiPrev = NULL;
    for (pbi = pbiHead; pbi != NULL; pbi = pbi->pbiNext)
    {
        if (fPtrEqual(pbi->pb, pbToFree))
        {
            if (pbiPrev == NULL)
                pbiHead = pbi->pbiNext;
            else
                pbiPrev->pbiNext = pbi->pbiNext;
            break;
        }
        pbiPrev = pbi;
    }
```

(continued)

```
        /* If pbi is NULL, then pbToFree is invalid. */
        ASSERT(pbi != NULL);

        /* Destroy the contents of *pbi before freeing them. */
        memset(pbi, bGarbage, sizeof(blockinfo));

        free(pbi);
}




/*-------------------------------------------------------------
 *  UpdateBlockInfo(pbOld, pbNew, sizeNew)
 *
 *  UpdateBlockInfo looks up the log information for the memory
 *  block that pbOld points to.  The function then updates the
 *  log information to reflect the fact that the block now
 *  lives at pbNew and is "sizeNew" bytes long.  pbOld *must*
 *  point to the start of an allocated block; otherwise,
 *  you will get an assertion failure.
 */

void UpdateBlockInfo(byte *pbOld, byte *pbNew, size_t sizeNew)
{
        blockinfo *pbi;

        ASSERT(pbNew != NULL  &&  sizeNew != 0);

        pbi = pbiGetBlockInfo(pbOld);
        ASSERT(pbOld == pbi->pb);

        pbi->pb = pbNew;
        pbi->size = sizeNew;
}




/*-------------------------------------------------------------
 *  sizeofBlock(pb)
 *
 *  sizeofBlock returns the size of the block that pb points to.
 *  pb *must* point to the start of an allocated block;
 *  otherwise, you will get an assertion failure.
 */
```

```
size_t sizeofBlock(byte *pb)
{
    blockinfo *pbi;

    pbi = pbiGetBlockInfo(pb);
    ASSERT(pb == pbi->pb);

    return (pbi->size);
}
```

```
/*--------------------------------------------------------------*/
/*      The following routines are used to find dangling        */
/*      pointers and lost memory blocks.  See Chapter 3         */
/*      for a discussion of these routines.                     */
/*--------------------------------------------------------------*/
```

```
/*--------------------------------------------------------------
 *  ClearMemoryRefs(void)
 *
 *  ClearMemoryRefs marks all blocks in the memory log as being
 *  unreferenced.
 */

void ClearMemoryRefs(void)
{
    blockinfo *pbi;

    for (pbi = pbiHead; pbi != NULL; pbi = pbi->pbiNext)
        pbi->fReferenced = FALSE;
}
```

```
/*--------------------------------------------------------------
 *  NoteMemoryRef(pv)
 *
 *  NoteMemoryRef marks the block that pv points into as being
 *  referenced.  Note: pv does *not* have to point to the start
 *  of a block; it may point anywhere within an allocated block.
 */
```

(continued)

```c
void NoteMemoryRef(void *pv)
{
    blockinfo *pbi;

    pbi = pbiGetBlockInfo((byte *)pv);
    pbi->fReferenced = TRUE;
}



/*-------------------------------------------------------------
 *  CheckMemoryRefs(void)
 *
 *  CheckMemoryRefs scans the memory log looking for blocks that
 *  have not been marked with a call to NoteMemoryRef.  If this
 *  function finds an unmarked block, it asserts.
 */

void CheckMemoryRefs(void)
{
    blockinfo *pbi;

    for (pbi = pbiHead; pbi != NULL; pbi = pbi->pbiNext)
    {
        /*  A simple check for block integrity.  If this
         *  assert fires, it means that something is wrong
         *  with the debug code that manages blockinfo or,
         *  possibly, that a wild memory store has trashed
         *  the data structure.  Either way, there's a bug.
         */
        ASSERT(pbi->pb != NULL  &&  pbi->size != 0);

        /*  A check for lost or leaky memory.  If this assert
         *  fires, it means that the app has either lost track
         *  of this block or that not all global pointers have
         *  been accounted for with NoteMemoryRef.
         */
        ASSERT(pbi->fReferenced);
    }
}
```

```
/*-----------------------------------------------------------
 *  fValidPointer(pv, size)
 *
 *  fValidPointer verifies that pv points into an allocated
 *  memory block and that there are at least "size" allocated
 *  bytes from pv to the end of the block.  If either condition
 *  is not met, fValidPointer will assert; the function will
 *  never return FALSE.
 *
 *  The reason fValidPointer returns a flag at all (always TRUE)
 *  is to allow you to call the function within an ASSERT macro.
 *  While this isn't the most efficient method to use, using the
 *  macro neatly handles the debug-vs.-ship version control
 *  issue without your having to resort to #ifdef DEBUG's or
 *  to introducing other ASSERT-like macros.
 *
 *      ASSERT(fValidPointer(pb, size));
 */
flag fValidPointer(void *pv, size_t size)
{
    blockinfo *pbi;
    byte *pb = (byte *)pv;

    ASSERT(pv != NULL  &&  size != 0);

    pbi = pbiGetBlockInfo(pb);              /* This validates pv. */

    /* size isn't valid if pb+size overflows the block. */
    ASSERT(fPtrLessEq(pb + size, pbi->pb + pbi->size));

    return (TRUE);
}


#endif
```

C

ANSWERS

This appendix contains the answers to all of the questions in the "Things to Think About" sections in the book. Note that the open-ended PROJECT ideas aren't treated in this appendix.

CHAPTER 1

1. The compiler catches the precedence bug because it interprets the expression as

```
while (ch = (getchar() != EOF))
```

In other words, the compiler sees an expression being assigned to *ch*, assumes that you've mistyped == as =, and warns of the possible assignment bug.

2a. The simplest way to catch accidental "octal bugs" is to use an optional compiler switch that would cause the compiler to generate an error anytime it ran across an octal constant. The work-around: Use decimal or hexadecimal instead.

2b. To catch cases in which programmers mistype & for && (or / for / /), the compiler could apply the same test that it uses to catch the case in which you mistype = for ==. The compiler would generate an error when you used & (or /) in an *if* statement or a compound conditional without explicitly comparing the result against *0*. So this would generate a warning:

```
if (u & 1)            /* Is u odd? */
```

but this would not:

```
if ((u & 1) != 0)     /* Is u odd? */
```

2c. The simplest method to warn of unintentional comments is to have the compiler issue a warning whenever the first character in a comment is either a letter of the alphabet or an opening parenthesis. Such a test would catch the two questionable cases:

```
quot=numer/*pdenom;
```

```
quot=numer/*(pointer expression);
```

To silence the warning, you would make your intentions clear by separating the / and the * with either a space or an opening parenthesis:

```
quot = numer / *pdenom;
```

```
quot=numer/(*pdenom);
```

```
/*But note:  This comment generates a warning.*/
/* This one does not because of the leading space. */
/*-- -- -- -- --Nor does this comment.-- -- -- -- --*/
```

2d. You could have the compiler detect possible precedence errors
     by having it look for troublesome operator pairs that are used in
     the same unparenthesized expression. For example, program-
     mers occasionally introduce precedence bugs when they use
     the << and + operators together, so the compiler would issue a
     warning for this code:

```
word = bHigh << 8 + bLow;
```

The compiler would not issue a warning for the statements below because they make use of parentheses:

```
word = (bHigh << 8) + bLow;
```

```
word = bHigh << (8 + bLow);
```

A less ad hoc approach would be to use a heuristic such as
"If the two operators have different precedence and they are not
parenthesized, then issue a warning." That heuristic is too
simple to be practical, but you get the idea. Developing a good
heuristic would require running a lot of code through the compiler and tweaking the heuristic until the compiler produces useful results. You certainly wouldn't want to get warnings for
these common expressions:

```
word = bHigh*256 + bLow;
```

```
if (ch == ' '  ||  ch == '\t'  ||  ch == '\n')
```

3.   The compiler could alert you to possible dangling-*else* clauses by
     issuing a warning whenever it encountered two consecutive *if*
     statements followed by an *else* statement:

```
if (expression1)               if (expression1)
    if (expression2)               if (expression2)
        .                              .
        .                              .
else                           else
    .                              .
    .                              .
```

To silence the warning, you would use braces around the inner *if* statement to make the binding of the *else* explicit:

```
if (expression1)              if (expression1)
{                             {
    if (expression2)              if (expression2)
        ⋮                             ⋮
}                                 else
else                                  ⋮
    ⋮                         }
```

4. Putting constants and expressions on the left-hand side of your comparisons is useful because it provides one more method of automatically detecting bugs, but unfortunately, it works only when one of the operands is a constant or an expression—the technique is worthless if both operands are variables. Another problem with this method is that programmers must learn and remember to use the technique as they write code.

    If, on the other hand, you use the compiler switch, the compiler would alert you to every possible assignment bug. Even better, the switch would work for programmers straight out of CS 101 who have never learned the benefits of reversing operands in their comparisons.

    If you have the compiler switch, use it; if you don't, put your constants and expressions on the left-hand side of your comparisons until you get a more helpful compiler.

5. To prevent undefined preprocessor macros from generating unexpected results, the compiler (really the preprocessor) should have a switch that allows programmers to turn uses of undefined macros into error conditions. There is little need for undefined macros to be "defined" as *0* now that ANSI C compilers support both the old *#ifdef* preprocessor directive and the new preprocessor *defined* unary operator for use in *#if* expressions. Instead of using undefined macros in *#if* expressions,

```
/* Set up target equates. */

#if     INTEL8080
        .
        .
#elif   INTEL80x86
        .
        .
#elif   MC680x0
        .
        .
#endif
```

which would generate an error if you used the optional switch,
you would use the *defined* unary operator:

```
/* Set up target equates. */

#if     defined(INTEL8080)
        .
        .
#elif   defined(INTEL80x86)
        .
        .
#elif   defined(MC680x0)
        .
        .
#endif
```

The switch should not give a warning if you use an undefined
macro in an *#ifdef* statement, since that use would be intentional.

CHAPTER 2

1. One possible implementation of the *ASSERTMSG* macro could
    have the macro take both an expression to validate and a string
    to display if the assertion fails. For example, to print the *memcpy*
    message, you would call *ASSERTMSG* this way:

    ```
    ASSERTMSG(pbTo >= pbFrom+size  ||  pbFrom >= pbTo+size,
            "memcpy: the blocks overlap");
    ```

    In the implementation of the *ASSERTMSG* macro shown on the
    next page, you would put *ASSERTMSG*'s definition in a header
    file and the *_AssertMsg* routine in a convenient source file.

```
#ifdef DEBUG

    void _AssertMsg(char *strMessage);     /* prototype */

    #define ASSERTMSG(f,str)        \
            if (f)                  \
                NULL;               \
            else                    \
                _AssertMsg(str)

#else

    #define ASSERTMSG(f,str)  NULL

#endif
```

And here's the routine, in another file:

```
#ifdef DEBUG

    void _AssertMsg(char *strMessage)
    {
        fflush(stdout);
        fprintf(stderr, "\n\nAssertion failure in %s\n",
                strMessage);
        fflush(stderr);
        abort();
    }

#endif
```

2.   The easy solution—if your compiler supports it—is to throw the optional switch that tells the compiler to allocate all identical strings in the same location. With that option enabled, your assertions may declare 73 copies of the same file name but the compiler will allocate only one string. The drawback to this approach is that it will "overlap" all identical strings in your source files, not just assertion strings, and you may not want that extra behavior.

An alternative is to change the implementation of the *ASSERT* macro so that it intentionally references the same file name string throughout the file. The only difficulty lies in creating the file name string, but even that is no great difficulty—you can bury the details in a new *ASSERTFILE* macro that you use once at the start of each source file:

```
#include <stdio.h>
    .
    .
    .
#include <debug.h>

ASSERTFILE(__FILE__)
    .
    .
    .

void *memcpy(void *pvTo, void *pvFrom, size_t size)
{
    byte *pbTo   = (byte *)pvTo;
    byte *pbFrom = (byte *)pvFrom;

    ASSERT(pvTo != NULL  &&  pvFrom != NULL);
    .
    .
    .
```

You can see that the call to *ASSERT* is unchanged. Here is the code to implement the *ASSERTFILE* macro and the version of *ASSERT* that works with it:

```
#ifdef DEBUG

    #define ASSERTFILE(str)         \
            static char strAssertFile[] = str;

    #define ASSERT(f)               \
            if (f)                  \
                NULL;               \
            else                    \
                _Assert(strAssertFile, __LINE__)

#else

    #define ASSERTFILE(str)
    #define ASSERT(f)  NULL

#endif
```

Using this version of *ASSERT*, you can gain a lot of memory. For example, in the small application I used to test the code in this book, the new implementation cut 3K off the data area.

3.   The problem with the assertion is that the test contains code that should remain in the nondebug version of the function. As it is, the nondebug code will enter an endless loop unless *ch* happens to equal the newline character when the *do* loop is executed. The function should be written this way:

```
void getline(char *pch)
{
    int ch;          /* ch *must* be an int. */

    do
    {
        ch = getchar();
        ASSERT(ch != EOF);
    }
    while ((*pch++ = ch) != '\n');
}
```

4.   The simplest way to detect bugs in *switch* statements that have not been updated is to include assertions in the *default* cases to alert you to unexpected cases that pop up. In some instances the *default* case should never be invoked because all of the possible cases are explicitly handled. When all cases are handled explicitly, use

```
        :
        :
default:
    ASSERT(FALSE);        /* We should never get here. */
    break;
}
```

5.   By design, the pattern for each entry in the table must be a subset of the corresponding mask. For example, if the mask is *0xFF00*, the pattern must not have any bits set in the low byte; otherwise, it would be impossible for any instruction, once masked, to

match the pattern. The *CheckIdInst* routine could be enhanced to verify that the pattern is a subset of the mask:

```
void CheckIdInst(void)
{
    identity *pid, *pidEarlier;
    instruction inst;

    for (pid = &idInst[0]; pid->mask != 0; pid++)
    {
        /* Make sure that pat is a subset of mask. */
        ASSERT((pid->pat & pid->mask) == pid->pat);
        .
        .
        .
```

6. Use assertions to verify that *inst* has none of the problematic settings:

```
instruction *pcDecodeEOR(instruction inst, instruction *pc,
        opcode *popc)
{
    /* Did we get a CMPM or CMPA.L instruction by mistake? */
    ASSERT(eamode(inst) != 1  &&  mode(inst) != 3);

    /* If nonreg mode, allow only abs word and long modes. */
    ASSERT(eamode(inst) != 7  ||
            (eareg(inst) == 0  ||  eareg(inst) == 1));
        .
        .
        .
```

7. The important point in choosing a backup algorithm is that it be a different algorithm. To verify that *qsort* is working, you could scan the data after a sort to verify that the order is correct. Scanning is not sorting and therefore qualifies as a different algorithm. To verify that the binary search is working, follow it with a linear search to see whether the two searches give the same result. Finally, to verify that the *itoa* function is working, take the string it returns, reconvert the string to an integer, and compare the value to the integer originally passed to *itoa*; they should be equal.

Of course, you probably don't want to use backup algorithms for every piece of code you write—that is, unless you're working on code for the space shuttle, a radiation machine, or any other device in which a coding bug could be life threatening. But you probably should be using backup algorithms for all of the major engines in your application.

CHAPTER 3

1. You can make it easier to distinguish between code that uses uninitialized data and code that continues to use released data by using different debug values to destroy the two kinds of memory. For example, *fNewMemory* could destroy new, uninitialized memory using *bNewGarbage*, and *FreeMemory* could destroy the memory it releases using *bFreeGarbage*:

    ```
    #define bNewGarbage      0xA3
    #define bFreeGarbage     0xA5
    ```

    fResizeMemory creates both types of garbage—you could use the two values above, or you could create two more values.

2. One way to catch "overfill" bugs is to periodically check the bytes following each allocated block to verify that they have not been modified. But while that test sounds straightforward, it requires that you remember what all those trailing bytes are, and it ignores the potential problems you might run into by reading from memory that isn't part of the allocated block. Fortunately, there is a simple way to implement the test, provided you're willing to allocate 1 extra byte for every block that you allocate.

    For example, when you call *fNewMemory* with a size of 36, you could actually allocate 37 bytes and store a known "debugging byte" in the extra memory location. Similarly, you could allocate and set an extra byte in *fResizeMemory* when it calls *realloc*. To catch the overfill bugs, you would then put assertions in *sizeofBlock*, *fValidPointer*, *FreeBlockInfo*, *NoteMemoryRef*, and *CheckMemoryRefs* to verify that the debugging byte has not been touched.

One way you could implement the code is shown below.
First, you would define *bDebugByte* and *sizeof DebugByte*:

```
/*  bDebugByte is a magic value that is stored at the
 *  tail of every allocated memory block in DEBUG
 *  versions of the program.  sizeofDebugByte is added
 *  to the sizes passed to malloc and realloc so that
 *  the correct amount of space is allocated.
 */

#define bDebugByte 0xE1

#ifdef DEBUG
    #define sizeofDebugByte 1
#else
    #define sizeofDebugByte 0
#endif
```

Next, you would use *sizeof DebugByte* to adjust the calls to *malloc*
and *realloc* in *f NewMemory* and *f ResizeMemory,* and you would
use *bDebugByte* to fill in the extra bytes if the allocations are
successful:

```
flag fNewMemory(void **ppv, size_t size)
{
    byte **ppb = (byte **)ppv;

    ASSERT(ppv != NULL  &&  size != 0);

    *ppb = (byte *)malloc(size + sizeofDebugByte);

#ifdef DEBUG
    {
        if (*ppb != NULL)
        {
            *(*ppb + size) = bDebugByte;

            memset(*ppb, bGarbage, size);
                :
                :
```

(continued)

```
flag fResizeMemory(void **ppv, size_t sizeNew)
{
    byte **ppb = (byte **)ppv;
    byte *pbNew;
    .
    .
    pbNew = (byte *)realloc(*ppb, sizeNew + sizeofDebugByte);
    if (pbNew != NULL)
    {
        #ifdef DEBUG
        {
            *(pbNew + sizeNew) = bDebugByte;

            UpdateBlockInfo(*ppb, pbNew, sizeNew);
            .
            .
```

Finally, you would put the assertion below into the *sizeof Block, f ValidPointer, FreeBlockInfo, NoteMemoryRef,* and *CheckMemoryRefs* routines that are in Appendix B:

```
/* Verify that nothing wrote off end of block. */
ASSERT(*(pbi->pb + pbi->size) == bDebugByte);
```

With these changes, the memory subsystem would catch bugs in which code writes past the end of your allocated memory blocks.

3.   There are many ways you could catch the not-so-dangling pointer bug. One possible solution would be to change the debug version of *FreeMemory* so that it wouldn't actually free the blocks it receives, but would instead build a list of free but allocated blocks. (The blocks would look allocated to the system but would look free to your program.) Modifying *FreeMemory* this way would keep a "free" block from being reallocated before the memory subsystem could be validated with a call to *CheckMemoryRefs*. *CheckMemoryRefs* would then validate the memory system and finish up by taking *FreeMemory*'s "free" list and releasing all the blocks.

Now, while this solution would catch not-so-dangling pointers, you probably shouldn't use it unless your program suffers from such bugs. The reason: The solution violates the

suffers from such bugs. The reason: The solution violates the
principle that debug code is extra—not different—code.

4.   To validate the sizes of the objects that your pointers reference,
     you must consider two cases: pointers to entire blocks and point-
     ers to suballocations within blocks. For pointers to entire blocks,
     the strongest tests you can make are to verify that the pointers
     reference the starts of their blocks and that the block sizes match
     what the *sizeofBlock* function would return for them. For pointers
     to suballocations within blocks, the tests should be weaker: The
     pointer must point into a block, and the size must not reach be-
     yond the tail end of the block.

     So instead of using the existing *NoteMemoryRef* routine to
     mark both suballocations and complete blocks, you could use
     two functions to mark the two types of blocks. For sub-
     allocations, you could extend the existing *NoteMemoryRef* func-
     tion by adding a *size* argument, and for marking full blocks, you
     could create a new *NoteMemoryBlock* function.

```
/*   NoteMemoryRef(pv, size)
 *
 *   NoteMemoryRef marks the block that pv points into as
 *   being referenced.  Note: pv does *not* have to point to
 *   the start of a block; it may point anywhere within an
 *   allocated block, but there must be at least "size" bytes
 *   left in the block.  Note: For entire blocks, use
 *   NoteMemoryBlock -- it provides stronger validation.
 */
void NoteMemoryRef(void *pv, size_t size);

/*   NoteMemoryBlock(pv, size)
 *
 *   NoteMemoryBlock marks the block that pv points to as
 *   being referenced.  Note: pv *must* point to the start
 *   of a block that is exactly "size" bytes long.
 */
void NoteMemoryBlock(void *pv, size_t size);
```

These two functions would let you catch the bugs posed in
the question.

5.   To improve the integrity checks in the routines in Appendix B, you
      would first change the reference flag in the *blockinfo* structure to a
      reference *count*, and you would then update *ClearMemoryRefs* and
      NoteMemoryRef to handle the counter. That part is straightforward.
      The question, though, is how do you modify *CheckMemoryRefs* so
      that it will assert when some blocks have multiple references but
      won't assert for other blocks?

      One solution to this problem would be to enhance the
      NoteMemoryRef routine so that it would take a block ID tag in
      addition to the pointer to the block. *NoteMemoryRef* could then
      store the tag in the *blockinfo* structure, and *CheckMemoryRefs*
      could come along later and use the tag to verify the reference
      count. You can see the code to implement this change below. For
      header comments, see the original functions in Appendix B.

```
/*  blocktag is a list of all of the types of allocated
 *  blocks maintained by the application. ClearMemoryRefs
 *  sets all blocks to tagNone. NoteMemoryRef sets the
 *  tag to a specific block type.
 */

typedef enum
{
    tagNone,
    tagSymName,
    tagSymStruct,
    tagListNode,        /* List nodes must have two refs. */
      .
      .
      .
} blocktag;


void ClearMemoryRefs(void)
{
    blockinfo *pbi;

    for (pbi = pbiHead; pbi != NULL; pbi = pbi->pbiNext)
    {
        pbi->nReferenced = 0;
        pbi->tag = tagNone;
    }
}
```

```
void NoteMemoryRef(void *pv, blocktag tag)
{
    blockinfo *pbi;

    pbi = pbiGetBlockInfo((byte *)pv);

    pbi->nReferenced++;

    ASSERT(pbi->tag == tagNone  ||  pbi->tag == tag);
    pbi->tag = tag;
}


void CheckMemoryRefs(void)
{
    blockinfo *pbi;

    for (pbi = pbiHead; pbi != NULL; pbi = pbi->pbiNext)
    {
        /*  A simple check for block integrity.  If this
         *  assert fires, it means that something is wrong
         *  with the debug code that manages blockinfo or,
         *  possibly, that a wild memory store has trashed
         *  the data structure.  Either way, there's a bug.
         */
        ASSERT(pbi->pb != NULL  &&  pbi->size != 0);

        /*  A check for lost or leaky memory.  If there are
         *  no references at all, it means either that the
         *  app has lost track of this block or that not
         *  all global pointers are being accounted for
         *  with NoteMemoryRef. Some types of blocks may
         *  have more than one reference to them.
         */
        switch (pbi->tag)
        {
        default:
            /* Most blocks have a single reference. */
            ASSERT(pbi->nReferenced == 1);
            break;

        case tagListNode:
            ASSERT(pbi->nReferenced == 2);
            break;
            .
            .
            .
        }
    }
}
```

6.   MS-DOS, Windows, and Macintosh developers normally test out-of-memory conditions by using a tool to gobble memory until the application's memory requests begin to fail. That approach can work, but it is not very precise—it causes some allocation request somewhere in the program to fail. The technique is not very useful if you want to test an individual feature. A better technique is to build an out-of-memory simulator directly into the memory manager.

But notice, memory errors are just one type of resource failure—you can have disk errors, out-of-paper errors, the-phone-line-is-busy errors, all sorts of errors. What's really needed is a general tool to fake failures.

One possible solution would be to create a *failureinfo* structure that would contain information to tell the failure mechanism what to do. The idea is that programmers and testers would fill in the *failureinfo* structure from an external test and then exercise their feature. Microsoft applications often have debug-only dialogs that allow testers to use such systems, and in applications such as Excel, which have macro languages, debug-only macros allow testers to automate the process.

To declare the *failureinfo* structure for the memory manager, you would use

```
failureinfo fiMemory;
```

Then to simulate out-of-memory errors in *fNewMemory* and *fResizeMemory*, you would insert a small block of debug code into each function:

```
flag fNewMemory(void **ppv, size_t size)
{
    byte **ppb = (byte **)ppv;

#ifdef DEBUG
    if (fFakeFailure(&fiMemory))
    {
        *ppb = NULL;
        return (FALSE);
    }
#endif
    :
    :
```

```
flag fResizeMemory(void **ppv, size_t sizeNew)
{
    byte **ppb = (byte **)ppv;
    byte *pbNew;

#ifdef DEBUG
        if (fFakeFailure(&fiMemory))
            return (FALSE);
#endif
        .
        .
        .
```

With these changes, the failure mechanism is in place. To make it work, you would call the *SetFailures* function to initialize the *failureinfo* structure:

```
SetFailures(&fiMemory, 5, 7);
```

Calling *SetFailures* with *5* and *7* tells the failure system that you want to call the system five times before getting seven consecutive failures. Two common calls to *SetFailures* are

```
/* Don't fake any failures. */
SetFailures(&fiMemory, UINT_MAX, 0);

/* Always fake failures. */
SetFailures(&fiMemory, 0, UINT_MAX);
```

Using *SetFailures*, you can write unit tests that call the same code over and over but each time call *SetFailures* with different values to simulate all possible error patterns. A common test is to hold the second "fail" value at *UINT_MAX* while the first "success" count is progressively bumped from *0*—"always fail"—to some number that is deemed large enough to test each successful call to the system.

Finally, there are times when you will want to call the memory system, disk system, and so on, and you definitely won't want any fake failures; this is often true when you're allocating resources from within other debug code. The two nestable functions on the next page allow you to temporarily disable the failure mechanism.

```
DisableFailures(&fiMemory);
    do some allocating
EnableFailures(&fiMemory);
```

The code below implements the four functions that make up the
failure mechanism.

```
typedef struct
{
    unsigned nSucceed;    /* # of calls before failing  */
    unsigned nFail;       /* # of times to fail         */
    unsigned nTries;      /* # of times already called  */
    int      lock;        /* If > 0, disable mechanism. */
} failureinfo;



void SetFailures(failureinfo *pfi, unsigned nSucceed,
                 unsigned nFail)
{
    /* If nFail is 0, require that nSucceed be UINT_MAX. */
    ASSERT(nFail != 0  ||  nSucceed == UINT_MAX);

    pfi->nSucceed = nSucceed;
    pfi->nFail    = nFail;
    pfi->nTries   = 0;
    pfi->lock     = 0;
}



void EnableFailures(failureinfo *pfi)
{
    ASSERT(pfi->lock > 0);
    pfi->lock--;
}



void DisableFailures(failureinfo *pfi)
{
    ASSERT(pfi->lock >= 0  &&  pfi->lock < INT_MAX);
    pfi->lock++;
}
```

```
flag fFakeFailure(failureinfo *pfi)
{
    ASSERT(pfi != NULL);

    if (pfi->lock > 0)
        return (FALSE);

    /* Pin nTries at UINT_MAX. */
    if (pfi->nTries != UINT_MAX)
        pfi->nTries++;

    if (pfi->nTries <= pfi->nSucceed)
        return (FALSE);

    if (pfi->nTries - pfi->nSucceed <= pfi->nFail)
        return (TRUE);

    return (FALSE);
}
```

CHAPTER 4

There were no questions in Chapter 4, although some projects were suggested.

CHAPTER 5

1. *strdup* has a risky interface because its error return value is disguised as a *NULL* pointer where, like *malloc's*, it can be overlooked. A less error-prone interface would separate the error condition from the pointer output to make the error condition obvious. One such interface would be

```
char *strDup;      /* pointer to the copied string */

if (fStrDup(&strDup, strToCopy))
    successful -- strDup points to the new string
else
    unsuccessful -- strDup is NULL
```

2. A better interface for *getchar* than *fGetChar*'s interface would be
    one that returns an error code instead of a *TRUE* or *FALSE*
    "success" value—for example,

```
/* These are the errors that errGetChar may return. */

typedef enum
{
    errNone = 0,
    errEOF,
    errBadRead,
       .
       .
       .
} error;

void ReadSomeStuff(void)
{
    char  ch;
    error err;

    if ((err = errGetChar(&ch))  ==  errNone)
        success -- ch has the next character
    else
        failure -- err has the error type
       .
       .
       .
```

This interface is better than *fGetChar*'s interface because it allows
errGetChar to return multiple error conditions (and multiple success conditions, for that matter). If you don't care about the specific kind of error being returned, you can eliminate the local
variable *err* and revert to *fGetChar*'s interface style:

```
if (errGetChar(&ch)  ==  errNone)
    success -- ch has the next character
else
    failure -- we don't care what kind of error we have
```

3. The trouble with *strncpy* is that it is inconsistent in its behavior:
    Sometimes *strncpy* terminates the destination string with a null
    character, and sometimes it doesn't. *strncpy* is listed along with
    the other general-purpose string functions, and programmers
    may erroneously conclude that *strncpy* is itself a general-purpose
    function. It isn't. *strncpy* really shouldn't be in the ANSI stan-
    dard, given its unusual behavior, but was included because of its
    widespread usage in pre-ANSI implementations of C.

4. C++'s *inline* function specifier is valuable because it allows you to define functions that are as efficient as macros—if you're using a good compiler—yet don't have the troublesome side effects that macro "functions" have in evaluating their parameters.

5. The serious problem with C++'s new & reference arguments is that such arguments hide the fact that you are passing the variable by reference, not by value, and that can cause confusion. For example, suppose you redefine the *fResizeMemory* function so that it uses a reference argument. Programmers could then write

```
if (fResizeMemory(pb, sizeNew))
    resize was successful
```

    But notice, programmers unfamiliar with the function would have no reason to believe that *pb* might be changed during the call. How do you think that will affect program maintenance?
        A related concern is that C programmers often manipulate the formal arguments to their functions because they know those arguments are passed by value, not reference. But consider the maintenance programmer who fixes a bug in a function he didn't write. If that programmer fails to notice the & in the declaration, he could modify the argument without realizing that the change won't be local to the function. & reference arguments are risky because they hide an important implementation detail.

6. The problem with *strcmp*'s interface is that its return value leads to unintelligible code at the point of call. To improve *strcmp*, you would design the interface so that the return value is easily understood, even by those unfamiliar with the function.
        One possible interface is a minor variant of the one that *strcmp* already has. Instead of returning arbitrary negative and positive values for unequal strings—which forces programmers to make all their comparisons relative to *0*—you could change *strcmp* so that it returns three well-defined named constants:

```
if (strcmp(strLeft, strRight) == STR_LESS)

if (strcmp(strLeft, strRight) == STR_GREATER)

if (strcmp(strLeft, strRight) == STR_EQUAL)
```

Another possible interface would be to use separate functions for each type of comparison:

```
if (fStrLess(strLeft, strRight))

if (fStrGreater(strLeft, strRight))

if (fStrEqual(strLeft, strRight))
```

This second interface has the advantage that you can use macros to implement it on top of the existing *strcmp* function:

```
#define fStrLess(strLeft, strRight)      \
        (strcmp(strLeft, strRight) < 0)

#define fStrGreater(strLeft, strRight)   \
        (strcmp(strLeft, strRight) > 0)

#define fStrEqual(strLeft, strRight)     \
        (strcmp(strLeft, strRight) == 0)
```

You can increase readability even further by defining macros for the <= and >= comparisons. The result would enhance readability without any loss in size or speed.

CHAPTER 6

1. The portable range of a "plain" 1-bit bit field is simply *0*, which is not too useful. The bit field does have a non-zero state—you just don't know what it is. The value can be either *–1* or *1*, depending upon whether your compiler defaults to signed or unsigned bit fields. You can safely use both states of the bit field if you restrict all of your comparisons to *0*. For example, if you assume that *psw.carry* is a plain 1-bit bit field, you can safely write any of these four tests:

```
if (psw.carry == 0)              if (!psw.carry)

if (psw.carry != 0)              if (psw.carry)
```

But the following tests are risky because they depend upon the compiler you are using.

```
if (psw.carry == 1)            if (psw.carry == -1)

if (psw.carry != 1)            if (psw.carry != -1)
```

2. Functions that return boolean values are like "plain" 1-bit bit
    fields in that you cannot safely predict what the *"true"* return
    value will be. You can rely on *FALSE* to be *0*, but programmers
    often return any convenient non-zero value for *"true,"* which of
    course does not equal the constant *TRUE*. If you assume that
    fNewMemory returns a boolean value, you can safely write

```
if (fNewMemory(...) == FALSE)

if (fNewMemory(...) != FALSE)
```

Or, even better,

```
if (!fNewMemory(...))

if (fNewMemory(...))
```

But the code below is risky because it assumes that *fNewMemory*
will never return a non-zero value other than *TRUE*:

```
if (fNewMemory(...) == TRUE)      /* Risky! */
```

A good rule to remember is *Never compare boolean values to* TRUE.

3. If you declare *wndDisplay* as a global *window* structure, you give
    it a special attribute that no other window structure has: It is a
    global. That may seem like a minor detail, but it can introduce
    unexpected bugs. For instance, suppose you want to write a rou-
    tine to free a window and all of its children. This function will do it:

```
void FreeWindowTree(window *pwndRoot)
{
    if (pwndRoot != NULL)
    {
        window *pwnd, *pwndNext;

        ASSERT(fValidWindow(pwndRoot));
```

(continued)

```
for (pwnd = pwndRoot->pwndChild; pwnd != NULL;
        pwnd = pwndNext)
{
    /* Get "Next" pointer before freeing it. */
    pwndNext = pwnd->pwndSibling;
    FreeWindowTree(pwnd);
}

if (pwndRoot->strWndTitle != NULL)
    FreeMemory(pwndRoot->strWndTitle);
FreeMemory(pwndRoot);
}
}
```

Now notice, if you want to free every window, you can safely pass *pwndDisplay* because it points to an allocated *window* structure, but you can't pass *&wndDisplay* because the code will try to free *wndDisplay*, which is impossible because it's a global. To make the code work correctly with *&wndDisplay*, you would have to insert

```
if (pwndRoot != &wndDisplay)
```

before the call to *FreeMemory(pwndRoot)*. If you do that, you tie the code to a global data structure. Yuck.

One of the best ways to keep bugs out of your code is to keep arbitrary design quirks out of your implementations.

4.   The second version is much riskier than the first for several reasons. Because *A*, *D*, and *expression* are common code in the first version, they are going to be executed—and therefore tested—no matter what the value of *f* is. In the second version, the *A*'s and *D*'s will be tested separately, and unless they're identical, you risk missing bugs in one case or the other. (The *A*'s and *D*'s would not be identical if they were optimized specifically for use with *B* or *C*.)

In the second version, you'll also have problems keeping the *A*'s and *D*'s synchronized as programmers fix bugs and enhance the code. That's particularly true if the *A*'s and *D*'s are not identical. So use the first version unless calculating *f* is so expensive that the user will notice the difference. Here's another good rule to remember: *Minimize the differences by maximizing the amount of common code.*

5. It's risky using similar names such as *s1* and *s2* because it's easy to type *s1* when you mean *s2*. Worse, the code will compile without issuing an error. Using similar names also makes it harder to spot bugs where you have swapped the names by mistake:

```
int strcmp(const char *s1, const char *s2)
{
    for (NULL; *s1 == *s2; s1++, s2++)
    {
        if (*s1 == '\0')    /* Match to the end? */
            return (0);
    }

    return ((*(unsigned char *)s2 < *(unsigned char *)s1) ?
            -1 : 1);
}
```

The code above is wrong because the test in the return statement is backwards, but it's hard to see the bug because the names have no meaning. If you use descriptive and distinct names such as *sLeft* and *sRight*, the odds of having either the mistyping or the swapping kind of bug drop dramatically, and the code is more readable too.

6. The ANSI standard guarantees that you can address the first byte following a declared array, but it does not guarantee that you can reference the byte that precedes such an array. Nor does the standard guarantee that you can address the byte preceding a block that you allocate using *malloc*.

    For example, the pointers for some 80x86 memory models are implemented using *base:offset* pairs in which only the unsigned offsets are manipulated. If *pchStart* is such a pointer and it points to the start of an allocated block, its offset is *0*. If you assume that *pch* starts out with a value of *pchStart+size*, *pch* can never be less than *pchStart* because its offset can never be less than *pchStart*'s offset of *0*—it wraps to *0xFFFF*.

7a. Using *printf(str);* instead of *printf("%s", str);* will cause bugs if *str* contains any % signs; *printf* will misinterpret them as format specifications. The trouble with *printf("%s", str);* is that it can so "obviously" be optimized to *printf(str);* that unwary programmers will occasionally clean up the code and introduce bugs.

7b. Using *f = 1–f;* instead of *f = !f;* is risky because it assumes that *f* is either *0* or *1*, whereas using *!f* clearly shows that you are flipping a flag and works for all values of *f*. The only reason to use *1–f* is that it may generate slightly more efficient code than *!f*, but remember, local efficiency improvements rarely have any overall effect on a program's performance. Using *1–f* merely increases your risk of having a bug.

7c. The risk in using multiple assignments in one statement is that it may cause unexpected data conversions. In the example here, the programmer was careful to declare *ch* as an *int* so that it could properly handle the *EOF* value that *getchar* might return. But notice that *getchar*'s value is first stored in a string, which means that the value is converted to a *char*, and it is the converted *char*—not the returned *int*—that is assigned to *ch*. This unexpected conversion re-introduces the *getchar* bug we covered in Chapter 5, despite the fact that *ch* was so carefully defined to be an *int*.

8. In a typical case, a table simplifies code by making it smaller and faster, which increases the odds that it will be correct. You get a more balanced view of this question, though, when you consider the data in the table. The code may be small, but the table takes memory, so overall, the table solution may use more memory than the nontable implementation. The other problem with a table is risk—you must ensure that the data in the table is correct. Sometimes that's easy, as it is in the *tolower* and *uCycleCheckBox* tables, but in a large table like the one in the disassembler in Chapter 2, it would be easy for a bug to creep in. The rule is *Don't use a table unless you can validate the data.*

9. If your compiler doesn't make such basic optimizations as converting multiplies and divides to shifts (when appropriate), you must have far worse code generation problems to worry about; you won't notice an improvement by using a shift instead of a division. Don't make minor efficiency tweaks to overcome the limitations of a poor compiler. Instead, keep your code clean and get a better compiler.

10. To guarantee that it's always possible to save the user's file, simply allocate the buffer sometime before the user changes the file. If you need one buffer per file, allocate a buffer every time you open a file. If the allocation fails, open the file as a read-only document, or don't open the file at all. But if you need just one buffer to handle all open files, you could allocate that buffer during program initialization. And don't worry about "wasting" memory by having that buffer hanging around most of the time doing nothing. It's much better to waste that memory and guarantee that you can save the user's data than to let him or her work for five hours and then fail to save the data because you can't allocate the buffer.

CHAPTER 7

1. The code below modifies *pchTo* and *pchFrom*, both of which are inputs to the function:

```
char *strcpy(char *pchTo, char *pchFrom)
{
    char *pchStart = pchTo;

    while (*pchTo++ = *pchFrom++)
        NULL;

    return (pchStart);
}
```

Modifying *pchTo* and *pchFrom* doesn't violate the write privilege associated with those arguments because they are passed by value, which means that *strcpy* receives duplicates of the inputs, and *strcpy* is therefore allowed to change them. But note that not all computer languages—FORTRAN is one example—pass arguments by value. This practice is quite safe in C, but it can be hazardous if you use it with other languages.

2.   The trouble with *strDigits* is that it is declared as a static pointer, not as a static buffer, and that subtle difference can cause problems if you use a compiler option that allows the compiler to treat all string literals as constants. Some compilers that support the "constant string literal" option store all string literals with the other constants in your program, and because constants don't change, such compilers tend to scan all constant strings and throw out duplicates. In other words, if both *strFromUns* and *strFromInt* declare static pointers to a string like "?????", the compiler may allocate one—not two—copies of that string. Some compilers are even more thorough and combine strings whenever one string matches the tail portion of another, as *"her"* matches the tail of *"mother"*. Changing one string will change the other.

It is much safer to treat all string literals as constants and restrict your code to reading from them. If you want to change a string, declare a character buffer, not a string pointer:

```
char *strFromUns(unsigned u)
{
    static char strDigits[] = "?????";
```

But even this code is risky because it relies on the programmer to type the correct number of question marks and it assumes that the trailing null character will never be destroyed. Nor is using question marks as space holders such a smart idea. Is the string really five question marks, or do trigraphs affect it? If you're not sure, you understand why you should use a different character as a space holder.

A safer implementation would be to declare the size of the buffer and replace the assertion with a store:

```
char *strFromUns(unsigned u)
{
    static char strDigits[6];    /* 5 digits + '\0' */
        .
        .
        .
    pch = &strDigits[5];
    *pch = '\0';                          /* Replaces the ASSERT. */
```

3.   Using *memset* to initialize adjacent locals is both extremely risky and inefficient compared to using the straightforward

```
i = 0;                    /* Set i, j, and k to 0. */
j = 0;
k = 0;
```

or using the more terse

```
i = j = k = 0;           /* Set i, j, and k to 0. */
```

These pieces of code are both portable and efficient, and they are so obvious that you don't even need the comments. The *memset* version is another matter.

    I'm not sure what the original programmer was trying to gain by using *memset*, but I'm sure he or she didn't get a good return on the effort. For starters, on all but the best compilers, the overhead alone of calling *memset* is more expensive than explicitly clearing *i*, *j*, and *k*. But let's assume that the programmer was using a smart compiler that inlines small fills when the fill value and length are known at compile time. That doesn't improve things much: The code still assumes that the compiler will allocate *i*, *j*, and *k* adjacently on the stack, with *k* lowest in memory. The code also assumes that *i*, *j*, and *k* abut each other without any extra "pad" bytes to align the variables for efficient access.

    But who says that the variables even have frame storage? Good compilers routinely perform life-span analysis and use the information to keep locals in registers for their entire lives. The locals *i* and *j* may be allocated in registers and spend their entire lives there, never getting frame storage. The variable *k*, on the other hand, must be given frame storage because its address is passed to *memset*—you can't take the address of a register. In this scenario, *i* and *j* would remain uninitialized, and $2 * sizeof(int)$ bytes following *k* would be erroneously set to *0*.

4.   You face two risks when you call or jump to a fixed address in your machine's ROMs. The first is that the ROMs may never change on your own machine but they will almost certainly change on future models of your hardware. But even if the ROM

routines never change, hardware vendors sometimes fix bugs in their ROMs by using RAM-resident software patches that are invoked through the system interfaces. If you bypass the interfaces, you bypass the patches as well.

5.   The problem with not passing *val* if it isn't needed is that the caller is making an assumption about the internal workings of *DoOperation* in much the way that *FILL* was making assumptions about *CMOVE*. Suppose that a programmer enhances *DoOperation* and in the process rewrites it so that it always references *val*:

```
void DoOperation(operation op, int val)
{
    if (op < opPrimaryOps)
        DoPrimaryOps(op, val);
    else if (op < opFloatOps)
        DoFloatOps(op, val);
    else
        .
        .
        .
```

What happens when *DoOperation* references the nonexistent *val*? That depends upon your operating system, but the code could abort if *val* is in a read-protected portion of the stack frame.

You can make it difficult for programmers to play tricks with your functions by forcing them to pass placeholders for unused variables. In the documentation, you could say, "Pass *0* for *val* whenever you call *DoOperation* with *opNegAcc*." A well-placed assertion would help keep programmers honest:

```
case opNegAcc:
    ASSERT(val == 0);                    /* Pass 0 for val. */
    accumulator = -accumulator;
    break;
```

6.   The assertion verifies that *f* is either *TRUE* or *FALSE*. Not only is the assertion unclear, but more important, there is no reason to be so fastidious in debug code; after all, the code will be stripped from the ship version. The assertion would be better written as

```
ASSERT(f == TRUE || f == FALSE);
```

7. Instead of doing all the work in one line, declare a function
    pointer and break the work into two lines:

```
void *memmove(void *pvTo, void *pvFrom, size_t size)
{
    void (*pfnMove)(byte *, byte *, size_t);
    byte *pbTo   = (byte *)pvTo;
    byte *pbFrom = (byte *)pvFrom;

    pfnMove = (pbTo > pbFrom) ? tailmove : headmove;
    (*pfnMove)(pbTo, pbFrom, size);

    return (pvTo);
}
```

8. Simply put, the code calling the *Print* routine relies on the inter-
    nal implementation of the *Print* code. If a programmer changes
    the *Print* code without realizing that other code calls *Print* by
    jumping 4 bytes beyond the entry point, that programmer may
    modify the code in a way that breaks the *Print+4* callers. If you
    find that you must write code with entry points into the middle
    of a routine, at least make the entry points apparent to mainte-
    nance programmers:

```
              move   r0,#PRINTER
              call   PrintDevice
              .
              .
              .
PrintDisplay: move   r0,#DISPLAY
PrintDevice:                         ; r0 == device ID
              .
              .
              .
```

9. Jumping into the middle of an instruction was popular when
    microcomputers had such small amounts of memory that every
    byte was precious. Using this trick usually saved a byte or two.
    Such nonsense was a bad practice then, and it still is. If people on
    your team still write code like this, politely ask them to change
    their ways, or ask them to leave your group. You don't need the
    headaches that come with such code.

CHAPTER 8

There were no questions in Chapter 8, although there was a suggested
project.

REFERENCES

These books are explicitly referenced in the text.

American National Standards Institute (ANSI). *Programming Language-C*. New York: American National Standards Institute, 1990.

Apple Computer, Incorporated. *Inside Macintosh*, Volumes I–VI. Reading, Mass.: Addison-Wesley, 1984–.

Cialdini, Robert B. *Influence: How and Why People Agree to Things*. New York: Morrow, 1984.

Kernighan, Brian W., and P. J. Plauger. *The Elements of Programming Style*. 2d ed. New York: McGraw-Hill, 1978.

Kernighan, Brian W., and Dennis M. Ritchie. *The C Programming Language*. Englewood Cliffs, N.J.: Prentice Hall, 1978. Second edition 1988.

Knuth, Donald E. *T$_E$X: The Program*. Menlo Park, Calif.: Addison-Wesley, 1986. Reprinted with corrections 1988.

Lynch, Peter, with John Rothchild. *One Up On Wall Street*. New York: Penguin Books, 1990.

Motorola. *M68000 16/32-Bit Microprocessor Programmer's Reference Manual*. 4th ed. Englewood Cliffs, N.J.: Prentice Hall, 1979.

Plauger, P. J., and Jim Brodie. *Standard C*. Redmond, Wash.: Microsoft Press, 1989.

Plauger, P. J. *The Standard C Library*. Englewood Cliffs, N.J.: Prentice Hall, 1992.

Robbins, Anthony. *Awaken the Giant Within*. New York: Summit Books, 1991.

Simonyi, Charles. "Meta-Programming: A Software Production Method." Thesis, Stanford University, 1977. Also issued as CSL Report 76-7. Xerox Palo Alto Research Center, December 1976.

INDEX

Special Characters

& (address of)
   C++ & reference arguments, 108, 233
   in explicit optimizations, 144
&& (logical AND) expressions
   assignments in, 4–5
   errors in, 10, 214
   stepping through, 79, 82–83, 85
<< (shift left), precedence bugs and, 215. *See also* shift operators
>> (shift right), 135. *See also* shift operators
= (assign), mistakenly typing, 4–5, 11. *See also* assignment statements
== (equals), typing = for, 4–5, 11
() (parentheses)
   with mixed operations, 138–39, 142
   precedence bugs and, 215
+ (plus), precedence bugs and, 10, 137, 215
?: (conditional) expressions
   avoiding nested, 127–29, 142
   stepping through, 79, 82–83
   use of, 161–62
¦¦ (logical OR) expressions
   assignments in, 4–5
   errors in, 10, 214
   stepping through, 79, 82
   use of, 162
680x0-based computers
   validating environment assumptions, 24–27
   validating pointers, 64–66
80x86-based computers, pointers and, 49

A

AddChild function, 122–27, 142, 235–36
address of (&). *See* &
algorithms
   table-driven, 117–18, 129, 144, 238
   validating with backup algorithms, 33–38, 44, 221–22
ANSI C standard. *See also* C language
   data types in, 112–15
   function prototypes in, 5–6
"APL syndrome," 161–62

Apple computers. *See* Macintosh computers
arguments
   argument bugs, 5–6
   passing, 167, 168, 239–40, 242
arithmetic operators, 137
arrays, naming, xxvii, xxviii
ASCII characters. *See* strings
assembly language, calling functions in, 169, 243
_*Assert* function, 17–18
assertions, 16–44
   for assumptions, 26–27, 43
   checklist for, 200–201
   in code libraries, 21, 41, 43
   and converting integers to strings, 121
   in defensive programming, 29–33, 43
   detecting impossible conditions with, 28–29
   documenting, 21–23
   for illegal conditions, 22, 42
   in Microsoft Word code, 20
   for NULL pointers, 13, 14–18
   overview of, 13–14, 42–43
   parasitic functions and, 158
   in startup checks, 38–42
   vs. stepping through code, 75–76
   strings in, 43, 218–20
   for undefined function behavior, 19–21, 42
   validating algorithms with, 33–38
ASSERT macro
   calling functions in, 38
   redefining *assert* as, 17
   vs. *assert*, 17–19
assert macro, 16–19
ASSERTMSG macro, 43, 217–18
assignment bugs, 4–5, 10, 11, 216
assignment statements
   compiler warnings for, 4–5, 10, 11, 216
   multiple vs. separate, 144, 238
assumptions, assertion macros for, 26–27, 43, 220
atoi function, 159–60
attitudes, 171–94
   blaming testers for bugs, 188
   cleaning up code, 177–78, 193
   "cool" features, 179
   disappearing bugs, 172–73, 193

About the Author

Although Steve Maguire has a degree in electrical and computer engineering from the University of Arizona, he has always been more interested in the software end of the computer business. He has been programming professionally for the past 17 years and has worked in Japan as well as in the United States. In the late 1970s Steve was active in the microcomputer arena and was a regular contributor to the Processor Technology and NorthStar users' groups, contributing programming tools, applications utilities, and the occasional video game. Since then, Steve has been responsible for numerous projects, including *valFORTH* in 1982, an award-winning FORTH development system that allowed Atari programmers to write high-quality graphics applications and video games.

In 1986, Steve joined Microsoft Corporation specifically to work on high-end Macintosh applications. In addition to working on Microsoft Excel, Steve led the development of Microsoft's Intel-hosted MC680x0 Macintosh cross-development system. He was the driving force behind Microsoft's switch to a cross-platform shared code strategy in its applications development and is perhaps best known in the company for his efforts to increase the utility and quality of shared code libraries.

Writing Solid Code is the first of several books that Steve is undertaking to give programmers practical guidelines for developing professional, high-quality software. Steve lives in Seattle, Washington, with his wife, Beth, and their Airedale terrier, Abby. He can be reached at *microsoft!storm!stephenm* or *stephenm@stormdev.com*.

The manuscript for this book was submitted to Microsoft Press in electronic form. Text files were prepared using Microsoft Word for Windows 2.0.

Principal editorial compositor: Cheryl Whiteside

Principal proofreader/copy editor: Kathleen Atkins

Principal typographers: Jean Trenary and Carolyn Davids

Interior designer: Kim Eggleston

Principal illustrator: Lisa Sandburg

Cover designer: Rebecca Geisler

Cover photographer: Robert Barros

Cover photo editor: Rick Bellemy

Cover color separator: Color Control

Indexer: Matthew Spence

Text composition by Microsoft Press in Palatino with display type in Palatino using PageMaker for Windows. Composed pages were delivered to printer as electronic prepress files.

Printed on recycled paper stock.

Register Today!

Return the
Writing Solid Code
registration card for:

✔ a Microsoft Press catalog

✔ exclusive offers on specially
priced books

Fill in information below and mail postage free. Please mail the bottom half of this page only.

NAME

COMPANY

ADDRESS

CITY   STATE   ZIP

Your feedback is important to us.

Include your daytime telephone number and we may call to find out how you use
Writing Solid Code and what we can do to make future editions even more useful.
If we call you we'll send you a **FREE GIFT** for your time!

(   )

DAYTIME TELEPHONE NUMBER

1-55615-551-4A   A1L